CRAIG BRAIN

An invitation to wrestle with and discover life alongside a man who is doing the same.

Craig Gross with Levi Macallister

Published in Pasadena, CA, by Fireproof Ministries. Fireproof Ministries titles may be purchased in bulk for educational, business, fund-raising, or sales promotional use. For information, please e-mail info@fireproofministries.com.

Craig Brain illustration David Leutert
Cover by Ashton Owens
Editor Jeanette Gross (I love you)

The Library of Congress Cataloging-in-Publication Data is on file with the Library of Congress
ISBN: 978-0-578-52608-9

DEDICATION

Mom,

Chapter 36 is for you. I made you wait a while because it's good for us in the Gross family to have some patience.

I didn't just write that chapter for you. I wrote the whole thing for you. This is my 13th book, and inside are the most important words I have ever put down on a page, detailing the biggest discoveries, turns and shifts that have taken place in my life these past few years. I hope you enjoy it as much as I have enjoyed being your son.

TABLE OF CONTENTS

On Life & Living It

INTRODUCTION & FORWARD

Chapter 1 – Craig's Introduction

I just completed forty episodes of a podcast called Craig Brain. As this project comes to an end, so – it seems – does an entire chapter of my life. But, as my wife's epilogue suggests, *the end is the beginning*, and in other ways, my world is brand new.

Now that Craig Brain is complete, I thought I'd back up and review it for what I hope will become the introduction to the shiny new book you're holding in your hands.

In December of 2018, while at the Hyatt Regency Spa in Huntington Beach, I heard the voice of God.

"How?" you might ask.

"What does it sound like?" you might ask.

I just know it was His voice, not mine.

I believe God to be a truth-teller when he proclaims, *"My sheep know my voice and do what I say."*

And so, I heard him say:

"You have worked hard for years at putting out everyone else's content. Next year, it's time to begin to share what we've been working on together. To pay forward what I've been teaching you."

And, as my friend Stephanie says, *"I was shook."*

Really.

If you picked up this book without knowing anything about me, I'll attempt a summary.

For the past eighteen years, I have been working on (and in) a ministry I founded: <u>XXXchurch.com</u>. We publish content and develop resources that help people break free from pornography and sex addiction.

To make a long story short: this year, after a long season of restlessness that I feared might never end, I realized that I was being released from what kept me at XXXchurch for such a long time, and I finally felt free to leave it. You'll read more about that before long.

I say that I *"finally"* felt free to leave because the instruction to do so first came to me six years ago, in 2013, in a small town just north of Anchorage, Alaska, during a profound encounter with God. At the time when I and a few friends flew to Alaska together, I had just lost my father, my health was failing, and I felt like my entire world was collapsing.

So *of course* I embarked upon a spiritual pilgrimage in the Alaskan wilderness.

I went to find healing. During an experience called a *"process"* – wherein I lay on my back, blindfolded for two hours sweating, crying, praying and being guided through the past and into my childhood – I heard the Lord say, *"Stop running XXXchurch."*

I kept it to myself.

I left it out of our "sharing time" and felt like I flew home with more secrets than the healing I hoped for. I only ever told my friend Levi – the co-writer on this project who is making my sentences legible.

How could I possibly leave the ministry I started?

Wouldn't leaving make me a quitter?

Who else could run XXXchurch?

Who else would even *want* to?

What would I do if I left?

How could I provide for my family?

To be honest, those questions were loud. *So loud.* Despite having clearly heard from Lord, my fear overruled my excitement. I wish I would have given it more time and thought…

Instead, I resisted, questioned and buried it.

I am a 9 on the Kolbe test for Quick Starts. If you're unfamiliar with this personality assessment, here's what that means for me:

When I have an idea, it is immediately followed by a website and an email to a few people who can help me develop it into a product that will ship a few weeks later.

Which is to say… *I move really, really fast.*

This time was different.

Probably, because it wasn't *my* idea. It was *His*.

Probably, because my ego was still in the way.

I heard that same voice in Venezuela as a kid. I was sixteen years old on a summer mission-trip just prior to beginning my senior year of high school. I raised my hand in response to a call. Not to get saved for the fifth time, but to go into full-time ministry.

I heard this call *very* clearly.

I came home and told my parents that I would be going to a Christian college. I wanted to become a youth pastor. Though surprised, they supported me. My grandma never got it though. She said that I should go into business *"like your Uncle Bill."*

But I knew what I was supposed to do.

Years later, in 2006, God told me to uproot my family from our California life and move to Grand Rapids where, after meeting Rob Bell and speaking at Mars Hill, I was to build the ministry of XXXchurch.

We did it.

Two winters on Lake Michigan were enough to push us back to warmer weather, and we spent a few years in Las Vegas, NV before circling back to Los Angeles and – today – Huntington Beach.

By 2013, the Lord found me eleven years into the ministry of XXXchurch. I was no longer a novice in this industry. Our nonprofit had grown and matured, and we had the great joy of watching as our work helped churches throughout the world normalize a conversation otherwise left to fester in closets where shame and secrecy crushed people too afraid to talk about their struggles.

This time, I didn't jump at the Lord's call. I barely gave myself room to sit with it at all, but I never forgot what he said.

"Stop running XXXchurch."

The words haunted me.

I struggled to figure out how it would be possible. Instead, I just kept my eyes open for new opportunities to tack onto an already-overwhelming workload.

Shortly thereafter, I met a kid named Jefferson Bethke. In 2011, he posted a poem on YouTube titled "Sexual Healing." It did well. A few million views. But in 2012, his video for "Why I Hate Religion, But Love Jesus" created opportunities that very few twenty-something year olds ever receive. At this point, that poem has *thirty-five million* hits, and afforded him book deals, speaking gigs and an entire internet-based entrepreneurial career.

Jeff and I became friends, and I started working with him. I helped him and his wife, Alyssa, create sellable e-courses that they'd be able to add to their wheelhouse so that they could get off of the road, step away from an income solely reliant upon speaking gigs and start a family. Our work together was good for Jeff, and it was good for me. It helped me realize how easy I found online promotion and sales to be – especially for someone with an audience like his.

And frankly, it was a whole lot more enjoyable than constantly talking about porn.

Over the next few years, I created ten-plus resources for the Bethkes. Books. Video courses. Even a membership site. We sold over two-hundred thousand books and hit over three million dollars in gross sales. Too bad *Ole Mark Zuck* took over a million of that from our Facebook Ads spends... but I learned a ton. Jeff and I even started a company together wherein we offered similar services for other thought leaders and artists like Jen Hatmaker, The Liturgists, Propaganda, Trey Kennedy, Jack Douglass and more.

I joined a mastermind with the world's best internet marketers.

Then I started two masterminds of my own – one for business owners and one other for social media influencers.

I turned my spare bathroom into an office. Yes, *bathroom*. And *half bath*, at that. More like a closet with a toilet.

Give me a computer and a quiet space and leave me to it.

That was my life.

Through all of this, I held on to XXXchurch. And I coached my son's soccer team. And I managed his work in the entertainment world. And I tried to be a dance dad to my daughter. And I tried to be a husband to my wife.

I remember sitting at Coachella in 2017 when I told Levi about the words from the Lord. Four years after I first heard them. He didn't give me much advice or direction at the time, but he asked a few questions, and it felt good to tell someone. Finally. These new projects and endeavors had begun to pick up pace, and I thought I'd begun to see my *out*. I even remember sitting next to one another at the spa that weekend, writing up a proposal for the Jen Hatmaker project. It was one of the first opportunities that I believed could tip the scale and allow me to transition into this type of work full-time.

As I worked on and grew the business, other aspects of life began to shift for me, too. I was introduced to cannabis in 2013 – shortly after that infamous Alaskan encounter – but didn't become a regular user until four years later, in 2017…

In February 2018, my family and I took a trip to Huntington Beach, where we happened across an apartment complex with spaces available for rent.

And I was ready for a change. By then, I'd become comfortable with crediting cannabis for slowing me down enough to realize that *#beachlife* would be good for me and my family. It'd take more than a location-change to change me, I knew, but perhaps it would be a step in the right direction.

We moved three months later.

And the beach did help.

The pace – slower than LA – did help.

And the office-bathroom went out the window as soon as I realized how stupid it was to move to the beach just to sit on a toilet in a cramped closet with no windows all day and pretend it was a healthy work-environment.

I started doing something unique – something beyond and outside of all my businesses projects – that I really enjoyed:

Being with people.

(As opposed to just emailing all of them.)

My wife and I started reflecting on who we'd become –
both individually and as a couple. As we approached our
twenty-year wedding anniversary, we were both thankful to
have made it much further than most of our friends…

At the same time, we knew we wouldn't last another two
weeks if we were unwilling to work on and change certain
unhealthy aspects of our lives.

We embarked on a three-day intensive with Kay and Milan
Yerkovich – marriage counselors and the creators of *How
We love* (here, you'll find a whole chapter dedicated to this
experience).

I purchased a spa membership at a resort around the corner
from our apartment within three days of moving to the
beach. To this day, it's been the best *hundred-and-fifty-
bucks-per-month* I've ever decided to invest in myself…

"Start sharing what I have been teaching you."

Hundreds of journal entries.

Disconnected thoughts and fragments of ideas so heavy I
can't often stand to reflect on them.

Share what? And with whom?

I only work with people who have blue checkmarks next to their social media handles, or a minimum of 100k followers attached to their names.

Would you like to know how many followers I have? Four thousand-ish. And no blue checkmark.

When I started <u>XXXchurch</u>, social media didn't exist. We grew our reach and influence prior to the world of social. We played catchup and built our numbers over the years:

- 700k on our FB page
- An email list of 150k
- 100 million visitors to our website over the last 18 years

Google my name and at best, you will find an article, a book or a video of me talking about porn. If you're lucky, you might find an old clip of me harassing telemarketers.

What I'm getting at is that I didn't believe that I had an audience big enough to warrant the release of personal content like what what you're holding in your hands today.

What I've realized is that my belief didn't matter in the end, because the idea wasn't mine to begin with.

One day, my friend Drew sent me a text asking for a few minutes of my time because "he needed some Craig-brain." I bought the domain (obviously), and then laughed to myself that day in the jacuzzi when I realized that's what I'd call my podcast.

The format I ended up using for Craig Brain was one that I'd previously pitched to an influencer who didn't take me up on the idea. Most people listen to podcasts during "found time" or when they're preoccupied with something else, so I wanted to follow mine up with a book that would contain chapters written in conjunction with this year's weekly releases that people could sit down and pay attention to.

Gary Vaynerchuck had just decided to share his MicroContent methods with a bunch of us, whereby one creates a single piece of pillar content that gets chopped up and blasted all over social media throughout the corresponding week…

So I thought, "Why don't I take that idea for my own stuff? Why don't I do this with Craig Brain?"

I explained it to my team. Admittedly, I felt weird trying to rally everyone around a project called "Craig Brain" (a weirdness that compounded given the fact that I had no idea about what would happen next).

I booked a podcast studio space.

I hired Levi to help me write this, and gave him access to all of my journal entries – every half-baked, out-of-order, broken-sentenced and often-undeveloped thought. I couldn't have done this without him. He is the younger brother I didn't have growing up, and I consider him one of my best friends. In many ways, we couldn't be more opposite from one another, but we've shared many of the same interests and passions throughout the years, and both of us lost our fathers way too early in life. He is a wordsmith and a poet – two words that *no one* would ever use to describe me. Levi has been a significant part of my journey, and the details that you'll hear more about in the coming months. Much of what I chose to divulge, he was familiar with. And some of it, he had his fair share of pushback on. Maybe that's part of what makes me feel like this project has been successful. The push and pull of honest critique and revision. What's more, he's familiar with me and my brain, and so I asked him to help me bring this project to life.

I won't lie, that part was scary. Uploading journal entries that had only ever been *mine* for someone else to see – in all of their private rawness – and make sense of…? That's a vulnerability that has only come to me through practice, but being known is worth the risk.

Levi helped me create order out of chaos. He organized every entry, breaking each up into sections that seemed to make the most sense for whatever it was I hoping to communicate:

- *On Balance & Being*
- *On Family & Friends*
- *On Marriage & Making It*
- *On Work & Workmanship*
- *On Life & Living It*

These are, quite simply, pieces of life that I don't want to forget. I chose to invite others into them, and decided that I would spend 2019 pulling back together all that I poured out during the past two years. I hope that whatever I have had to offer will impact those who have chosen to follow these meanderings, as well as you, here and now. Reflecting upon them has certainly had an impact on me.

To be clear, I never intended to write *most* of what you're about to read for *anyone* but myself, family or friends these entries were addressed to. Perhaps that's why I've come to believe that I can share these entries with a sense of freedom, and abandon. I'm not writing to influence or persuade an audience – I'm simply inviting you into my world – and after nearly twenty years of life spent in a ministry that has sought to champion openness and vulnerability, I know what kind of power *simply sharing a journal entry* can be to someone who needs it.

When I started this project, I didn't mention anything about cannabis.

Frankly, I didn't want to lose whoever might be willing to listen to me straight out of the gate because some ex-pastor I assumed they'd label *apostate* was getting woke off weed. But I did share it eventually. It is amazing what transparency will do for a person who has decided to stop hiding from the world.

I don't love cannabis. Rather, cannabis has helped me understand what and who it is that I love.

In March 2018, I decided I wasn't going to hide anymore, and I shared my experiences using cannabis with my family, friends and more.

I've learned.

I've grown.

I've experimented.

I've shifted.

The best word to describe it is *surrender*. Acceptance. Allowing myself to "live for the first time," and abandoning my lifelong need for control.

Life *does* seem clearer than it ever has. I can't deny that, either.

But it hasn't been without its consequences.

My friends – husband and wife – called me after I released Craig Brain Episode 6 and said, *"This is the best stuff you have ever put out."* I thanked them and responded, "Just wait until you hear Episode 7."

The following week, when I mentioned cannabis for the first time, they officially *unfriended* my wife and me.

After that, the *one* church that has ever consistently, financially supported myself and our ministry with XXXchurch throughout the years ceased all contributions.

Their senior pastor – my friend – publicly denounced me as a drug dealer before his congregation… without ever calling to talk to me. Neither will he answer me when I call.

My wife's best friend said that she would pray for her before cutting all communication with our family.

My business partner told me to repent, and his wife sent Jeanette and me a nine-page, handwritten letter filled with agony over the lost state of our souls.

I have received death threats.

I have been told I am going through a midlife crisis.

The hate-mail in my inbox is overflowing.

I've lost relationships.

It feels like every one of my movements is analyzed, and every motive misconstrued.

Consequence of telling the whole truth, I suppose.

I'm not playing the martyr, I'm simply telling my story.

I'm not writing *you* a prescription.

I'm.
Simply.
Telling.
My.

Story.

What you'll see is what you'll get. It's all of me. Right, wrong, or somewhere in-between, this is my journey.

What you are about to read is called Craig Brain, but I think you'll find more heart than head in these pages. The beating muscle inside of my chest would never have made its way into that microphone were it not for the progress I've made during the past two years, as follows.

I have experienced forgiveness, been released from a ministry that we worked hard to leave well, and fallen in love again with my wife all over again.

I am a changed man.

So, thanks for picking up this book. However you came across it. I know it is not by accident.

I don't expect you to agree with everything that I have to say. I don't expect to be fully understood. All I can tell you is that it's real. I've done my best to be vulnerable and put all of myself out there. It's new to me – vulnerability. At least, on this scale. But I hope you'll be able to take it in. Take what you may.

I hope it takes you inward.

I hope it takes you somewhere new.

I hope it encourages and helps you.

And I pray it lands.

Craig Gross

*Watch Craig expand on this chapter by scanning the QR code below.

Chapter 2 – Levi's Foreword

I met Craig when I was a nineteen-year-old child addicted to porn and writing poetry about it. His organization - XXXchurch - was resourcing people like me with internet accountability and filtration software so that those of us who didn't *want* to be addicted to porn could kick the habit.

At some point, a mutual friend introduced us to one another, and I began performing my poetry as a guest at the ministry's events. I had only ever talked to Craig over the phone. I don't think we met in person until I'd already completed at least three XXXchurch events *on my own,* overwhelmed and hoping I was - at the very least - *coming close* to representing their name well.

In the decade since, Craig has changed a lot, but I'll tell you what: it's still in his DNA to move so fast that he hires a man-boy he hasn't even met to run events for whatever the next thing is that he's doing. You and I might think that's something one might describe as - oh, I don't know… *ridiculous* - but Craig is a mover, and a risk-taker, and seems to function like some weirdo superhuman - *"faster than a speeding bullet."* My wife says that she doesn't know a single person on earth who *moves faster* than him. And it's not just in business. Try keeping up with him at the mall or something - the man may as well be a damn competitive power-walker.

But while Craig is still capable of being that *X-Men* character whose slow-motion is everyone else's steady pace, his strength - as goes the cliché - started to become his weakness (sometimes literally, which you'll read plenty about here), and it was as though the Lord forcibly imposed *rest* upon him.

I remember one of these "heavy-handed" moments - like "the bitter hand of God" that the Old Testament's *Ruth* describes - while attending a conference with the Gross family in San Antonio, Texas, circa 2013. At one point, Craig had to crawl on hands and knees underneath the souvenir table in an attempt to escape one of his oncoming headaches, and his wife Jeanette stood terrified at the possibility of this becoming yet another trip to the emergency room, full of yet another series of unanswered questions...

It tripped me up - seeing someone so previously unstoppable, *stopped* dead in his tracks - and yet, that season proved to become a catalyst for change that I doubt Craig could have *(or would have)* ever imagined...

For all intents and purposes, Craig and I are opposites. He moves incredibly fast, and I move breathtakingly slow (it's a real sight to see me sloth around). Craig tends to take risks, and I tend to worry about whether or not someone will be upset because I chose to write the word "damn" in a sentence four paragraphs ago.

We've had our fair share of disagreements throughout the years. I get nervous about stirring the pot, but he's always got a new ladle in hand like pot-stirring is his spiritual gift or something. It makes for an interesting relationship, at times, and as a person who has made "conflict" synonymous with "Satan is coming to kill me," I sometimes find it easy to get lost in the fear of separation that *pushback* threatens.

Nevertheless, I have learned a little something about pushback throughout the years (partially thanks to all of the great opportunities he's given me to practice), and I must say, he has never validated my fears. Quite the opposite, actually. Our friendship and the work that we've been able to do together has only grown stronger - largely because of the way that we compliment one another's strengths and weaknesses (i.e. - has learned to walk a little slower, and I've learned how to jog).

Last year, I introduced Craig to a book titled The Path Between Us by Suzanne Stabile. The author writes about the way that different personality types - according to Enneagram-speak - function together. Of *9s* (me) and *3s* (Craig), it essentially reads: *"Nines help threes relax, and threes help nines believe they actually have something meaningful to offer this world."*

We both laughed when we read it. If that isn't a spot-on snapshot of our relationship, I don't know what is.

I say all of that to say this: you don't need to be me - or to understand the foreign language that I am well aware *Enneagram lingo* is - to know that Craig loves to see people succeed. He is a helper, through and through. In all of his *quick-start* drive, he's always trying to pull others along with him, demanding that they see their potential, and hoping they'll develop the kind of confidence that he has in them for themselves. There's always a new text, a new resource, a new Voxer message, a new *something,* simply for the sake of helping others succeed.

What follows is evidence of it, and I'm proud to have been a part of helping him tell his stories - many of which I was present for, living in tandem. Some of them stories that I wish we both could have avoided: the death of our fathers, minds exploding (or, in my case, *imploding*), and the consequences of our own respective proclivities toward workaholism, bar none.

I'm proud of him, too.

The Craig that I met ten years ago, from what I am able to remember, wasn't an especially vulnerable person. Granted, you should take my memory with a grain of salt, but I recall thinking that - and this is often the case for *anyone* - perhaps Craig was better at prescribing the cure than he was at taking it. After all, if it is true that the things we are most passionate about advocating *for also* just so happen to be the things we most deeply struggle *with*, then the gap would only be natural. But what Craig has chosen to divulge of himself in what follows is something different than any other pursuit I've seen him embark upon. In this place, he doesn't come as the teacher, or the leader, or the giver of monologues...

Here, he is the peer and the learner - the conversationalist. And if anything that follows is sermonesque, it is dialogical and open to discourse.

Each of these chapters began as a diary entry, or a private letter, or a personal reflection, and we could have made them anything we wanted. A simple shift in tone during the editing and rewrite process could have transformed genuine questions and a man's wrestling with God and self into teachable absolutes and pithy definites. It's amazing how easy it would have been to make these process-pieces into *Your New Guru's Ten Steps Toward Success*, or some other title from a photoshopped author, primed for clickbait.

After all, the final touch on *expertise* is as easy as clicking "delete" on a few inconsistencies before you go to press.

We're keeping them in. Life is *all of it*, not just the pretty bits.

Craig Brain is more *memoir* than anything else. It is an invitation to discover and wrestle with and alongside a man who is doing the same.

This is a conversation. Feel free to engage. Whether you "boo" or applaud, Craig is living out his desires to be *not just* a hearer, but a *doer* - and especially when it comes to exemplifying the openness, transparency, and accountability he has long encouraged millions of others to champion in their own lives.

So, love it or hate it. Or - if you're like me - sit with it for a while in the murky middle, and the tension that everything worth engaging on this planet seems to be. If you are able to remember it along the way, keep in mind that disagreement doesn't have to be synonymous with discord.

We're all works in process, trying and failing and succeeding and switching and starting and quitting and *living,* and waking up to new mercies each and every morning.

CraigBrain is not *YourBrain* or *MyBrain,* but neither must unity be predicated upon uniformity, and I would not be the person that I am today without the gross (pun intended), squishy alien matter inside of this dude's skull. Take a peek.

*Watch Craig expand on this chapter by scanning the QR code below.

Chapter 3 – Spa Day (Or, Sin City Jesus)

Journal Entry: January 20, 2017

I've always wanted to have a relationship with Jesus, but growing up as a "Christian" kid in a "Christian" school whose "Christian" *Quiet Times*™ (yes, that's sarcasm) were forced upon me left me feeling jaded.

Years later, I continued my education at a Christian college. I suppose it was my choice. Rather than igniting a passion for God and His word, though, I found myself studying the Bible for the sake of course grades and a ministry degree, which only proved to perpetuate my lifelong experience "in relationship" to Jesus as… *more school work.*

Throughout the course of my life, I have spent innumerable hours – days, even – digging into the Bible for a sermon, blog or book, but truth be told: I've always lacked the passion and desire to spend time with God just *for me.*

On June 13, 2016, I was packing my bags for the eXXXotica Expo – a adult entertainment convention that our ministry, XXXchurch, sponsors each year – and a box fell on my head from the top storage area in my garage.

I knew I had a concussion, but I didn't stop what I was doing. I grew sluggish as the day progressed, my head pounding inside of my skull. The pain didn't go away – not that day, or the next, or the next. I wore sunglasses around the house for a week in an attempt to keep the migraines at bay.

Things never got better.

Eventually, I got an MRI. I went to a doctor, and in November – five months later – found a concussion expert in the Valley.

The specialist led me through a series of "impact tests," and I failed one of them. He advised that, for two full weeks, I was to do the most difficult thing he could have asked of me:

nothing.

I left his office knowing that it would be next to impossible.

Before that fateful day, I know that I felt the Lord's pursuit in this area of my life, by which I mean: my *time*, my *attention* and my *focus*.

I run fast. I oversee a ministry, work on the side, and manage my son Nolan's career. Beyond occupation, I am involved in Nolan's soccer teams. I help my daughter Elise with dance, and am engaged in many other activities, interests and pursuits with my wife, Jeanette.

I'm thankful for the life I've been allowed to lead, and while I'm able to recognize Who it comes from, *I kept putting off the time to stop and reconnect with the Lord.*

I know that you only make time for the things that are important to you.

I know that I've given a hard time to plenty of men who don't date their wives, or spend time with their kids.

You make time for the things that matter, and I wasn't making any for Jesus. What else is there to say than to admit that my desire for the Lord was based more out of guilt than want or passion?

This past year, I made it a goal to work out. To set aside time for it: one hour a day, three-to-five days per week. I have never committed to something like it before, and no one forced me to do it. I do it because I want to, and the more I do it – the more I see the resultant changes in my body and my health – the more excited I get about it. If I'm honest, I don't *really* enjoy working out, but I see how *working at it* is working for me, so I continue.

Did God give me a concussion? *No.*

Did God use my concussion to get my attention? To slow me down? To refocus my priorities?

Does he redeem the painful parts of our lives?

I believe so.

After my meeting with the concussion specialist, I told my wife, our long-time ministry partner Michelle and a few other friends about the doctor's recommended *off time*, to which they responded, "When are you going to do it?"

"Later," I said, "maybe over Christmas."

When December arrived, a new friend invited me to a private screening of *The Shack* – a film adaptation of William Paul Young's New York Times bestselling novel, which allegorized God's trinitarian nature in profound ways. I said yes. I hadn't read the book, but – whether for its critical acclaim or condemnation – was familiar with the story, and I was stoked. In my opinion, the movie was incredible: an awesome [motion] picture of the trinity personified. I left the film that day, wondering, *"Maybe God is sending me a note to meet him at The Shack...?"*

Spoiler Alert: If you aren't familiar with or haven't read the book, the story's main character loses his daughter. Later, in the midst of a life that has come to be defined by grief and anger, he discovers a note in his mailbox, left there by God, inviting him to this place called *The Shack*. He accepts, and throughout the course of the story, his eyes are opened to realities that he never saw or understood before. For lack of a better descriptor, the man goes on a *"healing journey"* to deal with his pain. His issues with forgiveness. His self-blame and blame-of-God for the loss of his daughter. The movie does an excellent job of showcasing his journey. Eventually, through these encounters with God, what the man first discovered as a weathered, beat down and dilapidated ruin is then revealed as a glorious retreat.

A place of rest.

A garden.

It was a beautiful story, but I didn't connect the dots. I can string a line between them now, but at the time – in the busyness that doesn't allow for reflection – life was moving too fast to catch the pattern.

It's funny – the way that God seems to function. I think He does it all the time: hints at healing we're too busy to accept. We move too fast. We move from one thing to the other, mindlessly, and we miss what God is attempting to show us because we don't – *can't,* maybe – stop and let it sink in.

My family spent a week in Oregon for Christmas that year.

I went into it thinking that – fingers crossed – it might be a slow week. Maybe I'd have time there. As it turns out, between year-end reports and a book project that wasn't edited correctly, one thing led to another... led to another... led to another… and our time away was *anything* but a peaceful break from work or stress.

I was without relief as we entered into the new year, but surprisingly, about halfway through January 2017, my symptoms disappeared. I felt better. I went back to the gym. Back to my normal routines. I told everyone (including myself) that I didn't need a two-week break from work or life.

As it stands, my symptoms still haven't returned. I'm thankful for it, but my emotions are mixed, as well. I feel relief and sadness, simultaneously. I am grateful for the Lord's healing, but it is combined with the sting of regret for not having heeded His invitation to spend time together had I actually pried myself away from the work that consumed my life. If I'd have taken the recommended break, perhaps I could have heard his voice more clearly.

The thing about the Lord, though, is that He's relentless. He never stopped – and never will stop – pursuing me.

And he'll never stop pursuing *you*.

I headed to Las Vegas' AVN Adult Expo on Tuesday, January 17. We had an amazing team helping us with the ministry that year, and it helped offload some of the burden that normally falls on me throughout the convention. I didn't have to be at the booth all day, for one, and it allowed me the freedom to cut away for work, meetings or whatever I needed (or, frankly, wanted) to do...

So, I did just that. On Wednesday, Thursday and Friday afternoon, I snuck out for a bit and spent $35 bucks on a day pass to the spa at the Cosmopolitan Hotel. I needed to get away. I needed some time alone. I didn't feel bad about it, and I didn't tell anyone where I was going.

I also didn't go there expecting to get what I got out of it.

I like nice hotels. Maybe you love the outdoors, and the thought of a spa day bores you. My friends joke and laugh about how, if I had my way, I'd never step outside to see the town – just enjoy the facilities. I wouldn't go so far as to say *that*… but they're onto something.

That day was quiet and still, and I was finally alone. I turned my cell phone off, and my music on. I'm a huge Justin Vernon fan, and playlisted a mix of Bon Iver and some of my favorite worship songs, and let it run all afternoon.

I sat in a jacuzzi.

I sat in a steam room.

I lied down on a lounger.

I talked to no one.

The spa's quiet transformed what had historically been one of the loudest, busiest weeks of my year into a retreat, and I found the opposite: stillness and rest.

My eyes were opened.

Out of nowhere and everywhere, God began to speak to me. Bible verses that I memorized to boost my grades in high school suddenly returned to me. This time, though, they felt like life – different and complete, offering respite.

"Very early in the morning, while it was still dark, Jesus got up, left the house and went off to a solitary place, where He prayed."

Mark's gospel accounts for this truth: even Jesus would slip away.

Jesus would pull back – go somewhere for Himself – to meet with His Father.

That Wednesday afternoon – the first of three that I would spend pursuing the Lord, and my own mental, emotional and spiritual well-being – I looked out at the view from the Cosmopolitan and thought, *Why wouldn't I come here every day?*

I thought, *Each day, I need to find my retreat. Each day, I need to find a place, and give myself the freedom to slip away to it.*

I told the Lord, "I'll see you back here tomorrow."

To press pause in the middle of the day... in the middle of the week… in the middle of the Vegas Strip… It was an incredible afternoon, unlike anything I'd ever experienced before it. All I wanted was to get back to that place.

And I did go back. Same spot. Same playlist. And a similar experience regarding the clarity the Lord – giver that He is – had been longing to provide.

I say "similar" as opposed to "same" regarding my time with the Lord that Thursday, because one thing did change:

I left my phone on vibrate.

I worried that if someone needed me, I would have to be available. While that's all well and good, I also learned a valuable lesson:
I shouldn't do to the Lord what I wouldn't do to another person had I been meeting Him in the flesh – over dinner, perhaps, or across the table from me in a meeting.

Perhaps you are *that person* who can never shut down your phone… even when you are with someone else, face to face. There are plenty of them out there. (And yes, I did just make an "us vs. them" distinction.) I try to be present when I am with someone. I try to put my phone somewhere I won't look at it – where I won't be distracted if we're engaged in a conversation.

When I meet with the Lord, why shouldn't I implement those same rules just because I can't see Him?

I found myself distracted, somehow trying to intermingle urgent texts and emails and task lists into my time with the Lord.

Disclaimer: it doesn't work.

The next day – Friday – I went back and kept my phone on airplane mode. By that time, I sensed the dots connecting, and I wanted to draw lines between them. I wanted to write down what I'd begun to learn: thoughts, ideas for the future, things I needed to change, practices I needed to implement.

Friday's time was much more about chronicling what I'd been told.

Writing helps solidify the thoughts that float around inside. Writing grounds the lesson.

So, I started writing, and much of what I wrote that day became what you just read. I saw these lessons begin to make sense, and I decided to make some changes in my life...

If I can find time to work out (something I still don't like, but I love what it is doing to my body) each week, why can't I find time to slip away? To retreat and meet with the Lord? To sit in the silence? *Even Jesus did this* – and not because He was forced to. He wanted to spend time with His Father.

I learned that if nothing changes… *nothing changes*.

God doesn't want to meet with you out of obligation.

God doesn't force your hand.

What would my life be like if I lived it with a greater sense of awareness and intentionality?

What if I did something that I love every day?

What if I did something that the Lord loves every day?

He *loves* time with you and me.

Practically, then, the question becomes: *how to create it?*

I like lists. *Need them*, actually. Whether it's a meeting outline or an agenda for the day, I need a sense of order. For example: a friend of mine who works with me remotely comes to town once a month. We use a project-management tool called Basecamp to create running lists of the topics and conversations we want to tackle during our time together. If we run out of time, we roll the leftovers into the next meeting, in addition to adding new ideas, tasks and discoveries to our list of changes, pursuits and implementations along the way.

Knowing myself and the ways I work best, I began to honestly apply the same type of pragmatism to my time with the Lord. What's on our list? What do we need to tackle? Where are we going to meet?

I didn't have all of the answers perfectly squared away, and I didn't perfectly keep to the agendas I created, but I did start to write them down…

- "Find a place without distractions."
- "Find a place I want to be."
- "Bring a pen and paper (or phone... *if* you can handle not looking at anything else while you're on it)."

- "Schedule it like you would any other time, gym session or meeting."
- "Block it out on iCAL."
- "Stay focused. (For me, that means bringing music and sticking to the agenda.)"

I also wrote out a topic for each day of the week – something or someone to hone in on – whether that was a specific person's name (Jeanette, Nolan, Elise, or another member of my family), my friends, myself or a particular area of my life about which I was searching for wisdom. I tried to align myself and my new appreciation for this *quiet time* (now attractive, unforced and wholly mine) with the Lord's invitation in Psalms 55:22, which reads:

"Give your burdens to the LORD, and he will take care of you. He will not permit the godly to slip and fall."

Bring what you've got to the Lord and ask Him for direction, guidance and "next steps." Don't try making sense of it – He is the one writing this story behind the scenes. Maybe he'll give you the gift of clarity – of *answers* – or maybe he'll sit with you and allow his presence to be your comfort.

Find your retreat.

Find your rest.

When I started writing this, I was unsure about what it might become (assuming it needed to become *something…*

anything). Is it a blog? A podcast? A chapter in a book? All of the above?

What I now know with certainty is this:

It was a start. It *is* the start.

It was a renewal and a stirring, and it continues to be those things to me when I retreat to silence and listen for the voice of my Lord, Who has called me "friend."

I can't force you to do what I am doing. I can't force you to spend time with the Lord. Frankly, neither will He, but that doesn't mean Jesus isn't jealous for your attention.

Jealous for your time.

Jealous for *YOU*.

Because *you* are who He wants.

For what it's worth, Craig Brain wouldn't exist without what I believe was the Lord's intervention at the spa that day. Without having met me in Sin City, smack-dab in the middle of one of the world's largest porn conventions. In fact, my entire life changed after our meeting at the Cosmopolitan...

This journal entry was the start of it all. It reminds me – in my own, small way – of Jesus' promise to make all things new. He has certainly been remaking much of my life since then and, invariably, my family's. Speaking of: we even uprooted our lives and moved away from what was comfortable for the sake of discovering what else is in store (and yes, I attend a spa regularly – a luxury, I know, for which I'm thankful – in order to get myself in a frame of mind that will allow for the silence I need to hear the Lord's voice). The time spent with Him in those quiet places has proven to seep out and into every decision we've made, whether that be personally, occupationally, socially… fill in the blank.

What follows in this series of "Craig Brain" podcasts, blogs and – eventually – a book is exactly that: a peek into the fruit of prayer growing in my life. To be frank, I can't believe I'm actually going to share much of what you'll hear throughout the course of this year (or read, whenever that happens). I've not been, historically, a particularly vulnerable person, at least in the public eye. It has taken me a lifetime to understand myself, and I know the process is nowhere near complete. You will not find perfection in these pages, and many of them scare me to share, but I take comfort in knowing that He who has authored my story will someday perfect it, and bring it to completion…

Welcome to Craig Brain.

*Watch Craig expand on this chapter by scanning the QR code below.

Chapter 4 – Turn Your Damn Phone Off (A PSA from Old Man Craig)

[July 5, 2017]

Turn.
Your.
Damn.
Phone.
Off.

Or at least… *turn your damn notifications off.*

Alright, I don't think I'm *that old* yet, but I know for a fact that I am capable of delivering what can only be considered an exquisite *old man* rant.

Listen up! Pappy's got somethin' to say, and it just might change your life.

Have you ever gotten stuck next to someone painting their nails on an airplane?

Or some idiot about to eat a tuna sandwich?

Somebody passing gas? *(That was me.)*

What about those people so aloof (or inept) that they *still* have their phone's keyboard noises set at full volume so that *you* – lucky human that you are – can listen to every text, type, and click pound into the screen?

Have you ever been on a screen-sharing conference call with people who don't turn off their notifications, guaranteeing that you *know* they're not paying attention and that they have *zero* idea about what's actually going on?

Have you ever watched a grown ass man "work" on his computer with a screen so full of notifications about everything from how much his favorite sports team sucks to Twitter updates and Facebook *likes* to the next Nordstroms sale email?

Oh, you haven't?

That's because the grown ass man *isn't working*, because he *can't work*, because he *can't see whatever he is supposed to be working on* anymore.

Those people aren't productive people. How do I know that? Because one cannot focus with endless distractions, and if all of our stupid notifications are *anything*, they are certainly: *endlessly distracting*.

Also, lest you assume that I'm *only* screaming from atop my high-horse, I've been this person, too.

It's an annoying person to be.

Certainly, you have friends (or are the friend) who can't put their phone down during your entire meal together, or who can't stop checking each and every inbox pushing alerts into your periphery.

I'm tired of it. It's annoying, it wears me out because it makes me feel like I'm always *on* and it guarantees I get *nothing done.*

My friend Aaron works at Apple, so I asked him how to turn text and iMessage off on my phone. I hate the dinging. That damn text *ding!* takes me, you, and everyone else away from whoever we're spending our time with, or supposed to be focusing on.

As if that isn't *old man* enough for you, I ranted at him, too.

I told him I want to go back to the days of answering machines, where you had the option of returning people's calls, but only when you got home, if and when you actually listened to their message. I wanted to get away from the expectation that I must respond to everything immediately.

That damn text *ding!* takes you and your focus away from whoever you're spending time with, or supposed to be focusing on. Even if you just read the text and don't respond, it takes your attention away from being present and gets you to think of the message and response.

A few minutes later, Aaron smiled and said he had it.

God graced this old man with an angel who knows how to turn text notifications off.

My messages are still there, but they don't have a red number next to them on my home screen (in fact, I removed the iMessage app from my home screen altogether), and now I hear the sweet sound of silence instead of *The Damn Ding!*™.

My point?

We live in a world where Amazon delivers literally anything you can dream up *that day*.

We live in a world where everyone is connected on social – watching everyone else's lives – at the expense of missing out on their own.

We live in a world where we both *record* all our moments and *miss them* at the exact same time in order to capture them for someone else to watch on a screen when that person could be living their life, instead of envying (or laughing at) yours.

We live in a world where emojis and text messages have replaced phone calls *(and God, I HATE emojis)*.

We live in a world where most people don't even turn off their phones to sleep, and where people interact (tap, type, swipe, click) with those *always on* phones over 2,617 times per day.

These things are drugs, triggering dopamine spikes, that hook us on endless loops of information overload, and between the internet (and every social media giant it hosts) and text-messaging, we can instantly gratify our incessant desires for *more*.

Want to talk to someone right away? Send a text. They'll respond in a few seconds.

Want to look something up? Google it.

Want to see what your colleagues are up to? Linked In.

The addiction is effortless. Your brain says "seek," gets rewarded when you "find," and urges you to repeat.

So, *Old Man Craig* made some changes recently. Here are a few of them:

1. Call me if you want to talk.
2. If it's work-related, I'll get to it when I am in front of a computer – working. Until then, *The Damn Ding!*™ is turned *off*.
3. My daughter sorted my apps by color, which has proven to help me spend *less* time on my phone (everything is so hard to find now that I just give up instead).
4. I moved everything that *isn't* crucial away from my phone's home screen, so when I turn it on, I'm not tempted to look at anything.
5. I deleted the Facebook app from my phone, Twitter sucks (it bores me), and I enjoy Instagram…on the toilet.
6. My family and I downloaded a private text messaging app that we only use between the four of us to communicate if and when we don't want to talk.

7. This list is growing. I recently sold my computer
    and decided if I can't do it on my iPad Pro, I
    shouldn't be doing it anyways.

I don't have a home-phone line at my house. If I were a
better old man, I would. Maybe that's the next step in my
own personal evolution. When I do get one, I'll give you
my number – you can leave me a message on my answering
machine and wait *God-knows-how-long* for a response like
we used to when I was a kid...walking to school, barefoot,
and backward through six feet of frozen rain and snow.

You do what you want with your own damn phones, but
this is what I've done.

If you do anything, though, try something new *(or old)*,
because what we are doing with technology isn't working.

With some combination of love and hate, sincerely,

Old Man Craig

*Watch Craig expand on this chapter by scanning the QR code below.

Episode 5 – A Gross Christmas

(December 24, 2018)

To my family...

I am writing this letter to you on Christmas Eve and –
 depending upon whether I'm able to articulate what I think
I want to – I'll read it to you in the morning *(so…now, I
guess, if I decided to go through with it – it's weird thinking
about how to write something into the future).*

Maybe this letter is something I write once, or maybe I
make a tradition of it, the way our friend Matt used to. Do
remember the way that he'd send Christmas cards every
year? I wish he still did. I gave him a hard enough time that
he promised to bring them back this Christmas, but he only
wrote one for me. I guess I should be flattered, except…he
sent it on email.

I look forward to Levi's *end-of-the-year* album reviews and
Jamie's *top-songs-of-the-year* playlist. Maybe my
Christmas Eve letter will become one of those things you
guys look forward to reading each year. Or maybe this will
simply be a *One-Hit Wonder…*

Time will tell.

This year has been wild. I guess you know that. When it
began, I never would have imagined all that has unfolded
for each of us during the past twelve months – individually,
and as a family. Now, I'm sitting here on the night before

Christmas with a full heart, trying to articulate what I hope
will be a gift.

Nolan and Elise, I want you to know that I enjoy being your
father more than ever.

I am proud of each of you, and you are an unspeakable joy
to me.

At dinner tonight, I sat glued to my chair, dumbfounded at
how a thirteen-year-old and a fifteen-year-old are able to
articulate themselves and hold a conversation better than
most twenty-somethings. I am proud of the ways that you
display wisdom beyond your age. The ways that you carry
and conduct yourselves. The ways that you are able to
communicate with others, and share your perspectives –
your outlook on life.

I see a maturity in the both of you, far exceeding that of any
other kids I've ever known. I don't say it to blow up your
heads, but to honor you, and to let you know it's okay to
believe that *it's good to be a Gross*.

Remember when we made a list of the *Gross Goods* and
hung it on our kitchen wall?
We want our family to be good with:

- *God*
- *Marriage*
- *Family*
- *Friends*
- *Health*

- *Work*
- *Money*
- *Fun*

If those attributes are truly a reality in our lives, it's okay to be proud of them. It's good to live them out in the world around us.

Jeanette, I'm more grateful for your love and friendship than I have ever been able to express.

As I look back on this year, the one word that stands out is *CHANGE*. We did a lot of it.

We changed addresses.

We changed schools.

We changed schedules.

We changed the way we live, the way we eat, the way we exercise, the way we work…

Personally, I'm aware that *you're aware* of the changes that have been happening in me, too. 2018 was full of them, and I'm writing this letter as a man who is better than the one I saw in the mirror a year ago. I hope that you see that reflected in me as a father and husband, as well, and I hope that I'll be able to say the same a year from now on December 24, 2019, too.

I learned a lot about myself this year, and that's part of why I'm writing this tonight: to share some of it with you.

I recently had a talk with Nolan about what I was dealing with when my dad died, like why I wasn't at his bedside when he breathed his last. I missed it.

I missed it.

Nolan showed me compassion and understanding beyond his years. It made me realize that you guys are at an age where we don't have to keep things from you because you "can't handle them."

So, I'm going to share with you, freely.

I like learning. I like growing. I like new things and new opportunities… but I always end up *DOING*. I've never understood why I just keep *doing* until I burn out. What do I have to prove, and to whom? I don't know. I've always just *done* it to provide for our family, and to provide for others.

This year, I've been honest with you about struggling with work – with what to do. And should we move? And where? And what will that mean for me, for you, for us? We talked through it all while we figured it out together, but there was more to the *why*…more to the story.

Before we moved to Huntington, mom told me that she couldn't do twenty more years like this.

She's said it before, I never believed her. In the past, I'd simply promised to slow down… and *not*. For our entire marriage, I'd promise to change – to do something different – but I never did. I just kept adding to the plate until it overflowed. I kept *doing more.*

This time, mom meant it.

I turned her promise into a challenge. A literal, thirty-day day challenge. I asked her to give me thirty days, and swore that this time would be different. We made the decision to move during a time when I needed something different and drastic to happen if I was going to save our relationship. I needed a new location – new sights and new sounds – and a break from old routines and bad patterns. And I needed to begin to *think* differently: *What do I do? What do I keep? What do I quit?*

You probably remember me during this time, although you weren't yet aware of the circumstances. I showed you both a video after I picked up from school one day – a recording of me…*not knowing what to do.* I flew to Salt Lake City, randomly. I was scrambling…

How the hell am I supposed to fix this in thirty days?

I was trying to make shit up. It's what I do. I make shit up. Sometimes it works, and sometimes it doesn't.

But this *had* to work.

I wanted to win your mother back. I couldn't lose her. I couldn't lose you.

This has to work.

We moved.

We met with counselors and dinner at their house.

We went to marriage conferences.

We went to marriage intensives.

We discovered the Enneagram.

We remembered that we never finished the *How We Love* stuff that we began years ago.

Our friend Tom reached out during this time – my old mentor – and I offered him a job just for the sake of having him in my life, if nothing else...

Elise, you can dance to *absolutely anything* you set your mind to, but you don't love hip-hop, and you're discovering how incredible you are at ballet…and how much joy it brings you.

Nolan, you can accomplish *absolutely anything* on your computer, but you love creative expression, and you want to express yourself through works of art.

I know these things about you, and you know them about yourselves – even at such a young age.

I am forty-three years old today, and only in this past year have I begun to realize the things that I truly love.

I can *do* a lot, but I only *love* a few of the things that I do.

When I discovered that truth, I continued to change. I shifted my role at Fireproof. I shut down Aloha & Rain.

I turned down people I said I would work with.

I've been trying to replace the things that I hate (or, at least, the things that aren't a *hell yes)* with the things that I love.

I started my mastermind group.

I launched betterandbetter.co and have been able to help other people through it.

I discovered that I only like the office in the bathroom at night when I am writing and dreaming and *not* in the day, grinding away behind a computer screen.

I discovered what I am good at.

I helped a lot of people this year go from *stuck* to *unstuck*…

It has been fun. But my God, it has been hard. Apparently, a learning curve is exactly that, and some of the realizations that arise in the process are difficult to face.

I learned that much of why I do what I do can be traced all the way back to my childhood. I grew up trying to fix everything from my parent's marriage to my dad's struggling businesses. Somehow, even as a kid, *I was the parent*, and their approval was nonexistent. When I became an adult, I turned to work and success as a way of receiving the approval of others – the approval that my parents never gave me – and I've gone long and hard after the praise of others in an attempt to fill a void that keeps leaking out at the bottom.

Mom and I learned that stuff in counseling together, and while we're far from perfect, we hope that we don't repeat our parents' mistakes. Those kinds of burdens aren't yours to shoulder, and we want to give you a better life than the ones we had growing up.

I want you to chase things that you don't think are possible. *Anything and everything.* They *are* possible, and you've seen some of them come true this year – from Nolan getting to do the Nike project he pitched, to Elise getting called out in her dances.

Don't be afraid. Or, in your fear, be courageous.

Do you remember when I joined Jeff Walker's Mastermind? That was almost a year ago, now, and just *getting in* was a massive turning point in my life. In fact, I believe it's the very reason that I have finally learned this lesson, because getting into the group felt like a miracle –

or the completion of a dream that began as an impossibility.

When Carl and I first attended one of Jeff's *LaunchCon* events, Walker straight up told the room that no one else could get into his mastermind, and that's exactly what challenged me to try.

"Carl, not only am I going to get into this group, I'm going to speak at this conference."

That's what I told Carl that day. In hindsight, he probably thought that I was crazy, and maybe I did, too. I had no personal connections to the room, which meant no chance of getting into the group, and certainly no chance of ever speaking at their conference.

The whole process – from how to ask for an application, to filling it out, to filling it out *again*, to coughing up a *30k* membership fee, to being accepted – *all of it* was nerve-racking for me.

But do you know what I did have? What proved to be all that I needed?

CONFIDENCE.

I was confident that I deserved to be in that room, and on that stage. I believe that I am capable – excellent, even – at the things that I know how to do. The things that I have done. The way that I am able to deliver a message with the same kind of confidence needed to get into the room in the first place.

Of course… that doesn't mean I don't experience insecurity. When I got in, I was nervous – out of my comfort zone with fifty-two new people (zero of which were friends) and not one connection – but I did it. (Ironically, though, after all of that…I skipped the first "fun" day and went to the spa by myself. Three days of nonstop interaction with brand-new faces was *so* hard on me.) I pushed through. I went back. I tried to discern how to navigate a brand-new experience.

When do I speak up? When do I *ask* and when do I *tell?* Who do I introduce myself to? Do I approach them, or wait for them to approach me? Will Jeff ask something of me, and when?

I've learned a lot in Jeff's group, and the Lord's direction hasn't returned void. Financially, it's a pricey place to be, but the returns have far exceeded my investments. More than monetary gain, though, is the relational component…

I've been able to learn from guys that I want to be like – some of them doing things that I was doing already, but in other areas, things that I didn't yet know how to do.

They've helped me reshape my thinking.

I watched Stu tell stories and love his wife like no one I've ever known – ways that challenged me to be a better husband to your mom – and then got to spend two days with them in Canada.

Jeff told me that business (and life, for that matter) isn't about chasing revenue…it's about chasing lifestyle. I watch him work with his son, Daniel, in ways far more patient than I do with you, Nolan. I watched him trust his entire family with his business and – at the same time – saw how he refuses to let his business run him and his family.

Today, one of the "big names" in our group posted a question that might prove to be one of the best things that I've interacted with all year…

He asked about how to sell 100k copies of a book using Facebook Ads.

I know, I know – it probably sounds boring to you, or way out in left field with no connection to everything that I've been writing about thus far, but hear me out…

Almost every day on our Google group, at least one person posts *something* – a question, a comment, a tip. Throughout the entire year, I have only commented on *maybe* 5 of 300 posts on our thread... and I have only started one thread, myself. I read them all, though, and I watch the interactions that take place.

Today, though, in between all of our Christmas bagel eating, I saw the notification on my computer and just…*started typing*.

I included a few links. I included a proposal that I had previously assembled for a client, revealing our sales model and a few suggestions for the guy. I hit "send" and laughed, thinking, *You chose Christmas Eve to* finally *engage in a post for this group? No one is going to see - let alone read - what you have to say.*

And I was right…I got to public messages from anyone, praising my response with digital back-claps.

What I did get, however, was a *personal* email from Jeff Walker, asking me to *PRESENT* the topic – and my methodology – at our next Mastermind.

I'm not going to lie – I freaked out inside. I haven't been in that group for a full year yet. Jeff assigns two-to-four people per group-meeting to share, and he wants me to be one of them. I couldn't be more excited to put my presentation together, and crush it. If all goes well there, I might even have the opportunity to speak at *LaunchCon* someday (something Jeff offers to the best of his mastermind presenters so that they can pay forward, publicly, what they've contributed to his private group)...the same event that I told Carl I'd speak at someday.

This morning's email from Jeff is just the second step in a process that – as such a fast-moving person – has admittedly taken longer than what I'm used to, but I've begun to recognize that perhaps the best things in life are worth the wait. Maybe patience is a virtue I haven't always possessed, but it feels like the Lord has begun to provide a path for me to walk into the dream he gave me. Jeff's response encouraged me. It gave me confidence that *this is happening*, and it feels like a win.

You know me… *I like to win*. When I set out to do something, I want to see it through. It's fun for me.

At the same time, as the saying goes, *our greatest strengths are also our biggest weaknesses*.

Bloomberg – a business and marketing company – recently wrote an article about my uncle Bill, who just sold his stamp collection for ten million dollars (yeah, I can't believe, either). In short, he basically said that, *"Once you win by having nothing else to buy, the game is over."*

He "won," sort of. He won the stamps game, apparently, but he hasn't won in life. He lost two marriages. Two people who loved him, and who he loved. I don't know if he can trace his longings for affirmation back to childhood the way that I can, but he still has something to prove.

We all want to keep playing, even when we've won, and it makes me wonder what *"winning"* means.

Tom Brady is better at forty-two than twenty-two. He wants to play forever.

Lebron isn't done.

Steve Jobs worked all the way to his grave.

My uncle Bill kept working through and beyond both failed marriages.

Winning is fun. Accomplishing new things is fun.

But when is enough *enough?*

I am not quitting or retiring at forty-three, but this year, I have learned that I have to set better boundaries. I have to slow down. I have to learn to enjoy the life that's been give to me, and the people that I've been blessed to live it with.

Nolan and Elise, I hope you both continue to chase after the things that you love. You don't have to have it all mapped out, but you do have to start. You'll never reach them unless you start.

At the same time, I need you to remember what's most important, and I'm not sure that whatever I've always thought *winning* meant…is, anymore.

I don't win if I lose mom.

I'll be honest with you…I'm not there yet. I've asked mom for plenty of extensions since that first scare last May. But I'm trying, and she's being gracious to me. I hope that, pretty soon, I can stop asking. I hope that she'll be able to see that my changes are real, and lasting.

I don't know quite how to explain it, but I've begun to *feel* more this year. It's been hard, but it's been helpful – trying to discern and understand who I am, and how I feel about things both *good* and *bad*.

I think I'm getting closer, whatever that means. I think I'm figuring stuff out.

The email I got from Jeff today ended not with some other business plan or proposal, but with a note about his family's holiday celebration:

> *We're about 60 minutes from having 60 people show up for a Christmas Eve party. :-)*
>
> *But the best part is that tomorrow it will just be the four of us all day... so blessed that our kids want to hang out with us when they're adults. I cherish these days.*

He reminded me that I'm not his group to feed my need for validation (although, of course, I'm thankful for what I got), but to be reminded of the type of family goals I want to have…that, simply, you guys would just want to *be* with us.

Earlier this year, a guy named Sam Parsons told me that, *"He saw his wife with the eyes Jesus had for her,"* and encouraged me to do the same.

I offered to help him publish a book, and I'll be honest: it wasn't primarily because he needed me…it was because I needed him.

I wanted to learn how to love mom like I saw Sam love his wife.

I told Jeanette that I wanted to see her the way that Jesus did. I wanted to act like Jesus would toward her.

I've tried. I might even be making progress, but let's be honest...I don't know much about being like Jesus.

I know him, but being like him is just...hard.

Really hard.

It can be really hard to know what that means.

It can be really hard when you don't want to be.

It can be really hard when you don't think someone is being fair.

But I am trying to do life better.

And I think I like where life is going for all of us.

Elise, I love the spirit that I see in you. I love the way that you love just *being here* with us – with your family and with Churro. I want to spend more time with you. I mean that, and I will work on creating that time this year. I will work on finding the time for us to have our "things" – even if it simply means walking through Westminster Mall together every week...I am fine with that. Whatever it takes. You are growing so fast despite all of your longing to stay young, and you are absolutely beautiful. Your friend Ashley says that she hears all day long about how much she looks like her mom and frankly...? That's not a good thing - *haha*. But you? You look more like mom in so many ways, and that *is* a good thing. You are stunning in your photos, and in the movie we just watched together.

Nolan, I don't know what to tell you that I haven't told you already. Looking at you is like having a mirror pointed right back at me. Sometimes, it reflects the things that I'm proud of, and sometimes I find myself unable to look into your eyes for the way that they scare me. I don't know how to describe that other than to say that this year, I want to look you in the eyes more, and enjoy your youth. Your spirit. Your love for life. You hold so much of it within you, and I think I need to be overwhelmed by it. I watch you worship and it inspires me. Don't ever stop. I want to worship like you someday but right now, I can't. Whether because of my own strict upbringing, or something else, I'm not sure, but even though I haven't gotten over whatever it is yet, I'm practicing again, and I hope that eventually I can let go the way that you can.

Jeanette, I am sorry. For what? That list is longer than any I have ever given you. I want to love you and try to see you as Christ sees you every single day. This is my prayer, and I want to ask you to make it yours, as well. Please. Pray that I might have those eyes. I like our future. I don't mind our past. It's what's got us here and *here, now,* is better than where things were last year. We have persevered through so much pain. Next year, I want way more good days than bad days. I don't want *any* bad days, and I know that has got to start with me.

So…what about *2019?*

It's going to be a good one for us, and I have a few things to say about it.

If 2018 was about *CHANGE,* then I believe that 2019 is going to be about *LESS.*

They say *less is more.* Ironically, I think I even wrote an entire book about that. It seems as though I could stand to benefit from re-reading it and – perhaps – even sharing more of the lessons I learned during that time as I re-learn them, myself.

Knowing me, I'll probably make us all create a *"LESS LIST,"* but here's what I've got for the time being:

- *Less Struggle:* in marriage.

- *Less Things:* I've committed not to buying anything unless I sell or get rid of something else, first.

- *Less Travel:* I've committed to no more than 25 trips…the first time ever talked to mom about putting a cap on how much I'm away from the family.

- *Less Responsibility:* I don't want to do less work, but I need to scale back the amount of responsibility attached to the work that I do. I hired a full-time executive assistant to work alongside me, and all my *stuff*, and I hope that will release me to do *less*.

- *Less Resistance*: I hate routine, but need it. I need to lean in to stuff mom knows and does, and trust her to help me with my days.

I don't know what other *LESS* is going to make the list, or how each of you will see that word, or use it this year, but I wanted to share it a week *ahead* of 2019 – as opposed to hoping I'll have accomplished enough reduction to write about it in a yearbook at year's end.

And that is what made me think of writing this letter to you.

It's like picking up that yearbook and reading all the things that happened…before they did. This way, we can be a part of making them a reality.

Frankly, if I do create a tradition of family letter-writing, I hope that next year's will be much shorter. Partially, that's because I can't believe you're still listening to me talk right now but also, it's because our family can do a better job of communicating with one another in the moment. We can share our dreams and aspirations with one another as they come. We can ongoing conversations, as opposed to hindsight reminiscences.

What do you want this year to look like, and what can we be talking about as a family? And let's ask one another: *why?* Why do we want to hit the goals that we've set? What are our reasons, and are we keeping one another's ego in check (or, at the very least, are you checking mine)?

How can we be intentional about checking in with and supporting one another? How can we celebrate the wins better together? How can we come alongside one another in our losses?
Asking each other why we want the goals and checking our reasons for that to keep our egos in check or at least mine.

I need you, I love you, and I am so thankful for the gift that each of you is to me.

Merry Christmas.

*Watch Craig expand on this chapter by scanning the QR code below.

Chapter 6 – A Letter to My Son (And You)

[December 13, 2018]

Nolan,

Let me start by saying how proud I am of you – not for what you have done, but for *who you are,* and who I see you becoming.

Your youth leader told me that you feel more like his friend than his student. I know that I still have to parent you (and, I guess, be your driving coach at some point) but I feel the exact same way. Especially after a trip like the one we just had together.

Nolan, you will always be my son, but you're also becoming such a great friend.

It is *so much fun* to have you as a friend.

Our time in Vegas last Monday was *so fun*.

I was excited to share that kind of day with you. It's the kind of day that David Dean and I have made a tradition of each year (except we end up gambling, and you like higher-end window shopping than that Indiana-boy does…I suppose I have myself to thank for that). We visit the same restaurants I took you to, bet on the same games and just *hang out* and enjoy one another.

It's exciting for me to get to share something special – something that I love – with you like that. My favorite parts, though, were our conversations.

We went deep.

First, over dinner, it was our conversation about forgiveness. About making peace. After that, your cousin Mike came up - and I know things have been hard there. Mike's story somehow lead to me telling you about *my* dad, and the way I wasn't there for him when he died.

I wish so badly that I could have been.

I didn't have fun with my dad when I was young. We didn't get along, and I didn't see him much. Not enough to know him, anyway. He was too busy trying to provide for us, which might sound noble, but it pulled him away from our family.

I've had to learn a lot about forgiveness and making peace, too, Nolan. I'm so thankful that I was able to make peace with him. We finally became friends seven years before he died. I never knew how much I needed it until it happened, and my memories of him – of us together – are so special. Priceless.

I miss him.

It was nice – you asking me about that time in your life. About what was really going on, even beyond my dad dying. We took the same Vegas trip together, too, you know. I'm thankful that I got to be there with him – I as his son and friend the way that you are to me. Being there with you this week made me realize just how fast you are growing up. Time really is flying, and you are only a few, short years away from adulthood.

Then, I thought about how ours was technically a work trip for me. We haven't done one like it together since the year you were born, but this was something different. It wasn't the same as it has been in the past – you coming to listen to me speak before we peel out and play games somewhere. This was more like you entering into my world. Taking it in. Meeting some of the people you've always heard me talk about. It was first-hand view of the challenges we face in ministry, and the strategic conversations that exist in relation to the businesses I run.

I'll be honest: I was proud to show you off in those rooms, and I was proud of the responses demanded by your presence. No one could believe that a fifteen-year-old could actually carry himself the way that you do. And I'm proud of you for it.

You know I work hard. In fact, you know that I work too hard, and often spend too much time with my head buried in projects, but honestly? I hope you were just as proud to see me that room. I want you to be proud of me, too.

The next night, I got to jump into *your* world.

It wasn't *just* to see a band – it was to see your *environment*. Your world.

Watching girls pick-up on and take photos with you.

Watching you figure out how to be in the front row for LANY, or how to meet them afterward, deliberating over which of them you'd love to meet the most.

I was proud of the decision you made. It's who you are: someone who doesn't want to stand in front, but rather, someone who wants to stand beside others, and them beside you. The whole band loves you, Nolan. After something as special as that was, they talk about you for sure. There is no one else quite like you.

When we walked out and you told me the story of the model, I was stoked. I loved the way that you wanted to talk to me. The way that you trusted me with something. For what it's worth, I'm sorry that I paid part of that story forward when I now realize you probably weren't all that excited about it. I will learn to figure out what not to say, and when, but I was just excited that you talked to me like you would your friends.

Thank you for being willing to talk to me like that.

Remember when I asked you what was *one thing* that stood out to you during Jeff Walker's two-day conference?

You responded, *"A lack of confidence."*

And you're right. The only difference between myself, Mark, and Jeff Walker – as compared to the other people in that room – is confidence.

I am not smarter than everyone else in the room.

I don't have a better business mind than everyone else in that room.

I don't study and prepare better than everyone else in that room.

I just believe in myself a bit more than they do, and I want you to remember that. Confidence will get you in the room. Sure, if your confidence turns into cockiness, it can also get you kicked *out* of the room, so you have to learn how to use that gift. You have it. I know that you have it, and when confidence is paired well with a personality like yours, I swear you'll go far, Nolan.

I want to help you build that confidence. I want to do it for Elise and Mom, too. I hope you see me doing that with all of the people that I work with.

The Bible says, *"Train up a child in the way he should go and when he is old he will not depart from it."*

- I want you to be confident now and forever, and to know where it comes from – who you are in Christ. It's not you, but He who is within you. And He who is within you is capable of accomplishing more than you could ever ask for or imagine.

- I want you to keep believing that anything is possible. Dream big. Compete for spots you want, even (and maybe especially) those that most would say are impossible to get.

- Don't settle. I'm talking about girls. I'm talking about your values. I am talking about your life. I know you're making a list…believe that you will find a girl who is everything on that list and more.

- Don't stay quiet. Your voice matters. Most people are scared of the microphone, Nolan – but you aren't. Don't be afraid to speak your mind, share your passions and stand out. Keep doing what you're doing. Keep being you. Show us something different than everyone else out there. Don't stay quiet.

- You are living your bucket list. It's okay to write your dreams down, but remember what we're always learning in church: your best life is *now*, here. Enjoy your youth. Enjoy this season of life while you still get to look forward to summer vacations, and fall breaks. Keep saying *yes* to the things that come your way, even when you don't think they sound fun. Even when you don't think you'll get your *yes*. Keep living, and keep inviting others in to live right alongside you. I'm glad you decided to take the road trip.

- Continue to care for and love your sister and your mom. Love them well now, and for as long as this life gives us.

That's all I got.

After the first trip that I took with my dad, he wrote me a
letter, too. I received it in the mail – his shitty, cursive,
almost illegible handwriting on a piece of lined yellow
paper – thanking me for sharing something with him.

He wrote me after every trip we took together. I always
thought it was crazy, because never in my life did I think it
would happen until, by some miracle, we became friends. I
can hear mom's voice perfectly, announcing their arrival:
"You got a letter from your dad on your desk."

For some reason, I didn't keep them. I thought I did, and
every time I'm in the garage, I look for them. To find just
one would be so sweet, but it hasn't happened yet.

Nevertheless, I wanted to tell you the same. Thank you,
Nolan.

It's late, and I'm still awake, thinking. After our trip, I
thought about the way my dad would write those letters,
and I wanted to do the same. I can't promise I'll do it after
every trip, but when I think about it, I will.

Do me a favor, though? Don't delete it, or erase it, or throw
it away. Keep it. You might never know why, or when
you'll read it again, but at least you will have it.

I look forward to many more trips with you. I look forward
to watching you grow old (and myself grow older).

I love you Nolan.

Dad

P.S. I've spent too much of my life *thinking* about all of the things that I *could* say to people, and I think a lot of those same people spend their lives in the same way. I wish we'd all learn to speak. This letter is – in a way – my attempt at speaking. I remember Levi challenging people to *love the ones they love out loud.* I love you out loud, Nolan. Try to do the same for others, too.

P.P.S. Since you're keeping this letter forever, I have an answer to the question we've been asking, *"What does Nolan do better than anyone else I know?"* It might be rough, but I pulled all of my thoughts into a one-liner:

"Nolan's vast creative knowledge and interests allow him to relate to people of any age, race, or gender, which causes him to discover new interests, and pushes him to learn new things…that is why you are the best 15-year old I know."

Put better – You *love, learn, relate* and *create,* and to circle all the way back around…

I am proud of you.

*Watch Craig expand on this chapter by scanning the QR code below.

Chapter 7 – The Godforsaken Devil's Lettuce (Saved My Life)
Journal Entries Circa 2013 - Present

I have smoked a total of ten cigarettes in my lifetime, and the closest I've ever come to *enjoying* smoking is an occasional vanilla-or-chocolate flavored cigar (which – I'm willing to bet – doesn't even appear as a blip on the radar of a true connoisseur).

I got drunk *once* on my 21st birthday, and never again. If and when I do drink now, I try to make sure my beverage is sweet and fruity enough to come with an umbrella.

I didn't try any drugs until I was 37 years old, and before you judge me on that one, it was legal.

In other words, when it comes to physical health, I'm perfectly *bland*. I've never even broken a bone.

Shortly after my dad's passing, though, it seemed as though all my good luck had finally run out on me.

The year was *brutal*. I lost my father, my wife Jeanette was diagnosed with stage four endometriosis necessitating surgery, and then – one weekend in Amarillo – I thought I was dying (and no, that's not the name of a bad country song).

I don't mean "dying" in the *Texas is humid and I'm gonna keel over* sense. It was more like, *Oh my gosh, my brain is exploding inside of my head.* I even recorded an "I love you" video for Jeanette and the kids while the ambulance rushed me to the emergency room, genuinely unsure about whether or not I was going to make it.

I did make it. The pain went away almost as suddenly as it came, but it always returned with a vengeance and continued to come and go many times throughout the ensuing nine months that it took for me to find a solution.

June 7, 2013, marked the first of what became a series of these blinding headaches. They would appear unexpectedly, wrapping my brain in their vice-like grip, buckling my knees and paralyzing me for hours until – for reasons as unexplainable as their appearance – they disappeared.

I became a hospital frequent-*er*, landing in emergency rooms and doctors' offices in Texas, Arizona, Nevada, and Illinois. I called 911 three times, and two of them turned into ambulance rides.

Hospitals don't mix well with the unknown. Each visit turned into test after test after test to try to discover what was going on with me. I had more blood drawn out of my body than I ever realized it was capable of holding.

I had X-rays, CAT scans, and spinal taps.

I had an MRI, MRA of the brain and chest, and was screened for diseases like multiple sclerosis. I saw over twenty doctors and specialists – including a rheumatologist, a neurologist, a cardiologist, and other *-gists* that I can't even pronounce, let alone spell.

You name it. I did it. Or rather, I had it done to me. I sat beneath microscopes and had exams out the wazoo, many of which hurt as badly as the headaches.

And every single time, they told me I was fine.

No worries.

On paper, I was in perfect health.

"Here," they'd inevitably say, scribbling on a pad, "This is a prescription to help you with the headaches." Then they'd hand me a slip of paper that I could trade in at the pharmacy for Ibuprofen 800, Prozac, Oxycontin, or some other migraine medication.

I never filled any of them. I didn't want to cover up what was going on in my head. I wanted to discover the real issue. Plus, I'm not comfortable with the side effects and/or dangers that some of these medicines threaten (which is *not* to indict anyone who *does* or *must* go the pharmaceutical route – only to say that, I chose not to). Instead, I maxed out my insurance plan going from doctor to doctor, trying to figure out what was wrong with me.

I sought out psychiatric help. Maybe it was – no pun intended – all in my head? But meeting with them only served to convince me further that this was a medical issue, and that I didn't want to treat it with the pills I'd been offered. Call it fear or call it wisdom – there was just too much potential for side-effected wreckage than I was comfortable with.

That said, let me tell you about my experience with God's forsaken Devil's Lettuce.

One night, while my wife Jeanette slept in our bed next to me, I was watching CNN and Dr. Sanjay Gupta's documentary, *Weed,* came on.

I was fascinated. I hadn't been paying much attention to our nation's pot legalization debates because it never held much of my interest. I've never messed around with marijuana in my life. It wasn't even on my radar. But I was drawn in by the special, and the perspective it offered of this little plant and what it's capable of, as well as what other countries are doing with it.

The special ended with the story of a five-year-old girl from Colorado. She was dying until her parents looked into medical marijuana, extracted it into a liquid form, that ended up saving her life. Her 300+ seizures a week had been reduced – literally – to *one*. Plus, she was now able to talk.

Best of all, it seemed like the side effects were mild, especially when compared to the crazy stuff I'd been reading about the other pills available at my local pharmacy.

Could this be what I needed?

I began to consider everything I had tried to cure what was ailing me – tests, medicines, therapies – each with little to no results. I started to consider trying something a little less mainstream.

Was pot the cure I'd been looking for?

The next day I applied for (and received – yes, things happen fast in California) my shiny, new, state-issued medical marijuana license.

I'm not going to lie; the "doctor's office" was *sketchy*. Although, the licensers did share their space with a foot-fungal specialist who would perform surgeries in the office, so that had a lot to do with it. (Public Service Announcement: try *not* to visit pot-docs who co-rent spaces with foot lovers.)

The system is strange, absurd even. It took all of twenty minutes to have a Skype conference with the doctor (he wasn't even there in person, a receptionist ushered me into a room with a busted-up Windows desktop to discuss my symptoms with *whoever* he was, *wherever* he was). Seventy bucks and a couple of signatures later, the receptionist's printer pushed out my card, which gave me the legal right to possess up to eight ounces of marijuana and grow up to twelve plants. For what it's worth, that's *a lot* of weed, and this dumb piece of plastic with my name on it was the only thing separating my allowances from those of a person caught without it, who would've been subject to harsh fines and – potentially – imprisonment.

Like I said – absurd. Almost as crazy as the first dispensary I visited that same afternoon.

It had no name and no signage – just a red door on some building across the street from a *76* gas station. A friend of mine – someone with a past more, uh *"colorful"* than my own – joined me for the day's excursions. After our cards were verified, a woman at the front counter buzzed us through the doors separating the lobby from the back room, where the actual shopping experience took place.

I was expecting a clean, well-lit and minimalistic space – something like an Apple store for potheads – but this was *not that*.

Instead, I entered a cramped, crowded, *illegal*-feeling room packed with pot paraphernalia, complete with bizarre names rivaling some of the best (or most ridiculous) porn star monikers I've heard during my years as "The Porn Pastor."

The place looked *nothing* like what I saw in Gupta's CNN special, and even though my presence there was entirely legal, the atmosphere perpetuated all my preconceived, religiously-inspired notions about *Reefer Madness*, and made feel like I was doing something wrong.

But I had been desperate to find a cure for my headaches – desperate enough to skip church and end up *here* on a Sunday morning. I wanted to experience some normalcy in my life again, so I chose to brave the unknown. After all, I'd already come *this* far.

I had no idea that marijuana could be ingested in so many different ways. I spoke to the budtender (yes, they're actually called *budtenders*) – a pleasant Russian woman behind the counter – about my condition and what I was trying to medicate, searching my memory for the terminology Dr. Gupta used in his documentary.

Something about high CBD and low THC? Was that right?

Jeanette told me ahead of time that she wouldn't tolerate me smoking, so something like a traditional flower or a pre-packaged joint were out of the question, and I wasn't about to be sold on some weird, phallic-looking bong anyway. I do love candy and chocolate, though, and it just so happens that *edibles* aren't limited to gummy bears *(who knew)?!* I chose a cannabis-infused cake pop, a couple of brownies and chai tea.

It was lunchtime when we finally wrapped up the morning's activities, and I decided to get extra stereotypical for the family: I ordered two extra-large pizzas so that I'd have leftovers that night, just in case I got the munchies (you know, I'd heard about them on TV).

I don't know what I was expecting that first night, my virgin-self now tainted by a drug that had always been demonized, but it's safe to say that my experience was *underwhelming.*

I didn't know what else to do, and I also didn't understand a single thing about marijuana, or what it meant that different strains have different effects. My headache didn't go away (yet), but I was determined to find something that worked.

In the midst of all of this, stacked atop the unknowns in a world I'd never experienced before, was the creeping condemnation of a world I *was* intimately familiar with - the one I grew up in. The one I am still very much a part of. Like most Christians, I had always associated what I was beginning to dip my toes into as an enemy of the faith and inherently sinful.

What's the Christian's responsibility when it comes to this stuff?

I have a pastor friend who takes Zoloft, and no one bats an eye. Should it be okay for me to consume weed? Would it be okay if I didn't smoke it, but instead got it through a brownie or a cup of tea?

Did anyone have any definitive answers? Anything I could trust?

Anyone?

I only medicated with cannabis maybe fifteen to twenty times over the next four years. I told no one – save a few friends – opting to avoid the controversy that I was convinced it would cause, especially because of my ministry work, where I feared people wouldn't understand.

One day, though, I came across some infused mints that looked like Altoids (and tasted like them, too). Each mint contained a small dose – 5 mg – of THC, and they ran about twenty bucks for one-hundred of them. Little did I know, this "microdose" was the perfect amount for me, and that little can of mints ended up changing my life.

Shortly after my discovery, in January 2017, I flew to Las Vegas for the annual AVN show that our ministry, XXXchurch, attends every year. There – amid a break from the convention at the Cosmopolitan hotel – the Lord met me in ways more powerful than I have ever known in my forty-two years on this earth.

My head stopped spinning, and I heard His voice. I got clarity. I got direction. I got out of my head, and I let God into my heart in a lasting, visceral way.

You might remember my full, spa day experience.

When I returned from Vegas, I told some of my close friends about the incredible encounters I'd had with God, always carefully leaving out that – before each session – I would take one of my little "magic" mints.

I was scared to tell anyone because they were drugs, right? Drugs had been off-topic and taboo for my entire life. It never occurred to me that some drugs might *not be bad* (at least, not in-and-of themselves), let alone entertained the idea that they could ever be *good*.

Was weed helping me draw near to the Lord?

No, I thought. That's crazy talk. I'd better keep this to myself. And I did – for years – until, after an entire life spent encouraging others that transparency was a gift to be shared, I became convicted that this secret was no longer mine to keep. I did what all reasonable people do.

I recorded a Facebook Live video about my experience as the pastor "gone to pot." Frankly, the relative non-response to something that I had been previously terrified of sharing publicly left me wondering just what I had become so afraid of.

The more I began to unpack those experiences in my mind, the more I began to realize: *my life is busy.* Too busy. Marriage, two kids, insane work schedules, directing a non-profit, managing side-business projects, and each idea that I am constantly moving on.

Some days, I forget to eat. I don't stop working long enough to go to the bathroom. Sadly, I realized that entire days would go by without lifting my head for air out of whatever project was in front of me.

I could have been sitting in a room with my kids, or my wife, or *you,* but it'd always be clear that I was somewhere else.

I was there, but I wasn't *THERE.*

I haven't slowed down as I've gotten older. Instead, forty-two-me is running circles around twenty-two-me. I had the best year of my career in 2017 – new projects and growth in all the companies and ministries I am involved in.

At the same time, I almost lost my marriage in 2017.

Work never stops; there is *ALWAYS* something to do. Even with two virtual assistants at my disposal, there are not enough hours in the day.

So it probably doesn't come as much of a surprise that, out of nowhere, I started to get that feeling again:

My head was heading for an explosion.

Without going back into every shortcoming that I've already detailed in previous stories, I had to change. It was as though God was forcing change upon me. I had to apologize to my family for the unbalanced life I'd been living.

I had to tell them how I knew that I was heading for an explosion in my head again. I had to tell them how I had been failing, and all of my plans to change the path I was on.

But then I heard the Lord add, "Also…tell them about the dots you've been connecting to your moments of respite. Tell them about how you have come to hear my voice now more than ever."

Those damn mints.

I can't naturally shut off, and so I keep going. I'll sit down to meditate and pray and end up thinking about a to-do list, or trying to solve a work-related problem in my head.

It.

Just.

Never.

Ends.

I have a few friends in this with me. My good friend, Levi, wrestles with anxiety and depression. I don't know what that is like, specifically, but I can relate to being in your head way too much. I think that Levi and I have similar things going on, namely: noise and fog.

While I can't speak for Levi, I know that when I was able to take a small dose of marijuana, that noise and fog was lifted, and my path to God was made clear.

Eventually, I was convicted that I not only needed to share these things with my family, but I need to tell others about my experience, too.

I believe marijuana can be hugely, medicinally beneficial. It certainly has been for me. My health has never been better. Beyond that – and you might think I've gone crazy here – I've also come to believe that weed can be spiritually beneficial. It certainly has been for me.

I've become a better dad, husband, lover (sorry to gross you out, kids, but it's the truth), boss, business partner, and human being because of it.

I don't see a way for a person to be held accountable without him or her also being transparent. I've been involved in *everything you can imagine* related to accountability – from creating software to writing books and organizing groups – and am a huge advocate for living life *together*.

And yet, in full contradiction to all that I've dedicated myself to throughout the course of my adult life, I have somehow felt as though these are things that I can't share publicly, but deep down, I have no reason to believe that, save the fear that keeps me from speaking it out into the open.

So for now, I will not be ashamed of something that has done this much good in my life. Something that has brought me so close to the Lord. Something that I believe He, Himself, revealed to me.

Maybe weed *could* be a good thing – something that God uses to get our attention. It's certainly how he got mine.

Resorting to drugs? Using drugs? If the pharmacist at Walgreens were filling them, I wouldn't even consider the possibility of shame. So why the abashment just because I happened to fill mine at a store with a green cross over its entryway?

Call me crazy, but that little green cross pointed my eyes toward the real cross, and I finally saw it.

After having gone through this process, I have to say that most of my preconceived notions about marijuana have flown straight out the window. I haven't turned into a mellow stoner. I haven't begun to slide slopes slippery enough to find myself in gutters with track marks lining my arms.

I have learned, however, that suffering from a debilitating medical condition gets all the more frustrating when all the doctors and specialists in the world tell you that they can't help you.

I have learned that however cliche the phrase *God works in mysterious ways* is, that He certainly worked a mystery in me.

Now, when I wonder whether it's okay for me (or other Christians, for that matter), to consider myself "pro-pot," I tend to live in the kind of tension that I find in the Bible, and in the whole of the Christian experience.

We want definitive answers for controversial conversations, but definitive answers often evade us.

What was once so black and white might not be as clear-cut as it seemed. Perhaps there is room for color in the margins.

I'm not going to be anyone's ticket to ride or their permission slip. I'm fully aware of the fact that my experience isn't a universal one, but neither, it seems, is the image of madness and debauchery that so haunted every association with cannabis up until this point in my life.

Besides, as I said, I've had a front row ticket to the mysterious ways God works lately. I'm a slow learner, but I sometimes wonder…wouldn't it be just like Him to give us a life-changing plant, and wouldn't it be just like us to call it a weed?

*Watch Craig expand on this chapter by scanning the QR code below.

Chapter 8 – My Sunday Best (And All the Hurt Beneath It)

[March 22, 2018]

"It is far easier to be angry than vulnerable."

And I feel like I'm angry all of the time.

Not long ago, I discovered a book titled *How We Love by Milan and Kay Yerkovich*. It's probably the best marriage resource I've ever come across – not just for understanding your spouse, but for understanding *yourself*.

I've learned so much about myself lately. It hurts as much as it excites me.

When I discovered the Enneagram, it helped me to figure out who I am, how I function, how my brain works, and how it works in conjunction with other people like friends, family, and co-workers.

But the *How We Love* stuff-it's telling me more about the root of who I am, *why I am*.

What is the root of all of this anger?

Nolan lied to me a couple of weeks ago. I was furious. I felt *so* betrayed. I laid awake in bed that night dreaming about what I could do to get back at him-my son. I justified thoughts of retaliation by telling myself that he needed to learn a lesson. It's not *punishment*; it's *parenting*. But at the end of the day, I was thinking far more like someone who wanted an eye for an eye that I was willing to turn the other cheek, let alone *raise up a child in the way that he should go*. I wanted him to feel what I felt.

I could smash his phone in front of him, I thought. After all, I discovered the truth there. I legitimately thought it would be a good idea to use a hammer to smash his phone into pieces while he looked on. The problem was, I didn't know where we kept the toolbox, and I ended up doubting that Jeanette would think it as great an idea as I did if I asked her to find the hammer for me.

So then I thought, *I could avoid her altogether! I could throw his phone in the ocean!*

After a few hours of fuming, a question crossed my mind: *Do I want to create this kind of memory for my son to weep over when he's my age, thinking back on how angry and punitive a person his father was?*

What was it about *this* situation that had me so furious at Nolan? Did it even have anything to do with him at all?

I started crying.

I didn't stop for about an hour.

When I was a kid, anger was my dad's first response to everything. When I lied to him, he never tried to show me the importance of the truth; he just started screaming. I'm not sure what it was about his upbringing that made him feel so out of control, but I think that my faults made him feel like a failure. He carried that identity around everywhere he went, and into every aspect of his life.

I don't know if he knew how to feel anything other than anger, or if it was just too difficult – as I've discovered, myself – to be vulnerable.

But I'm trying.

When Nolan lied to me, I heard all the lies that my best friends had told me throughout the past couple of years – the ones that hurt the most – and I responded in the only way I've ever been taught:

Misplaced anger is residual pain that someone else inflicted upon me.

I'm still carrying it around. I thought I dealt with it. I thought it was resolved.

Think again, Craig.

Considering it now, it's incredible how much our *un-and-subconscious* "knowing" plays out in real life before we realize that it has anything to do with us.

A couple of months prior, I was struck with the idea that XXXchurch shouldn't be starting conversations about pornography with the issue of addiction, itself, but with the emotions that fuel dependency, and the pain beneath them.

I'm usually the first one to be skeptical of claims like this, but as I sat in prayer one day, I felt as though the Lord gave me one specific word to focus on for our ministry's audience:

Resentment.

At the time, I didn't think it had anything to do with *me*.

Think again, Craig.

Over the past couple of years, our ministry has begun to use the language of "medication" over and above "addiction" when it comes to helping people move beyond their unwanted use of pornography.

What "illness" are you self-medicating with pornography? What wound is this escape helping you assuage?

Not only do those questions completely reframe the conversation, but they get past the shame-filling, *"When's the last time you jacked off to your computer screen?"* condemnations, and spark empathy and compassion.

They get to the root.

So, as it seems that I am stuck with this *Craig Brain*, I made a project of Resentment. <u>We built a website</u>, hosted an event, made it into a video series, filmed it, integrated it into our current XXXchurch course trajectory, developed workbooks, and curriculum.

We wanted to talk about how pornography and other unwanted sexual behavior are ways of putting a band-aid on top of the real problem – the actual trigger, or pain point.

Sure, porn's a problem, but it seems as though we're always talking too much about the things that we run *to*, and not enough about the things that we run *from*.

We'd been asking people surface-level questions and beating our heads against a wall when they – who genuinely desire to move beyond addiction – remain unchanged by platitudes and behavior modification.

A tree can't help but grow out of the seed that gave birth to it. And what did Jesus have to say about the seed that must die to bear fruit?

My friend told me about a song lyric: *"If there's blood on the roots, then there's blood on the branches."* Those words seem pretty applicable here.

I, too, have resentments that I have been harboring, roots to deal with and pain that needs healing if I am ever to let go of the anger that drives me to sin.

I saw my dad cry twice in my life. Once was in Middleton, Ohio. I took him to the house that he grew up in, and the current homeowners were kind enough to let us have a look around. We found the blueprints to his childhood home – complete with his name written on them – and he stood in his old room, and he started to cry.

That memory will never leave me.

What I saw in him, as a sixty-eight-year-old man, was the child beneath his fury. I saw the pain. I saw why he was stuck in all of the anger that I received from him as a kid. I saw the origin story.

We've got to go deeper.

We've got to start asking *why?*

Why are we the way that we are? Why am *I* the way that I am?

Why are you?

Why do I get angry instead of vulnerable? Why is it that I defer to seeing that kind of emotional exposure as weakness, like the day my friend David began to cry in my presence, and I didn't know how to handle him?

And once we've uncovered the *why*, how do any of us start to heal?

I'm convinced it has something to do with beginning to learn to *feel*.

Levi turned me on to a book called *Emotionally Healthy Spirituality*. In it, author David Scazzero writes:

To feel is to be human. To minimize or deny what we feel is a distortion of what it means to be image bearers of our

*personal God. To the degree that we are unable to express
our emotions, we remain impaired in our ability to love
God, others, and ourselves well. To cut them out of our
spirituality is to slice off a part of our humanity.*

That's all well and good, but how can I start? How do
permit myself to feel? How do I express anything other than
the anger that comes so naturally to me?

I think we have to start with putting in the hard work of
understanding ourselves. How else will we ever know what
we need unless we have indeed found out who we are?

Am I an angry person? Is that my identity? Or have I
merely learned that anger is my default reaction because it
is easier to express than whatever lies beneath, or acts as a
salve atop the pain that I'm too scared to come to grips
with?

I've come to learn that I need comfort just as much as any
friend, family, or audience member I've ever sought to
serve, but *acknowledging* that need – let alone asking for
and receiving comfort – means accepting the pain
underneath.

That's the hardest part for me. That's the challenge.

But maybe the payoff is worth it.

After all, I did decide that this was going to be a year of
"less."

Could I be *less* angry? Could I experience *less* stress? Could I have *fewer* blow-ups that my family has to endure? Could I have *fewer* headaches? Could I have *less* chance of the heart attack that my friend Cameron just had?

What would be the best part? What would *less* give me – *us* – more of?

Could I receive the comfort I never did as a kid? Could that child still be saved?

Could you and yours?

Could our spouses comfort us? Could we comfort them?

Could the Lord?

Could we pay that comfort forward to our children and break the curses passed down for generations before us?

Could my kids grow up with an emotionally healthy spirituality? Could they grow to say that they felt secure in our home? That they saw parents willing to go through the sometimes-excruciating-but-wholly-worth-it work of understanding themselves, and one another, and are better equipped for this life because of it?

Could we trust God enough to relinquish control – to take a back seat to the work that I have to believe He is doing in us – and plead grace from the one who also knows what it is like to suffer and prevail?

The one who suffered and prevails on our behalf?

The one who authors and completes the work that he has started?

Now God has us where he wants us, with all the time in this world and the next to shower grace and kindness upon us in Christ Jesus. Saving is all his idea, and all his work. All we do is trust him enough to let him do it. It's God's gift from start to finish! We don't play the major role. If we did, we'd probably go around bragging that we'd done the whole thing! No, we neither make nor save ourselves. God does both the making and saving. He creates each of us by Christ Jesus to join him in the work he does, the good work he has gotten ready for us to do, work we had better be doing. – Eph. 2:2-7

I have hope.

For you and me.

It's going to take work and time, but it's going to happen. Life, it seems, tends to force itself upon us one way or the other, no matter what. May as well start now.

There are a lot of hurts to heal under our Sunday best.

*Watch Craig expand more on this chapter by scanning the QR code below.

Chapter 9 – My Nine Questions (Who Do You Listen To?)

[May 5, 2018]

I love to learn. I suck at reading fiction, but I am willing to bet that I've already read your favorite book on business or self-improvement.

Lately, I've been loving learning about myself. It's amazing how much a forty-three-year-old man *hasn't known* about himself up until this point in life – whether it relates to family and relationships, or business and occupation, or *whatever*.

College never taught me much about any of it. I don't believe in college.

I mean, I *believe* in college as a thing that exists – like a tree or something – but I don't think that college is worth the price you pay for it. Not unless you want to be a doctor or go into some profession that warrants that kind of niche expertise.

I saw a guy post something on Twitter the other day who said, *"YouTube is a college for free."*

That's probably an overstatement, but in our day and age, I do think that one can just as easily create her version of a trade school. She does that by following the experts who are teaching whatever she wants to learn, directly – maybe buying their e-courses and learning specifically about how to make her passions sustainable – without all the absurd prices of general education indebting people to the system.

Of course, my daughter wants to go to college because - as an Enneagram No. 1 - *it's the right way to do it.* So, despite what I think, God may decide to giggle and give me that thorn in the flesh.

Anyway, I'm getting off on a tangent that <u>I've already written about</u>, but the point is this:

Who do you listen to? Who do you learn from?

And not *only* when it comes to education specific to schooling, or what you do, or want to do.

What about *who you are?*

I've heard an author say that most people end up becoming more Human *Do*ings than Human Beings. This is the kind of education I've been most excited about lately, and it's a lot more about *who I am than what I do.*

Most people I know are learning about or working on a lot of what they're doing, but very few are invested in self-awareness or – if they somehow have *that* – doing anything about what they know.

They say that college is supposed to prepare you for life. Maybe that's another reason I'm skeptical. I went to college, but most of what I've learned has been self-taught and tested through trial and error, and over the past couple of years, I've begun to invest more in various types of atypical education, like people I trust.

I've paid for classes to learn from the best in the fields applicable to my business - copywriting, Facebook advertising, product launch formulas-you name it.

I've also paid for more counseling and therapy – in various forms (personal, marital, familial, spiritual, etc.) – than ever before.

I joined Jeff Walker's Platinum Plus Mastermind group so that I could replace *"trial and error"* with *"tried and true."* It's funny, I bought in for business, and though it has undoubtedly been helpful there, the invaluable lessons I've learned have had far more to do with family, faithfulness to them and the life we want to build and live together.

Years ago, <u>my friend Drew Melton</u> decided to start paying for a life-and-business coach. It completely transformed his world.

Over the years, I've come to realize that I, too, have become an expert (of sorts) in my field of work. For some reason, that feels like an embarrassingly egoic statement to make, but I'm only paying forward the words of other people in my life who have helped me accept it as true.

When I consider it, I do suppose that I have become a go-to guy for answers to questions that my friends have, especially – it seems – when related to business and family.

Last year, I applied for a position at a life-coaching firm. I love helping people fix problems and move past barriers in their lives, and had been a sort-of coach for a handful of friends for a while by that time, anyway. I was curious about what "going official" was all about. I wanted to try it. See what the process was like. See if I could be an educator, of sorts, in this kind of one-on-one, *licensed-stamp-of-approval* world. See if I'd like it at all.

It turns out; I didn't. It wasn't for me, but I'm glad I tried. Had I not explored the possibility, I would have missed out on one of the single-most impactful exercises I've ever undertaken in my life.

As a part of the application process, I was required to send a list of nine questions to a minimum of five friends or family members who I trust the most, and ask them for honest answers:

1. Why do you think I will make a good coach?
2. What do you see as my greatest challenges in becoming a powerful coach?
3. How could I get in my own way?
4. How would you rate my integrity?
5. Do you trust me?
6. Tell about a time I have hurt you or you have been frustrated or disappointed with me?
7. When have you seen me at my best?

8. My worst?
9. If you could wave a magic wand what would you want to see happen in my life that isn't currently happening?

To say that asking these questions – let alone reading the answers – was a vulnerable process is an understatement. It didn't take long to realize how invasive the responses might feel. Nevertheless, I paid them forward and – knowing how intimidating it might be for some of my friends-and-family members to respond truthfully – promised that my feelings would not be hurt by whatever they had to say.

I'm Michael Scott. Roast me, Dunder Mifflin.

What follows is a summary of what I learned, specific to each question asked.

1. **Why will I make a good coach?**

   I want to see people succeed – to see their dreams come true – and will do what I can to make sure that it happens. I can see the problem – whatever is holding someone back from success – very quickly, and I won't bullshit them about what needs to change. I take a big-picture perspective and cut straight to the point, challenging people to think outside the box and see what they might not currently be able to.

2. **What are my greatest challenges in becoming a powerful coach?**

By far, the most consistent feedback I received from everyone on this question was concerning impatience (which includes unclear communication), and a lack of empathy. It makes sense, and is – to me – a perfect example of the adage: *"Your greatest strengths are your greatest weaknesses."* The positive side of fixing problems quickly is, well, problems quickly get fixed. But not everyone works like me, and it comes across negatively when I see where people "should be," and get frustrated when it takes them too long to get there (whatever "too long" means). When it comes to empathy, I find it difficult to put myself in someone else's shoes. Sometimes, that leads to generalizing or misunderstanding the problem at hand and coming across as insensitive or dismissive.

3. **How can I get in my own way?**

The responses here were a bit more varied, but what stood out most to me were the descriptions *intimidating* and *lack of compassion*. That sucks to hear. I place a high premium on clear-cut, no-nonsense answers. I know I'm opinionated, too, which isn't inherently wrong, but if I think something or someone is *pathetic,* for instance, I could also stand to figure out a better word for expressing it.

4. **Am I a person of integrity?**

Yes. Flying colors, unanimously. So, that's encouraging.

5. **Am I trustworthy?**

Yes across the board.

6. **When have I hurt or disappointed my friends and family?**

These responses sucked to read. I know I'm nowhere near perfect, but asking for straight, specific answers to a question like this is hard. I suppose they come as no surprise, especially as I learn more and more about myself. I place too much pressure on my wife – spiritually, emotionally, relationally. I publicly berated a coworker and left him feeling incompetent. I dropped a relationship when I felt like it wasn't worth fighting for. I've joked at other people's expense. I've made dumb decisions and justified them instead of humbling myself and apologizing.

7. **When am I at my best?**

It's funny; this one seems to have the most to do with *presence* and *leadership*, particularly in a fatherly role (though it applies to both family and business). My wife told me that "it is has done wonders for our family to see you breathe and be present." Nearly everyone had something to say about the way that they've seen my anxiety lessening, and my ability to lead well increasing because of it, so nearly all of the "best times" are more recent experiences. That's encouraging and feels progressive like it will continue.

8. When am I at my worst?

Unfortunately, I received almost identical feedback from everyone in response to this question, all related to the way that I handle conflict. Words like "belittling," "insulting," and "intimidating" are *not* adjectives that a boss, father or husband wants to be described by, and although "playing the victim" – I suppose – makes sense in conjunction with the rest, it's equally disheartening. Coming face-to-face with your inconsistencies (or, your less-than-helpful consistencies) isn't comfortable, especially when every person you ask raises their hand in unanimous assent to that ugliness.

9. What would people make happen in my life that they don't currently see if they could wave a magic wand and see it appear?

I think the gist of these responses can be summarized by the same words people used to describe me at my best: *when I slow down*. My wife straight up said just that, whereas others had more nuanced ways of getting there. For example: "strategize instead of quick-starting everything."

I've got to slow down to do that. "Delegate tasks." As someone who is used to wearing every hat, I've got to take them all off (slow down) for long enough to know what or how to delegate, and then trust whoever takes over enough to *slow down*.

Sitting with everyone's responses at the end of this exercise was an eye-opening experience equal to any other form of education I've previously received. Here, laid out in front of me, was a series of answers from my closest friends and family about *who I am* and *how I function*.

When I say "eye-opening," it's not necessary to infer that I discovered something new, but rather: what I know is now confirmed. Bluntly, blatantly and unavoidable. There is even unanimity in the feedback, so I can't argue my way out of the discomfort, and now that all of these people know I'm in the process of understanding myself and progressing where change is needed, the question becomes:

What am I going to do about it?

After all, information is not synonymous with transformation.

When I switched glasses, so to speak, and began to look at all of this feedback through a pragmatic lens, I was able to come to concrete conclusions and start to implement change.

Practically, when it comes to my weaknesses:

- If people are telling me that I suck at communication over text and email, I'm going to start using Voxer – a voice messaging, walkie-talkie style app – and give them more context that way.

- If people are telling me that I am dismissive in our conversations because I've overbooked phone calls and meeting times for the day, then I'm going to start using Calendly to make sure that I am available and that they feel more appreciated, and less like a task box that needs checking off.

- An addendum to the above; it's great that I have a calendar system set up for phone calls, but what boundaries should I place on that? When and on what days those calls should take place?

- If I lack empathy, then I want to surround myself with people who are better at it and can help me say what I mean to. I hired Levi to help me with most everything – including what you're reading right now – because he's the best empathetic writer I know, and when he did this "Nine Questions" challenge, everyone responded the same.

- If I'm spread too thin, then I need to have some difficult conversations with people. I need to drop clients. I need to stop working on things – some of the perfectly fine and good things – that aren't my things. Like Greg McKeown says, "If it's not a hell yes, it's a no."

- If I'm overworking, then I'm probably not enjoying the life that I've created - and neither is my family. I need Sabbath. We need to rest. I'm not going to be good at what I am good at without the rest necessary to fuel my work. I need to create healthy rhythms to function inside of.

- If I tend only to change when life forces it upon me, then how can I learn to ask people for feedback before it gets so bad that we're devastated by it? Before my wife comes to me and says, "I refuse to live another twenty years like this. Change, or I'm out."

- If I'm not good at details, but Jeanette needs them to function, then how can we learn to lean into one another's strengths and work in complementary ways rather than feeling as though we're just taking on one another's shit leftovers, and things the other doesn't want to do?

On the flipside, this questionnaire also helped me confidently acknowledge my strengths. It became more comfortable for me to make these changes because I now have the affirmation of those who know me best saying, *"Do it, Craig. Pursue the things that you've been too afraid of stepping out in faith for because you **are** good at them. Our responses are staring you in the face, cheering you on. There's no excuse to hold back anymore."*

So, I've done a lot since then, including *doing less, more* and what I've kept or started, *better.*

I know that I'm good at connecting people, so <u>I created a mastermind of my own</u>, with the people who I love and think stand to benefit from that connectivity, most. I built a room. (And, I made everyone in that room pay these questions forward to five of their friends and family members, too. The snowball is rolling.)

I created *betterandbetter.co*, as well, which has allowed me to outsource many of the hats that I'd previously wear myself for our ministry endeavors, as well as other projects we run as subcontracted through that entity.

I've led our family through considerable changes in the way that we function – many of which I've already written about, and more than I want to share with people moving forward.

The question is this:

How do you find clarity?

What are the things that you *shouldn't* be doing?

What are the things that you *should* be doing?

This was an unspeakably clarifying exercise for me, and after suggesting that many more of my friends, coworkers and family members risk the susceptibility it takes to do the same and ask others for feedback, I'd like to recommend it to you, as well.

Trust me, from someone who has been *personality-typed* as having the most challenging time with vulnerability; I promise it won't return void. Not a few of my friends have commented upon it as the single most beneficial thing they've ever done. For their businesses? Sure. But more-so for themselves, and every relationship within their proximity.

Of course, not everyone wants to be a life coach, so let me offer an edited, more applicable version of these questions for you to use as you wish. This series has replaced "coach" with "leader," as *everyone* – in one way or another – leads *someone*. If you need to hone it in even more specifically for your circumstance, feel free, but for now:

1. **Why do you think I am a good leader?**
2. **What do you see as my greatest challenges in my business?**
3. **How could I get in my own way?**
4. **How would you rate my integrity?**
5. **Do you trust me?**
6. **Tell about a time I have hurt you or you have been frustrated or disappointed with me?**
7. **When have you seen me at my best?**
8. **My worst?**
9. **If you could wave a magic wand, what would you want to see happen in my life that isn't currently happening?**

Two more things (and this is me working on my empathetic side):

First, I've realized – through frustration at past challenges given to friends and left unfulfilled – that not everyone has five people close enough to trust with questions like these. Whether that is truth or perception, I've got to be gracious there.

I'd encourage you not to get stuck on a number. Send the questions to a couple of people, or *one* person. Hell, Levi sent his list to his mom. No one's *not the right person* if they have your permission to speak into your life this way.

Brene Brown says that "courage starts with showing up and letting ourselves be seen," and that, "vulnerability is the birthplace of love, belonging joy, courage, empathy, and creativity… our source of hope."

She also says that shame can't survive in an environment filled with understanding, and no matter how uneasy I was about the answers I might receive, I found that to be true, as well.

Healthy and authentic relationships, it seems, are built off of both the permission to be and the ability to receive things that are both tough and tender from one another. No matter how alone you may feel; *you aren't*. Maybe sharing these questions is an opportunity – a challenge, even – to risk the vulnerability necessary to start building the kinds of relationships you want to have in the first place.

Do it.

Oh, and finally: if you want to go to college; *whatever*.

Craig

*Watch Craig expand more on this chapter by scanning the QR code below.

Chapter 10 – Traditions & Staycations (You Pick up the Tab)

[August 20, 2018]

Our family hasn't ever gone *all-in* on Christmas. Up until recently, we haven't had specific traditions that we look forward to each year. We never told our kids about Santa or entertained the mythologies that many parents do, and gifts – though we still gave them – were never the crux of our holiday season.

I guess I'm not sure why December 25th always came and went without the luster that the rest of our world ascribes to it – at least, in the *accumulation-of-stuff* sense of the word "luster" (which doesn't hold much shine for our family). My wife grew up in a home that was crazy about Christmas, but none of them celebrated Jesus, so they missed the point. It was all gifts and niceties, and I think it burnt Jeanette out.

That said, we don't have a ton of annual go-to set in stone - whatever holiday we happen to be talking about. We try to spend Thanksgiving considering someone in need, and how we might be able to help them, but that's about it. (And before I get slammed as a *humble-braggart* – I'm more than happy to be an arrogant bastard on my own, without any pretense, thank you very much. It's just that this does so happen to be something that we try to do consistently.)

A few years ago, though, Jeanette and I decided to give our best shot at a new Christmas tradition.

We wanted to figure out how we could turn a holiday that had somehow become all about *getting* and *things* into *giving* and *experiences*.

I experimented with this idea a couple of times before when Nolan and Elise were young. They *weren't as excited about it as I was*. Not at first. I remember staying up on Christmas Eve with the idea that they could take a trip with me the following year. I was traveling a lot at the time. I wrote a note that said, "*One free trip with dad...,*" and dropped it in each of their stockings.

When they woke up the following morning, they were about as enthusiastic at the "*fun with dad*" ahead of them as they were about the lack of dolls and robots in their hands.

But then, the following year, *after* having joined me on the trip of their choosing, both said that they wanted *more* trips with dad. We bumped it up to two the following year. I, of course, *loved* their company, and Christmas ended up providing our family with a series of "gifts" to look forward to throughout the months ahead.

A couple of years ago, Jeanette and I decided to follow suit. The kids – now eleven and fourteen years old – could still buy presents if they wanted to, but we had to gift them *and* one another with something experiential.

That year, Jeanette got me a night at the Beverly Hills Hotel. People always give me shit for preferring a beautiful room over a hiking trail, but my wife knows me, and her gift came complete with a great atmosphere, great music, great food, great s-

Well, anyway.

She took Nolan to the Rose Bowl and – knowing how much he loves shopping – some of his favorite stores in Downtown LA, where he was allowed to pick out something for himself (on her dime).

She took Elise to see an *Aladdin* play in downtown LA, they stayed at the W Hotel, they spent the whole day together (and, Elise got a massage) and then ended it with dinner together that evening.

I took Jeanette to Waco so that she could visit Magnolia Farms. She loves following Chip and Joanna, and always tuned into their show *Fixer Upper* when it was still playing on HGTV. We all went as a family together and took a tour of their beautiful, mid-Texas world.

I bought four tickets to Coachella Music Festival for Nolan – one for the both of us, and two for our friends. Nolan is so artistic and creative. He loves music and fashion –, especially streetwear. What better place to experience both?

Elise and I drove up the coast of California headed to a dance convention in Monterey. We ended up at the aquarium beforehand. We spent that day and weekend together doing the things that she cares about.

Throughout our planning, we began to joke about how funny it would be to create *the worst* experience for one another.

I could make Elise have a *Fast & Furious* movie marathon with me, or make Jeanette a keynote speaker at a last-minute conference event. We could force Nolan to shop at Gap. They could make me watch a Travis Scott performance on repeat for seven hours.

We'd all hate one another.

It was all fun and games, but insightful in its own right.

These gifts provided us *not only* with an opportunity to create fun memories together but challenged us on how well we know one another in the first place. After all, if the point is to *gift an experience*, well it had better be an experience that *feels* like a gift. It would have been quite a different thing if I took Jeanette to the hotel *I* love for *her* present. That'd have been a gift for me on her behalf.

Gift giving – whether in the traditional sense or in our creating an experience for one another – requires self-forgetfulness, and genuine thought invested into what the other members of our family enjoy.

A gift becomes special when someone moves beyond "*last-minute-lazy-ass*" and puts time, effort and self-sacrifice into giving specifically – lovingly – to another.

And so, our family finally created a Christmas tradition of our own.

Fast forward a bit and – *you'll never believe it* – I woke up with a new idea.

What if we were to reframe our concept of "family vacation" in a similar way? After all, we could stand in solidarity with our southern species celebrating *Christmas in July*!

So, as one (often) does, I called for a family meeting and announced that starting *tomorrow* (yes, tomorrow – I'm a fast mover, remember?), the Gross's are going to begin a family staycation.

Here are the rules:

1. Each person must pick another member of the family, and then we're going to spend the next couple of hours planning out *their special day*, which we will all participate in, together.
2. *You* have to pay for the experience you want to provide.
    - Spend whatever amount you want, or spend nothing at all.
    - If you need help with flights, hotel points, etc., ask Dad to spot you.
    - Someone figure out what the hell to do with the dog.

3. We don't tell one another what we have planned until the night before our turn, when we sit down and share it with the family.

Here's what our week turned into:

Nolan picked me. He began the morning by gifting the family with Acai Banzai Bowls and Nitro-Brew Starbucks Coffee from the market down the street – both of which I love and buy way too often. Then he bought me a massage at the spa around the corner from our place – three to four hours of "me-time" to relax – before taking the family to an Ed Sheeran concert at the Rose Bowl that night. Even though Ed Sheeran isn't my favorite artist in the world, Nolan knows how much I love live music, and we've always been able to bond over it. It was the perfect day.

Jeanette picked Nolan. She took the family to Sidecar Donuts (Nolan's favorite and, *for your information,* the best in the world), all the cool shopping spots (where, similarly as before, he was able to choose an item that she covered), lunch, an afternoon at the beach, and then a "guy movie" that night that Elise absolutely hated.

Elise picked Jeanette. Because this mom and daughter are also best friends, this was the perfect pick for Elise. She purchased a manicure and pedicure for the family, dropping over one-hundred bucks at Happy Nails. Later that day, she gave us nap time, took us out to dinner, and treated everyone to a Broadway play that was in town – *The Waitress* – which Jeanette had been looking forward to seeing.

I picked Elise. Even though I swore I'd never step foot inside of Disneyland until I became a grandfather, Elise loves the place, and I learned – like Justin Bieber – *never* to say "never." After our family piled into the van, I picked up Elise's friends and drove us all to *The Happiest Place On Earth* (still skeptical, but...). We checked into Disney's Grand Californian Hotel, and *I spent all day in the Magic Kingdom,* which completely freaked her out, and – I think – meant a lot, mainly because of my past stubbornness about the whole ordeal.

The *Gross Staycation* was one of the best weeks we've ever experienced, not just because of what we did, but because we did it together, and we were challenged to serve one another, albeit in ways that proved fun for the whole family.

The experiment also gave us, as parents, a way to challenge our children's notions about value, and generosity, and what is truly important.

For example, Elise, at first, had a difficult time deliberating over whether or not she should spend any money on the family for the day that was her responsibility to plan for Jeanette. In the end, she decided to, thereby valuing people over dollars, and it was reciprocated to her when it was my turn to gift her with our day at Disney. The point *is not* that every gift or experience requires spending an excessive amount of money, but I do think my daughter would have had an internal problem that prevented her from truly enjoying *her day* had she not gone the extra mile beforehand on behalf of her mom.

How can you thoughtfully seek to deepen relationships between yourself and the ones you love the most?

If you are reading this as a parent, how can you develop these strengths – this *others-centeredness* – in your kids, and give them memories that they can look back on as beautiful when they're your age?

Ours is an example of an experiment that proved worthwhile. It might not be your cup of tea, but the point is to pay an idea forward. To get the wheels spinning.

Neither Jeanette nor myself had these kinds of experiences growing up, but neither did we have families that invested the nature of thought they require. That's not a demonization of our parents, it is merely to say that we want to cultivate a selfless and *others-centric* mentality in our *Gross* family, and because of it: love one another – and others beyond this unit – well.

The questions that I'd like to pay forward are these:

If you have a family, or – in their absence – if you've created an honorary one of your own, what can you do to bring everyone together in meaningful ways?

What kinds of traditions will you spearhead for your loved ones to cultivate a life-story defined by depth, generosity, selflessness, and genuine love for one another, which snowballs and extends into the world beyond your walls?

Good luck!

Craig

*Watch Craig expand more on this chapter by scanning the
QR code below.

Chapter 11 – The Gross Goods (Life over Revenue)

[January 29, 2018]

Years ago, Jeanette and I attended a marriage conference together. The weekend's theme was "family vision," and Jeanette came home asking me why we didn't have any.

That's not the way she asked it (but it is how I took it).

Regardless, a *vision* wasn't absent from our family, or parenting, or marriage. However, she was correct in that it wasn't clear. Although we had been intentional about working toward the hopes we have, our goals were relatively arbitrary. We had a general idea of what progress felt like, but nothing concrete about *what* we wanted, or *why*.

Enter: *The Gross Goods*.

The idea came to me as a manifestation of one of my favorite quotes: *"Live by design, rather than default."*

If we – as a family – were able to articulate our vision clearly, so would we be better able to understand what defines us? Our values would act as boundaries, filters determining what is essential, and what is not. They would act as motivators, spurring each of us into action and providing specificity on our journey together.

We would be able to make decisions based upon parameters that express what we hold dear, as opposed to a vague shrug of the shoulders, hoping that whatever we might do on any given day would somehow – magically – work itself out in our favor.

So, we put pen to paper and wrote out a list of eight categories that summarize what our family holds dear. Then we wrote subcategories beneath each, defining the whole of what we mean when we say we want to be – for example – *"good with God."* What does it mean to be good with God? Moreover, how do we put that into practice? How do we accomplish that goal?

Here, based upon our name, are *The Gross Goods*, along with a brief explanation about what each means *to* us, and *for* us, is what we came up with:

1. **GOD**.

    Church. We want to be committed to a local congregation and attend regularly. Additionally, Jeanette participates in a mid-week Bible study, and it's important for our kids to say yes and make room for youth events and retreats.

    Accountability. Vulnerability, transparency, and honesty are crucial when it comes to growth in our faith, and we want to surround ourselves with other believers who can ask us hard questions, and point us to Christ.

    Reading, studying and memorizing God's Word. Jeanette is on a three-year reading plan. I leave my

Bible out, which reminds me to read each day. We write verses we want to memorize on our refrigerator chalkboard and encourage our kids to be in the word themselves.

Meditation and prayer. The word "meditation" gets a bad rap but is deeply biblical. We all took meditation classes in an attempt to understand better how we can relax, focus and contemplate in God's presence. Physiologically, meditation helps with stress, our mental state, and overall health. That, combined with planned-and-spontaneous prayer time, should be a regular part of life.

Let others lead our kids. This one's for us, as parents. We're not spiritual gurus, and we're not the only ones who have value to offer our children. Often, others are much better at discipleship than us, and we have to be humble about it, and let them lead.

2. **MARRIAGE.**

Be intentional. Don't drift into auto-pilot. *Always* work on bettering our marriage. Don't neglect date night. Invest in one another's interests. Read marriage books. Go to marriage conferences. Listen to marriage podcasts and sermons. Talk more than we watch TV.

Keep growing (individually *and* together). Spiritually. Mentally. Emotionally. Read. Study. We have to surround ourselves with others who challenge and cheer us on. We shouldn't hide our emotions, and we should talk to the kids about who they are, and how to grow into emotional maturity as well.

Create marriage and family goals early on (even while dating). Oh, how I wish that we would have done this before now! It's never too late, but perhaps our kids – and others – can approach relationships with this in mind.`

No secrets. Full transparency. We will *always* tell the truth, and we all have access to one another's texts, emails, and internet search history.

Date for longer than you think you need to. Our kids should feel comfortable asking us what we believe. They know Jeanette, and I dated for close to four years before we were married. Dating is serious, and it's an opportunity to begin learning what marriage might entail. All of us know couples who ignored warnings, and it blew up in their faces; we will heed one another's advice.

Like one another (and what one another likes). Sometimes, *loving* one another is more natural than *liking* one another. Also, sometimes, we don't like what the other person likes. *Try*. That goes both ways, and every couple in every marriage has to figure it out. Most "big deals" are little things. Let them go, and remember what you *do like* about one another.

3. FAMILY

The four of us are all we have. We want to be close and like one another now and forever. We want to cultivate a family that our children and grandchildren will want to return to. Be kind, avoid infighting, look for and focus on what is positive in one another.

Find things that others in the family like, or are interested in learning more about. Find things that others in the family like, or are interested in learning more about. Every month, one member of the family gets to choose an activity or idea that the rest of us have to participate in. For example one time, someone decided that we weren't allowed to buy anything online. On top of that, we had to purge one item per week from our toy chest or closet and give it away to a person or charity. We encouraged one another to make the purge something that *felt* sacrificial (as opposed to a throw-away item). We want to remember that we already have everything that we could ever need, and generosity is important, even when it hurts. Another month, we had to learn to play poker. Another, we had to watch football each Sunday (you can guess who chose that activity).

Support one another in the activities we are involved in. We go to Elise's dance performances and recitals. We go to sporting events and cheer for each other. We ask about and show an interest in the things that others care about (whether or not *we* do ourselves).

Intentionality. A great family doesn't just happen. We stay on our kids about speaking kindly and positively to one another, assuming the best about the other, and considering activities that will help them bond, as opposed to drifting into their private worlds.

Experiences over gifts. For Christmas and birthdays, we're opting for *experiences* instead of gifts. As our kids get older, the connection gets harder, and considering what they love to *do* allows us to create opportunities to do it together. A great memory lives on for far longer than a great gift (which, inevitably, finds its way to Goodwill).

Circle time. This is related to intentionality. We want to sit down and ask one another questions – whatever the depth of interest is. This exercise teaches us how to ask good questions, creates incredible conversations, and helps the *asker* to understand the *responder's* heart.

Steal stuff from other great parents. This point explains itself, but to reiterate: we will not be shy about learning what we don't know from others who have helped to give, and wisdom to offer.

4. FRIENDS

Accountability. People need people. Our relationships will only grow and deepen through vulnerability, openness, and the creation of opportunities to receive and extend constructive criticism, prayer, and support.

Intentionality. Again, purposefulness is key. If you want better friends, *be a better friend.* Call people. Schedule them in. Hangouts don't happen by magic, and friendship takes work.

Talk > Text. How's about a *real life* friendship? Pick up the phone, or meet in person.

Serve. We want to use our time and resources to be generous with our friends.

You are who your friends are, and vice versa. You are who your friends are, and vice versa. Positivity begets positivity, and the same goes for the negative. It is said that we are the average of the five people we spend the most time with. Be aware of who those people are.

Run with people who run faster than you. Our family wants to surround ourselves with people who are pushing us further, encouraging us to pick up the pace and challenging our stride.

We will always have people at our house. We will always have people at our house. We want ours to be a home that welcomes *all* people, whether it's for a half hour or a whole night.

No selfie sticks. This one is hyperbolic because I think we have owned a selfie stick, but the point is that – usually – everyone's favorite subject is themselves. We want to learn about, ask questions and listen to others. God gave us two ears and one mouth for a reason!

Knowing people (and knowing yourself) is more important than knowing *stuff*. Period.

5. **HEALTH**

Be Active. Whatever that looks like do it four to five times per week. Our family likes Orange Theory Fitness, Hot Yoga and Egoscue. There's a great, free gym twenty feet away from our apartment and included in our living plan, so use it!

Eat well and moderately. Need we say more?

Go to the doctor for yearly or bi-yearly checkups. Keep notes about your medical health history, so when you are asked at the doctor, you know what you are allergic to, when your last period was, that you are anemic, what kind of vitamins you take, etc.

Go to the doctor when you are sick. Don't wait it out or put it off. You have nothing if you don't have your health, and we've been privileged to be able to go-so, *go.*

Know how to cook healthy, balanced meals. We try to teach cooking lessons to our kids in the summer when time allows.

Know how to order at a restaurant. Practice asking the server questions about the menu items, how things are prepared, and what your healthiest choices are. Just because we're eating out doesn't mean we're eating sloppily.

Practice moderation and self-control when it comes to eating sugary or unhealthy foods. And – for that matter – in every area of life.

Take care of our home. Learn to clean it properly; do the dishes, laundry, etc. Taking care of your living space will fall on you someday, you have to know how to take care of it because mom isn't going to be around forever to do it for you!

6. WORK

Find what you're gifted in and do it over and over. Maybe someday, you'll get paid to do it! Maybe someday, you'll get paid to do it! As a family, we took the KOLBE test, which is designed to reveal how one works best. We want to push one another to keep chipping away at the things that we thrive in, especially when it comes to our kids. Too many young people have *no clue* about what they want to do, let alone how to make a living doing it.

Never stop learning, and keep curiosity alive. Read. Watch YouTube videos. Seek the advice of others who are gifted in your skill set, and *NEVER* be afraid of asking questions. Asking questions is not a sign of weakness, but rather someone who is smart!

If you can, do what you love for work. If you can't, then work to afford yourself the time for what you love.

Find good people around your work/team. God is all about relationships. If you don't have good people around you – no matter what we're talking about in life – you will fail.

7. MONEY

Know how to save and spend.

Learn to make a budget. Practice discipline, and keep at it.

Understand the value of investment. Risk VS. Reward. We want our kids to learn what a 401(k) is, what age they should start putting money into it, what the rules are for the money in it and why they need to understand the long game (like penalties for early withdrawals, or the ramifications of divorce) and the benefits of having money set aside for the future.

Your time is money. It's worth every cent.

Be a learner. You're not the smartest person on the planet. Find someone who understand finances more than you do and be their student. Someday, you can be the teacher.

Be a generous giver. Cultivate a generous spirit. If there is a cause that you have a heart for, give to it. If a friend is having a slow month financially and you can buy them gas, do it. We pick up the tab when we go out with friends; we take cousins to concerts and Vegas without asking for a dime. Don't hold this over friends heads or think you need anything in return. Your generosity will spark generosity in them. God gave you all that you have, so share it, don't hoard it. At Christmas, we want to bless other families by providing gifts for them, and we've been doing it since our kids were old enough

to understand why. They put their own money into it
and lend suggestions for what our gifts should be.
Our memories – one of the best: giving a single
mom a car – is priceless, and will never be regretted.

Live on less than you make.

**Married couples are one, and so should their
bank account be.** We will be unified in everything,
including our financial lives.

**Tithe (to church or a para-ministry)
immediately.** Don't wait and don't stop. If you do,
it'll be exponentially harder to start again.

What do you want your life to look like? Make
proactive decisions with your money to make
whatever you want to happen – whether it's for your
wife to stay home with the kids, or saving money
for a vacation, etc. – *happen*.

8. FUN

Work hard, play hard.

"If it's not a *hell yes*, it's a no."

Write out your bucket list. Fulfill it.

Travel. Visit people that live far away.

It's okay to have and spend money on things without feeling bad about it. Fantasy football, Disneyland passes, etc.

Have hobbies and engage them frequently.

Have to have something to look forward to. Otherwise, life becomes mundane.

Value people over things, and use things for people. Use *stuff* strategically. When I travel for work, I want to bring one or all of my family members with me, and I want to add an extra day to the trip so that I can treat them to something fun. My work has allowed for almost every single one of our family's travel experiences – throughout the United States and beyond – but each of them has been about far more than work.

It took our family a while to develop these categories, but now that we've completed this "organizational process," we have points of reference from which to function, and these *Gross Goods* have been *very good* for us (to say the least).

What about you?

Do any of our new, family "pillars" inspire what yours could look like with a bit of thought and intentionality given to the values you hold, and the dreams you have?

Feel free to steal them.

That's what we did for plenty of these ideas, and it's not a bad time to be a thief (primarily when the door is held open in invitation).

A friend of mine, Donald Miller, once wrote a book titled *A Million Miles In A Thousand Years*. In it, he talks about our lives as a story, and says that the only way we're going to be able to write a better one is to *be intentional about creating it.*

In his narrative, Miller articulates his desire to ride a bike across America. While *desire* is all well and good, that trek would have never happened unless he planned for it, trained for it, and began to pedal his way across one state, and then another, and then another.

Life – *a great life, a life worth living* – doesn't just fall in the laps of most people (and frankly, the people who's grass we envy on "the other side of the fence" are likely seeing more massive shades of brown on their lawn than we are, anyway).

It's not enough to *wish* and *want* – we have to turn those wants into goals – parameters, essentials – and *work* toward them. Work on them. Work within them. It's like the old saying goes, *"Don't just wish for it, work for it."*

All that to say, it's your turn, and our family already created a resource to help you get started. In addition to this chapter, if you visit www.thegrossgoods.com, you'll find a video of our whole family explaining *The Gross Goods* in greater detail, an audio download filled with more of the *how* and *why* behind our process, and PDF document recapping what I've written about here. Including a step-by-step guide on how to create a mission and vision for your family, what questions to ask one another, and how to get the ball rolling.

Do you want to live a great story? *Start writing it out.*

*Watch Craig expand more on this chapter by scanning the QR code below.

Chapter 12 – Thanks Dad (Now & Not Yet)

For most of my life, my dad and I had a next-to-no relationship at all, and I had completely given up on the possibility until – one day – he called me and said, "*Let's start over.*"

Don't get me wrong, my dad always *took care* of me. He got me a car when I turned sixteen. Even let me pick it out: a teal Geo Metro Convertible.

When I was a kid, he would come to my soccer and tennis matches, and he supported me through every crazy idea and adventure I had.

Once, I remember him coming home from San Diego with a gift for me – a pair of shoes from a new, up-and-coming company…*Vans*.

I remember going to Niners games at Candlestick growing up. He loved the 49ers so I, of course, began to root for the Raiders.

As I grew older, so did the distance between us. I knew he cared about me, and I even liked him, but we never seemed to talk – let alone connect – on much of anything.

When I was fourteen, my uncle – an uber-successful investor – sent his brother enough money to purchase a restaurant business. Dad opted for candy and soda machines instead. I remember all of his machines, stacked in our garage. The first place that wanted them was a local strip club in Sacramento – *The Embers*. Problem was, they wanted the prices doubled from fifty cents up to a dollar, and my dad had no idea how to do it.

I learned instead. I changed every single dial on every single one of those old machines.

We delivered them together one afternoon, and I experienced my first strip club at fourteen years old. Well, sort of. We went before opening hours. The dials in the machines lasted about a month before they'd break, so my dad made a habit of picking me up from school and driving me back to fix them all over again. We thought it was funny and my friends thought it was cool. I never told them the only thing I ever saw was a man with a gun at the door.

When I went to college, I left Sacramento. I would visit, though. I'd still go back to help Dad fix his machines. But I hated it. I *absolutely hated* fixing snack machines, but I did it because I loved him, and I knew that he had no one else who could help him do it.

Beyond my visits, though, we never interacted. My dad never called me. We didn't talk on the phone one time between the day I left for college until I was thirty-one years old. I would talk to my mom, and she became our middleman, passing messages back and forth between us.

One day, the phone rang and it *was* my dad. I immediately assumed someone died. I was waiting for the news, praying it wasn't my grandma, who – out of everyone in my family – I had the best relationship with.

My dad spoke, *"I had a hip replacement and have been on my back for a week. I've had a lot of time to think. Can we let bygones be bygones and start over?"*

Before asking him what in the hell "bygones" were, I just said yes. He wanted to start over. What did that mean? Only six months prior, I told Jeanette that I wished I could travel with my dad, or enjoy time with him now that had sold the vending machine business and retired, but by that point, I had given up.

We spent a few minutes on the phone, and when I told Jeanette, she asked what I was planning to do.

I said, "I have to speak in Colorado soon… I am going to invite my dad to come."

He said yes.

I was nervous. What would we do? What would we talk about? How uncomfortable might it be to share a hotel room together?

What would he think of me?

The trip was amazing. We spent five days in *Colorful Colorado* together. We went to the mountains, the movies, and Red Lobster. Several times, he simply sat quietly and listened to me speak. I found out that my dad grew up in Ohio. I don't know how I lived an entire life without knowing that, up until that point, I never did know much about him. I guess it explains why he liked the Cincinnati Reds. He told me about his dad passing away when he was a young man. I enjoyed his company. I felt as though we were starting down a road that I never even risked imagining we'd walk together.

I take for granted the travel that my job affords me. Most people I know don't frequent airports as often as I do. They don't get to explore the world beyond their own. In all his life, my dad had never been to Colorado.

I started inviting him along with me more often.

Our next trip was to Akron, Ohio. I had a speaking gig, and afterward, we visited the Football Hall of Fame. When he told me that he grew up in Ohio, I had the idea that I should take him back to his hometown. We drove toward Cincinnati, and I pulled up curbside to the house he grew up in before his family moved to the Bay Area when he was a preteen.

The house *his dad* built.

We knocked on the front door and explained who we were, merely asking the current homeowners if they'd allow us to walk through my father's memories.

Initially, the man who answered the door said no. But you know me…*"no" doesn't suffice* and he finally allowed us in. He even found my grandfather's blueprints, and my dad stood staring down at them in the living room of the house he grew up in – the house he used to call home – and shed a tear.

It was the first and only time I saw my father cry. He didn't shed many like I do today, but I saw it happen.

I can't count the memories we've made together since the day my phone rang 13 years ago, and I heard the voice of the man who made me on the other end, seeking reconciliation.

Orlando.

Lakers Vs. Celtics NBA Championship game… on Father's Day.

Agassi Vs. John Mcenroe tennis match.

Nolan's soccer game.

Elise's soccer game.

The Grand Canyon by helicopter.

Sacramento Kings games.

Las Vegas.

Alcatraz.

Porn Debates.

The Super Bowl.

And the last game we saw live in January 2012, the NFC playoff 49ers Vs. Packers game for our last game at Candlestick Park.

The events were fun, but they were never the point. We were reconciled.

We were friends.

My dad never owned a computer (let alone scoured the internet), and rarely used a cell phone. After each trip we took together, he would mail me a letter – handwritten in cursive on yellow or white lined paper.

I wish I would have saved all those letters now.

These years have been unbelievable.

My dad died this morning.

The last time he was able to walk was on our Super Bowl trip. His brother gifted us the tickets. We sat in the second row on the Giants' sideline and took in an amazing game together. I wrote to my uncle to thank him, and to suggest that he and my dad should reconnect. I told him that my dad's health seemed to be in decline, and that life is short, and that – especially after the years we'd been given the gift of experiencing – family problems were worth working through.

I never thought my dad's health would turn as quick as it did. We've had a couple of severe scares between then and now.

My dad was never what I'd call a "healthy" man. He used to own a Sizzler, so I think the decline must have begun with that one-sided toast they used to serve. (Maybe they still serve it? I do my best to avoid Sizzler.)

He worked for Burger King after that. Then Long John Silvers. Then Showbiz Pizza. Later, he started a company of his own... the vending machine business. His favorite digestibles – for as long as I can remember – were Coke Classic and ice cream.

He never cared about what anyone had to say about it. He had diabetes for thirty years. He had two stints and a pacemaker in his heart. He had Myasthenia Gravis – an autoimmune disease that weakens the muscles that make breathing possible. He had several blood clots.

Last Saturday, my family and I drove to Sacramento to watch *this year's* Super Bowl with him. This was the game we wished we could've seen in person, a year prior, but either way, the 49ers were in, and we settled for the television. My son, Nolan, was in a Super Bowl commercial that day, as well, so we cheered for him between cheering for the Niners.

My dad was living in his own apartment. By then, my folks had split up and – unable to care for himself any longer – he had hired a twenty-four-hour caretaker. That Sunday, she told me that he was bleeding internally and needed to go to the doctor. But my dad was stubborn. He thought he knew his body. He thought he'd live to be 87 years old. For some reason, that was the specific number he had in his head.

I knew he wouldn't go to the hospital willingly, but thought that if we could make it through the game, I could convince him.

He wasn't himself that day. He could still yell at the TV when the Niners failed to punch the ball through the end zone, but he wasn't himself. As soon as the game ended, I called 911 and fought with my dad until he was too weak to argue any longer, and took him into the ER.

He underwent a blood transfusion, and the doctors needed an extra day to discover where the bleeding was coming from. His body couldn't handle the scope, and one day turned into two. The following night, despite their best efforts to find a reason for the hemorrhaging, he suffered a heart attack.

Those days are a kind of a blur to me now. I drove my family back home to LA on Monday morning, while my dad was still in the hospital. That night, I flew back to Sacramento. On Tuesday, I flew to San Diego for a speaking engagement, then back again Wednesday morning.

Yeah. I'm confused just *writing* it out.

My dad was unconscious by the time I made it back that midweek. He couldn't open his eyes and couldn't hear me. I must have said *"Dad, it's Craig"* thirty times into his ear. No response.

I knew right then that he was gone.

I was mad at myself for getting on that flight to San Diego.

I had lunch with my mom. She said that after he had a heart attack, she and my sister were there. She said that my dad was scared and in pain – two words that I would have never used to describe him in all of his life – but that they were there, holding his hands.

She said, *"That night, I saw the man I married 44 years ago."*

My sister also commented on my dad's behavior. Neither of them has had a good relationship with him for years – nothing like the one we'd been able to create – and I had been praying for them as he neared his final days.

When my mom called me the night his heart finally broke, I was in a hotel room with my two best friends, but I was furious that I wasn't in the hospital room with my dad, and my mom and sister. It was the worst night of my life. In hindsight, I don't know that I would have had anything to give to him, but it sounds like he had something left to give to them.

Maybe those last hours weren't about me. I had the last six years of my dad's life with him, and they were a dream come true. Maybe those final hours were about my mom and sister. I'm thankful that they were able to spend them together with him.

Time is short.

Life is short.

If your relationships are broken – especially those in your family, especially those in your home – *go*. Do everything that you can to fix them. Don't wait for the other person to call you.

People say that God works in mysterious ways. Trite as that saying has become, it's true. Before my speaking engagement that fateful Tuesday night, I shared a meal with a friend I never thought I'd speak to again.

I called him to reconcile – just like my dad called me – and we agreed to start over.

In the end, Jesus is still making all things new. This is what the cross is all about. God is continuing to give us new mercies each and every morning, inviting us to join him in the work of restoration.

Don't wait another day. No one knows if tomorrow will come, and *now* is the only promise you have.

Shortly after my dad and I decided to start over, my wife decided to reach out to her father. Her mom moved away with her and her two brothers when she was one year old, and Jeanette hadn't heard from him since. She paid $49 for an internet search and found his address. She wrote him a letter and – months later – he responded. It didn't turn into the kind of relationship that I was able to experience, but her father met our kids, and the risk she took has lent itself toward healing for both of them.

My dad reached out to me.

My wife reached out to her father.

It has to start somewhere.

Broken families and relationships and all of the hurt and pain and days and weeks and months and years attached to them will only spread out into decades and lifetimes until someone says *enough is enough*.

Pick up the phone.

Make the call.

*Watch Craig expand more on this chapter by scanning the QR code below.

Chapter 13 – For Elise (You're my A-Team)

[February 15, 2019]

Elise,

Wow.

You did *amazing* tonight.

I know it was you because I felt tears flooding my eyes during a Beyonce song (and God knows it wasn't the music that moved me). I can't stand Beyonce or any of her overplayed, twenty-year-old songs that all the girls dance to.

Nevertheless, *you* were terrific.

Tonight was the first time that I've ever watched you dance and been able to connect with you. To understand you. To be *so excited* for you and then to be so *physically upset* when your troop didn't win.

If you want to know the truth, I stayed upset all the way back to my car and, well…I'm still kind of upset.

You know how competitive I can be. You've seen me coach enough soccer games to realize it doesn't always bode well for the bystanders (or the kids in the league). Tonight, I wanted to be like Abby Lee and hunt down whoever made the wrong call to tell them the way it should've been.

Do you remember the referee calling foul on us during the Pink Jelly Beans soccer season? It was the wrong call, and I challenged it, and I was right. I know soccer, so I know a bad call when I see one.

But I don't know dance.

I know how *every* sport scores *everything*.

But I don't know dance.

It's one-thirty in the morning, and I decided that *right now* is an excellent time to teach myself. That probably doesn't surprise you. I want to figure out how scores work, and who decides what the scores are, and what makes a dance the winner.

More than that, I want you to know that I want to know *not* because your team lost.

I want to know because you care about dance, and I want to care about dance because I care about you.

Last year, your mom started watching football with me. It was weird, but it has made our relationship that much more *fun*. I don't know that she made that decision for me but – if this makes sense – it did feel like one made *toward* me. She still likes the Rams over the Packers, but I can work on that.

She knows I care, and she has begun to care, too. The trip we took together for the Super Bowl this year was one of the best mini-vacations we've ever had together, and trust me – it had *nothing* to do with the game. People are actually saying it was the worst game *ever* as far as the Super Bowl is concerned.

It's not about the game or the sport, it's about the connection and it's about the people you get to make those memories with. I was happy I got to experience that with your mom.

Do you remember when I took my dad to the Super Bowl? The next year, right after we took our trip to Sacramento together – right after that year's Super Bowl – he died. When I think of football, I think of my dad. I know you think I just like sports, and while that's true, my love for them – and football, especially – has a lot more to do with him.

I'm telling you that, I think, as a way of explaining why Nolan and I go to so many football games together. He loves them – which I'm happy about – but also: I want him to experience with me what I wasn't able to with my dad until way later in life.

I didn't really like my dad when I was your age. Sports were the only topic of conversation that I seemed to be able to tolerate having with him, so I learned all about them to build that connection.

Well…all of them except for golf. I'm not sure why I never tried to understand golf, but I do remember that – two months after my dad died – I turned on the T.V. in our old

Pasadena house, found the biggest golf tournament in the world, and began to cry when some guy who I knew absolutely *nothing* about won his Master's championship title. Maybe it's too little too late, but I started to learn more about golf after that because it makes me feel connected to my dad. When I visited our friend Brannin last month, we went to one of the most famous golf courses in the world together, and I bought a sweater just because I *know* that my dad would've freaked out if he knew that I ever stepped foot on those greens.

All of that to say…

Tonight, I started researching dance.

I Googled, *"What makes dancing great?"* Some internet person's answer responded with "connectivity to the music" and "technical work."

Okay.

So…

You guys did better than anyone else at both of those things. Therefore, I can say with complete confidence – after one early morning spent doing some exemplary dance research – that you guys deserved to win tonight.

After I was convinced enough of that, I started watching dance videos. A couple of hours have gone by since I began my research, and the excitement of seeing you perform again tomorrow has left me sleepless. You dance in twelve hours, and I can't wait to cheer you on again.

You are stunning on that stage, Elise.

I know I kept telling you how cute you were earlier this evening, but you're growing into something more than cute, too – into *beauty*. Even Grandma sees it. I showed her the photo I took following your performance, and she said that it's nerve-racking to see you all grown up beneath those lights.

If I'm honest, that scares me, too. I am getting used to it (at least, a little bit) with Nolan, but it feels *way* different with you as my daughter. It's frightening. I can't help but think of all the boys who will be in love with you one day. The boys who are staring at you while you dance. The boys who will be knocking on our door all too soon, asking to take you out.

I want to protect you. I want to keep you young. I know you've wanted that for so long, too, but as much as I wish that it were possible, we can't stop time.

You wowed me on stage tonight. I keep thinking, *If I got teary-eyed to Beyonce, how in the world am I going to handle watching Elise dance solo – let alone to a song that I'm so deeply connected to? A song that has brought me through tremendous experiences – both high and low and deep and wide – during the past two years.*

At first, I thought I dove into all of this late-night research because of how upset the loss made me, but then I realized that none of this is about winning or losing, or judging, or right calls, or bad calls.

This is about me *loving* you. This is about wanting to connect with you. With your heart. With my beautiful girl.

Dancing…

Shows us who we are and who we want to be,
helps us find our own truth,
allows us to invest in something new, and to explore something new,
and is an expression of our humanness.

Whereas artists want to make a better place for people to heal,
dancers are encouraged to just be themselves.
When that "being" happens,
the audience can – in turn – feel themselves.

I read that tonight, and it is precisely what you helped me – an audience member – experience.

Thank you.

I know I've shown you the videos of Bon Iver's collaboration with T.U. Dance. It's part of why I suggested his song, *Creeks*, for your solo dance tomorrow. Justin Vernon, the vocalist, described why he wanted to team up with a troop for a project like that in the first place:

"I have never been moved by dance before. After seeing this dance troop, I saw real pain and real struggle and real redemption, and I didn't know bodies moving around to simple music could do that much to me."

He said that he loves and is comfortable playing music and guitar, but that he wanted to make something with this dance troop because watching the movement of their bodies makes him uncomfortable. It felt like he had to fight for it, and he did. He gave it everything he had, and it became something marvelous.

Justin believes that art connects people physically and emotionally and that whatever that way may be, it means something. Before that collaboration, he had only experienced that type of art through music – never through dance – and wondered what might happen if he stepped out of the way and gave the stage to the dancers. What would the audience be able to see inside of themselves? What would he?

I just watched all of his videos again – everything he and the troop made available online.

I tried to watch it with new eyes. I tried to understand the story the dancers were telling.

If I'm honest, I struggled a bit with that part. I kept getting confused and had to look up their explanations, detailing what it all meant.

In one interview, the troop's choreographer said that there is a *sense of community – a beautiful and hopeful message. A journey that inspires. One that is supposed to make you "feel" in a time where "feeling" is desperately needed.*

From my limited perspective, I can't say that I see all of that yet, but I am still moved by watching it happen. Over time, I hope I get better at understanding. Watching dance right now feels – to me – sort of how I imagine learning math might feel to you.

Maybe you can teach me.

You told me that tomorrow will be the first time you perform *Creeks* in front of an audience outside of your own mirrored reflection.

You told me that the other girls' choreography is better than yours.

You told me that you are nervous.

You told me girls are supposed to dance to songs sung by female vocalists.

You worried that you might forget something.

I have something to say, too, and I want you to hear it:

The connection that your dance holds with the music you've chosen is special. It sets you apart. It's why I sat you down and showed you the videos I showed you. It's why I asked you to choose from the sixteen songs I gave you because those songs tell such in-depth stories.

I've enjoyed music as much or more than sports (if you can believe it) ever since I was your age. Most of the connections that I hold to the songs that I love are birthed out of personal experiences that they have played the soundtrack to.

Often, I've put the music I enjoy into separate boxes. Work music. Workout music. Driving music. Praying music. Singing music. Creating music.

Bon Iver's music, however, seems to transcend them all. Justin's creativity stirs up so much emotion in me. It helps me *feel*. It even helped me realize that *I have something inside* to feel in the first place. He is my all-time favorite musician, ever. I've never listened, seen or felt more connected to an artist in my life.

You are deeply connected to your mother, and it is something special to see. To be honest, I am jealous of it. But not in a bad way. More of an inspiring way.

I do think that different types of bonds exist between fathers and sons and mothers and daughters, but *different doesn't mean lesser*. Mom and Nolan – and you and me – can have just as strong of a connection and relationship, no matter how different it looks.

Mom and I talk about these things a lot. We know that, as we all get older, it will become harder and harder to have

time with you. We've tried extremely hard to build a solid
foundation with you both – as a family and individually –
so that we aren't sitting here alone one day, when you're
our age, wishing you wanted to visit us. Neither of us has
ever had the kind of connection with our parents that we
believe we have we with you, and we wouldn't trade it for
the world.

I want us to keep building these connections. It's easier to
do when you're young. I know you're looking older and
more beautiful every day, but you're still thirteen…my dad
waited until I was thirty-three.

I refuse to wait that long.

So here I am. Let's dance together. Maybe our dance isn't
literal - I think I might step all over your toes, and God
knows I can't bend in half like you can - but our connection
can be.

Tomorrow, don't be nervous. Don't look for a mirror. Don't
worry about your friends. Don't worry about their dances.
Don't worry about how yours will compare. I'm as
competitive as anyone, but in the end, it doesn't really
matter.

Tomorrow, look for me. That's all. That's the connection
that I want you to have with this dance tomorrow.

I know it's not the song your teacher gave you. I know she
might not understand it. I don't expect her to. She did the
best that she could do, but in the end, I asked you to dance

out of the longing of my heart's desire to connect with you, and wondered what it might be like if we were both to combine something that we love, together.

You fulfilled my wish.

Thank you.

That's what this dance is about: *one step each of us is making toward the other*.

I know you're going to be amazing. I have never been so excited to see you dance, and I am so proud of you.

I asked Dave Tosti to come and watch with me. He's one of my best friends, and he was the first person I showed that Bon Iver /T.U. Dance video too, and he was so excited when I told him about your solo. His daughter dances, as well, and he knows how special this moment is. If I'm honest, Dave does a better job of connecting the dots I can't connect – of feeling the feelings I'm learning exist inside of me – and I wanted to invite him to see you perform because joy demands to be shared with other people, and I am overflowing with it toward you.

I might cry. It will be hard for me to hold it in, but even that is something new, and I'm glad that I'm finally learning how to let go. So, maybe this time, if I do start to cry, I won't hold back. We'll see what happens.

I can't wait to see it.

I can't wait to see you continue to grow. Continue to dream. Continue to tell us all the things that you are going to go. The places you want to live in. I can't wait until you finally get to visit Australia. I can't wait to see all of the dances that you will create and perform.

Elise, you are a gift to our family, and your friends, and this world.

You are a gift to me.

Tonight, before you fell asleep, you told me, *"Thank you for letting me dance at The Rage."*

You're welcome.

It's exactly where you should be. Seeing you grow and progress the way you have is worth every cent. Plus, you love it, and it's fun – and I love seeing that lived out in you.

It's three o'clock in the morning now, and before I stop writing, I need to tell you something: I don't know if I can go to the awards for *Creeks*.

I keep going back and forth in my mind, and I haven't made a decision yet, but I need to say *I'm not sure.*

I didn't ask you to do this dance to win a trophy.

You are the trophy, Elise.

I don't need you to bring one home, but I do know that both of us want it. I know you deserve it, too. I also know the judges don't understand our story.

This story…the one I wanted to write out for you here, tonight.

I thought, perhaps, spending the time to explain in more detail might help you understand my heart in it, too.

My heart is for you.

If the dots connect, and the lines between them add even more to your dance tomorrow, good. But beyond *anything* that has to do with winning or losing, I want *us* to be connected, and this dance has – for me, in some way – deepened our relationship more than I ever realized it could.

I hope that you will agree.

I love you Queeny!

Have fun up there. Be yourself.

Dad

P.S. This letter was written to – and only ever *for* – Elise. Sometimes, I worry that my family or friends will think these kinds of letters, once shared, were only ever those "for you (but really for me)" gifts. That's never been the case. Not for a single one of them. That said, though…

One of the coolest opportunities I've ever had was to be able to hand this letter to Justin Vernon, himself. He was getting into his vehicle one night following an intimate show that I attended. I gave him the letter and said, *"Thank you for helping me connect with my daughter through your music and her dance."* His face turned into one big-ass smile as he shook my hand and thanked *me* for flying all the way to his hometown to thank *him*.

I met Michael Jordan (my childhood hero) when I was fifteen years old. My kids have already met their favorite people in the world. Now that I'm forty-three years old, much of that childhood excitement escapes me… but I don't want it to. It was fun to shake the hand of a guy whose music has had a significant influence in my life. (I felt like a child, too. I literally hid in the ice-machine room of this hotel, waiting for Justin to get to his car, while my friend Matt kept a lookout to make sure I didn't get caught. We laughed like teenage boys who had just met the lead singer of their favorite band. Minus the "teenage" part, I guess that's true.) It was a night I'll never forget, and Justin's kindness, care and excitement about my story made a significant impact in my life.

P.S.S. My friend Matt (the one I mentioned above) loves celebrities. His camera roll is full of folder that TMZ would *love.* (That's an exaggeration, but I give him a hard time because he runs into more celebrities than anyone I know and seems to spot them everywhere.

After I handed the note to Justin, he left – we thought – for good. As it turned out, the night wasn't over, and he came back to the hotel later that night. He walked right into the restroom where, of course, Matt happened to be using the urinal. Matt didn't take a photo (thank God), but he did strike up a conversation, and – despite breaking *all* men's restroom rules – it ended with a midstream fist bump over the dividing wall.

Though Matt didn't have a letter for Justin, he always swore that, one day, he'd ask the man where all of his creativity comes from. I laughed as I saw them talking outside the bathroom following their "bonding experience," and Matt finally had his opportunity.

Justin answered, *"I don't know, just trust,"* which has since spawned countless conversations between Matt and me (and others) in the weeks that have followed.

That said, in an upcoming Craig Brain chapter / episode, I am going to take what that answer – and those conversations – have taught me, and talk about the topic of *trust*.

*Watch Craig expand more on this chapter by scanning the QR code below.

Chapter 14 – Don't Sit on Your Gift (My One Thing)

[November 5, 2018]

[Ultimately, our family and our friends know us better than anyone. Throughout the next couple of weeks – Episodes 14-16 – I will be exploring the ways that my family and friends have spoken into my life, and what has come of it – both personally and professionally. How has our proximity lent itself toward clarity? How has their discernment altered the way that I understand myself, and what may come of this new understanding? How might I reciprocate it? If Solomon's insistence on, "wisdom in the counsel of many," stands true (which it does), then why not listen to and learn from the "many" that are our own? Consider the following three chapters a compounding mini-series on understanding self and others – each with our respective strengths and weaknesses – as discovered in and through a relationship with our loved ones.]

It all started with a simple question.

"Don't answer this right away unless you have an answer," my friend Matt said, and then asked, *"What does Craig Gross do better than anybody else?"*

I, of course, *did* have an immediate answer.

"I've got it! I know how to start something and make whatever it is happen better than anyone else," I said. *"What about you?"*

Matt replied, "I do business and relationships better than anyone. I mean, there are guys better at business, and there are guys better relationally, but *no one* (that I know of) who is better than me at *both*."

Over the course of the next twenty-four hours, I ran back through my response to Matt's question over and over again. The more I sat with it, the more of a clarifying impact it began to have on me.

I wonder if other people agree with my answer?

I paid the question forward to five other friends and family members:

"What do you think that I do better than anyone else?"

All five people responded with – more or less – the exact same answer.

I received the most concise response from my long-time friend and employee, Michelle, who is perhaps the only person besides my wife who's been on whatever bandwagon it is that I've been working to create for as long as she has.

"You get shit done and make things happen better than anyone I know."

I sat with that for another day. The answers moved beyond providing mere *clarity*. Their unanimity began to bolster *confidence* that I am, in fact, good at what the people closest to me say that I am good at. Which snowballed into a proper deconstruction:

- "Why am I doing anything *but* that?"
- "How much of my time do I currently spend doing *this?*"
- "Oh! *Others aren't like me* (that explains why they all drive me insane)!"

I asked Matt to conduct the same experiment, "Send your question to five of your closest friends. Let's see how closely connected their answers are to one another." Then, I paid the question forward to my friends Levi and Carl, and my wife Jeanette. Before that, though, I brainstormed what I thought their responses might be.

This is what my best guesses were, prior to talking to any of them:

Carl figures stuff out better than anyone.

Levi empathizes in his writing better than anyone.

Jeanette has more discipline than anyone.

Here are their actual answers:

Carl said, *"I get shit figured out and working."*

Levi said, *"I am an empathetic writer."*

Jeanette said, *"I have willpower and discipline."*

Pretty.
Damn.
Close.

And *pretty damn close* – if not *exactly on point* – is how this experiment has played out with everyone we've brought it to nearly *every damn time*.

Of course (as is the Craig Brain custom), my head almost immediately spun straight off of my body, carried away by the winds of excitement, URL's, e-courses and deliverables. Right then and there – at 1:30 am – I outlined an entire video course. I would've shot the whole thing, too, hadn't it been so damn late and my son was already asleep. I didn't even have notes. I just finally believed that I was good at what everyone affirmed in me, and was ready to roll. It's funny, I realize the things that excite me probably sound like pulling teeth to so many people.

I kept thinking, "Wow…*everyone* I've asked has said that I do this *one thing* better than anyone they know. And *everyone* I've asked to conduct the same 'test' has had the same experience with its results as I have.

I wonder how or what we might be able to learn from one another if we could better understand our differences? If we could learn *not* to be threatened by our weaknesses (which we are *all* too familiar with), but instead hone in on our strengths, and complement one another?

How could I teach my particular gift – *My One Thing* – to someone who doesn't possess it, but wants to learn, grow, and stretch themselves?

How could someone else?

How could we flex new muscles and – as I've somehow found myself in the middle of a cliche bodybuilding analogy – how could we become trainers who help strengthen one another's weak spots in actionable ways? How do we help one another progress and see that our hard work is paying off when gazing into our proverbial mirrors?

And by *we*…I really do mean *all of us*.

Not just KOLBE Quick-Start dudes with an overabundance of confidence and ten lessons mapped out before you can blink an eye.

Not just e-course gurus and – also – *not just* for sale.

Anyone and everyone.

My friend, Matt. My wife, Jeanette. Neither of which are front-facing people with social media followings. Neither of which are artists or influencers. Neither of which have a solid headshot. Neither of which with any idea how to register a domain, shoot and edit a video course, or list it.

And, frankly, neither of which with a desire to do any of that in the first place, let alone the belief that anyone else would want or could stand to benefit from their "expertise" (which they're not convinced of) if they did.

A few nights later, I was at the Grammy Museum in Los Angeles with my son, Nolan. His favorite band, *LANY*, was hosting a small concert for 200 fans, and they promoted it as including dedicated time for *Q&A* with them at the end of the night. We got in, and during the post-show session, someone asked the band about how they first got started.

In short, Paul – *LANY's* vocalist – had a struggling career as a solo artist. Their drummer, Jake, was a session drummer at a studio in Nashville. And Les, their multi-instrumentalist on guitar, piano, etc., was working at a Post Office before he came home to make and produce music after his shifts.

At one point in his response, Paul looked at Les and said, "To be honest, Les was *sitting on his gifts.*"

I texted Matt, who spurred this whole idea on, told him *I've got it!* And immediately registered the domain name.

Enter: www.sitonmygift.com

At this point, I would say it's an extension of the same experiment our friend-and-family groups have been exploring with one another. When you land on the website's homepage, you, too, are prompted to answer the question that Matt first asked me:

"What do *YOU* do better than anyone else?"

After you answer for yourself, you will be asked to share that question with five other people.

Then, you wait.

You wait for *clarity* and *confidence*.

Maybe these epiphany moments are all you'll need to recalibrate life in such a way that it – and your responsibilities therein – seems to flow more freely. Clarity of mind is a gift in and of itself, and I've found that, when coupled with greater self-discovery, many of the *stuck* end up working themselves out.

Whether or not a person has any interest in using their expertise to build a product isn't the point. As I have grown more introspective (a process I long to have learned earlier in life), I am discovering that it has been something like embarking upon a journey into the unknown that *I am*. Thankfully, the conclusion I have reached along the way is that – whether personally or professionally – I am who I am for a reason.

Understanding and becoming more of *that* person – the one who I was created to be – is resulting in such a sense of freedom that I can't help but overflow with excitement. I've heard it said that "excitement shared is joy multiplied," and much of this process has seemed to be something like the unleashing of a long-oppressed person who I didn't even know existed, finally unbarred and given the freedom to run, and inviting others along for the ride.

Trust me, it's a lot better than wandering around aimlessly, or vaguely dissatisfied without a finger on your own pulse.

Maybe you know what that feels like.

Let *me* ask *you:* **What do you do better than anybody else?**

Ask yourself. And hear my friend, Matt, when he says, "If you don't know right away, that's okay, but don't make it up." Think about it. It's deep work, and it's worth doing. Ask your friends. Ask your family.

"Where there is no counsel, purposes are disappointed; But in the multitude of counselors they are established."

Sit *with* it, but whatever you do, don't sit *on* it.

What is* your *One Thing?

*Watch Craig expand more on this chapter by scanning the QR code below.

Chapter 15 – On Clarity (And Creating Fun)

[Last week marked the start of a mini-series detailing the way family and friends have influenced my ongoing journey toward self-discovery (and how yours might, too). Whether it's work, play, personal, relational, fill-in-the-blank…those closest to us know us best, like it or not. I, for one, am learning how to listen and learn, and the wisdom I've garnered has changed my life for the better.]

Throughout the past couple of years, two questions have been particularly intriguing to me: *what?* And *why?*

It has taken me a long time to answer both, and in the past, I don't know that I gave much thought to either. I've always been able to accomplish whatever I needed to, and there are still plenty of *"whats"* to get done. Ever a checklist. Entrepreneurial work (and, I suppose, work in general) is a never-ending job. I've never had a punch card. Some people envy that, but also fail to realize that if you never punch in, you never punch out.

Last week, I wrote about *My One Thing*. When my friends and family unanimously affirmed what it is that I do best, it proved not only clarifying, but freeing and invigorating.

"You get shit done cland make things happen better than anyone I know."

Over the past two decades, I've worn every hat there is to wear. I've been the youth camp guy. I've been the marketing director. I've been visionary. I've been the Wordpress code learner. I've been the keynote speaker. I've been the changer-of-DNS-settings. I've been the blog writer. I've been the oh-my-God-how-did-I-accidentally-start-a-tech-company-pastor-guy. I've been a social media guru. I've been the CEO. I've been the overnight driver.

You name it, I've done it. Sometimes out of necessity. Sometimes out of pride. Sometimes because I'm naturally an independent person who has always struggled with delegation.

And so when I began to realize that I'd been *"sitting on my gift,"* I also began to feel free. *Here is what I'm good at…*

Starting. Launching. Strategizing. Connecting the dots.

I don't want to set up a server reroute in Cloudflare *ever* again (and I might just start screaming if someone asks me to).

I finally had a set boundary – something specific – and have been offloading and replacing the work that no longer fits ever since. One new rule I created is if I can't do it on my iPad Pro, I shouldn't be doing it in the first place.

In the years that lead up to sitonmygift.com, I moved my family from Pasadena to Huntington Beach. I've better-delegated tasks according to the strengths of the people on my team. I joined a mastermind group and launched two of my own. I created betterandbetter.co – a twist on traditional marketing agencies/publishing houses where I connect clients who need help formalizing, launching, and scaling their ideas to trusted subcontractors that *I* have personal relationships with. I began coaching, counseling people, and hosting strategization workshops. I started *Craig Brain*: this vodcast/podcast, blog, book, internet-takeover-*thing*.

And I've loved it. This has been, by and large, one of the most fun, most "successful" years of my life.

But, until recently, there has still been a missing component.

The *why*.

I shared *My One Thing* with David Tosti – one of my best, longest-standing friends – recently. He thumbed through the narrative and, while agreeable enough, gave it a passing shrug before concluding,

*"Yeah, Craig, that's great and all, but **when I think of Craig Gross, I think of a guy creating fun.**"*

That's when everything clicked for me. The problem is: I still function more from my head than my heart. I might be the best at the things that I do, but what happens if what I'm best at isn't what I want to be doing? What happens if what I'm best at isn't fulfilling me?

How do I combine *what* I do best with *why* I love to do it?

How can I make *fun* the mission? The umbrella? How can I use what I *do* best – practically – to foster fun?

For what it's worth, I know that life hasn't promised any of us these words that I keep repeating. *Fun. Fulfilled.* I can't just neglect necessary parts of living and working for a 24/7 fun zone, and plenty of our days exists in the mundane. The point is, though, that with *fun* as both the precursor and the goal, this little epiphany that David sparked has given me a lens through which to view not just my work, but all of life.

More often than not, when a person asks (or is asked) about what one does, the question triggers a work-related response. People always think business, occupation, or career.

Same goes for *My One Thing*.

"You're the best preacher ever."

"Best poet ever."

 "Quarterback, ever."

What about me as a father? What about me as a husband? A friend?

I'll put it this way: as a Christian, there are – generally – two styles of seeing God. Two methods of relating to both him and the world. He is a priority, or he is a centerpiece. Sometimes (and perhaps *hopefully*), he is both. But the two are distinct.

When God is a priority, perhaps he comes first in the day.
For those of us who grew up like me, that means *quiet times*
first thing in the morning. Maybe it means prayer and
meditation before we go on with our day. But it also tends
to say that – *once we've gotten on with our day* – his time is
over, and it's on to the next thing. He is reduced to a
checkbox.

What I mean by God as a *centerpiece*, however, is that he
the fountain from which *all things* – throughout the day, in
all of life – flow. To eat a bowl of cereal following your
quiet time, from this perspective, is just as holy an act as the
moments spent in prayer, prior because the lifeblood of God
is central to the whole. He is the heart, pumping oxygen to
the body. The lens through which we look. He has
transcended the "first moments" of the day and entered into
all moments. *"In Him, we live and move and have our
being…"*

I'll be the first to admit: I've only recently begun to learn
how to function from the latter perspective, and I use this
analogy as an explanation because I think *"Craig, the
Creator of Fun"* is the fruit of that shift as much as it is its
own lens through which to look at work and life.

There are certain people I want to work with simply
because it's fun to work with them. Most of the time, I
could care less about what we're working on, as long as I
know that we're having fun together, and creating fun for
others. It's not the equivalent of a hedonistic search for
instant gratification – and "fun" might work itself out

directly or indirectly – but it has helped me temper my "yesses" with an ever-fine filter.

To put *fun* in front of everything I do – the *why* in front of my *what: My One Thing* – has made all of the difference.

And it's definitely *not* just work-related.

My family members have bucket lists, and I've been trying to make their dreams come true. Last year I discovered that – for some ungodly reason – Jeanette has always wanted to spend New Year's Eve in New York, watching the ball drop in Manhattan. That sounded like a nightmare to me, but we rang in 2019 doing just that.

My son turned sixteen this year. I wrote him a letter for his birthday, detailing some of what I've written about here. I bought him a watch that was on his list, even though I know Jeanette and I agreed upon experience type gifts only. We still had a fun trip, too, but I broke my own rule because it was *fun* for me to gift something from Nolan's bucket list and it was *fun* for him to receive it, and cross it off of his list.

Once again, it's not so much the *what* but the *why*.

I've never had a bucket list, and I never wondered why until recently.

In part (and however haughty this sounds, it's not my intent), I've always just been able to buy whatever I wanted to buy. Somehow, the Lord has given our family the privilege of a life where the money is not an issue, and while we seek to be generous and sacrificial, I've also never had much need for a wish list that I couldn't just go out and fulfill on my own.

In part, though, I think it's also because I'm not good at merely *receiving*. I always want to reciprocate. I still feel indebted to the giver, and perhaps that also accounts for much of why it has taken me a lifetime to *be* with God simply, as opposed to continually drowning beneath the weight of *doing* something for him.

Nevertheless, I'm changing. My family sees it. My friends see it. Levi kicked off this entire project with a foreword that details the shifts.

I'm trying to partner with God in giving the ones that I love an abundant life because it's fun. Abundance in work, life, marriage, opportunity, parenthood, friendship…doesn't matter.

In my Collide Mastermind group, I built a room of CEO's, business owners, and solopreneurs under the guise of spurring one another on in our own respective companies. But at the end of the day, the most fulfilling aspects of our time together are spent on the deep work of relationship. Work is not all of life (and I've learned that the hard way), and if it used to be fun before the passion became a poison, then we've got to remember *why* we started in the first place.

In my home, I'm trying to teach my kids to *accept* better than I have ever been able to, but I'm also trying to show them that it truly is better – *more fun* – to give than it is to receive. I'm trying to hear my wife tell me how fun her life is again…how much she loves being alive. She said that during one of our last trips together, and my heart just about exploded for joy.

I'm learning a little bit more, day in and day out, about what it means to function less from the head that I've bashed through walls to keep up the grind for twenty years, and more from that beating center.

The last chapter, I asked you to define your *what?*

Today, I want to ask you *why?*

Craig

P.S. It has been a while since I started this experiment and as I hit publish on this episode here in June of 2019, I thought I would add something to this entry. One thing I found was the thing people told me I do the best is not the thing or the things that I enjoy the most. So, the last few months I have been on a journey to really connect some more dots. I wrote this the other day and put it on my website and thought I would leave you with it.

I enjoy creating fun, connecting people and launching products. I believe anything is possible and love instilling that belief in others.

*Watch Craig expand more on this chapter by scanning the QR code below.

Chapter 16 – Pioneers & Builders (And Our Thing)

[This is the third and final installment of a mini-series on family and friends and how they relate to and spur on personal growth and self-understanding. Two weeks ago, I began by detailing the ways those closest to me have helped me discern what it is that I do best. Last week, I took it a step further and tried to explain the "why" that most motivates me to do those things in the first place – the "why" that bookends the "what," so to speak. Today, before entering into our third section – On Work and Workmanship – I want to discuss the final piece that ties it all together.]

Years ago, Levi wrote <u>a public letter</u> to his wife and published it on their fifth wedding anniversary. Though well-intended, he should have thought it through a bit more. His wife is quieter and more concerned with their privacy than he is, and – given his profession as a memoir-style writer – she already felt as though her entire life had been on public display since she said: *"I do."* His gift, as you might imagine, didn't exactly go over the way he had hoped.

That's part of what this is about.

The other part of what it's about, though, is that Levi described his marriage back then in such a way that seems to resonate with the lessons *every marriage* (and, I think *every friendship)* must endure, as summarized in this question:

*How can **your thing** and **my thing** become **our thing?***

I will say that, after twenty years of both a marriage and a business partnership with my wife, the answer is not an easy thing to come by. The ego is a thick skin, and it's no easy task to uncover what lies beneath. I've heard it said many a time that there's nothing quite like marriage to teach a person just how selfish he is, and it's not just some pithy saying. Cliches always exist for a reason.

I wrote a letter to Jeanette (December 6, 2018) as I began to understand more about myself. Much (if not most) of that self-discovery is thanks to her. Here, at the risk of getting myself into the same trouble as Levi, is a part of that note:

> I'm an idea guy. Whatever size those ideas are, I've got too many flooding my mind day-in and day-out to know what to do with any of them.

> I go fast.

> I say *yes* more than I say *no*.

> I'm learning to say no…*slowly*.

> I moved our family to the beach, but then I went and built an office in the damn hallway-closet of a bathroom.

I add too many things to iCal.

I make too many meetings.

I don't plan breaks.

I don't write in time for meals.

I don't stop to pee.

I don't stop to eat.

I don't stop to work out.

I don't stop for the kids unless our time is planned beforehand.

I have a lot of *wants* too, though.

I want to do the things that I don't.

I want nothing on my schedule before 9AM.

I want to work out five days a week (and at least one of them at OrangeTheory with you).

I want all work removed from my schedule between 4-9PM on Mondays, Wednesdays and Fridays.

I want to have a planning meeting each weekend so that we know what we're doing the following week.

I want to schedule family time each day. Maybe that means I take Elise to dance on Thursday, or take Nolan wherever he's going on Tuesday, and pen in time with you on Friday.

I want to schedule a Bible class twice per week.

I want a minimum of three hours at the spa, once a week, to write, record, dream, and reflect.

I want to pray with the kids at night. I should never have stopped.

I want to be intentional about spending time working through *How We Love*. I want to schedule holding times and comfort circles.

I want to take a month off of work next summer.

I want to ride a bike or skateboard three to four times a week.

I want to be here with you more, and so I only want to plan 25 trips in 2019. I have 12 planned already, and I'm only allowing myself 13 more.

I want to set a *spending* rule for myself: no buying anything unless I've first sold something else. I want to budget better.

I want to set a *saving* rule for myself. I want to save more than ever for our family, and for the ministry.

I lead best when I have help, and when there are people helping me with implementation.

These – good or bad – are all *my* things, and I'm not going to detail Jeanette's, but I will stop to focus on that last line in light of what I know my wife excels at (which you might remember from a few weeks past): *willpower* and *discipline*.

The woman *has* to have willpower to put up with me, I suppose, and when I let down my pride, I know that she champions discipline and orderliness above and beyond anything that I'm capable of submitting for comparison, as well.

Her strengths compliment my weaknesses.

And, of course, vice versa.

We've worked harder than ever to understand one another better over the past two years, and that work has resulted in some of the most significant breakthroughs – yielded, if you will, the ripest harvest – as has anything in the two, married decades we've spent together.

Our time invested into the Enneagram, Strengths Finder, and How We Love – including the supplementary counseling and deep work we've pursued – has shown me just how vital a complimentary view of our relationship is.

Where I tend to be a risk-taking, quick-starting and frenzied mess, Jeanette is my balancing opposite. Where I'm always throwing variables into the mix, she's still trying to bring order to an ever-changing environment.

While I want to feel valuable, she wants to feel competent, and we have an opportunity to either provide that encouragement *for* or strip it *from* one another.

I've not always paid enough attention to fostering Jeanette's strengths. To be honest, especially when it comes to our work together, I've too often and quite merely: *given her the shit that I don't want to do.* The point is: dumping our "unwanted" tasks into the other's lap is a far cry from figuring out what we're best at – and might actually enjoy- and building a working and/or home environment that reflects our mutual respect for one another's strengths and weaknesses.

At one point, in a season where I remember feeling particularly overwhelmed, I told Jeanette to manage my email inbox, and about the only good it did was to pay my overload forward. I shouldn't have just given her all of my clutter to sort through – all of my work to try to figure out. Instead, I should have sought to recognize how we could work together so that she – who genuinely wants to help – might do so by using her strengths to make sense of it all.

These days, then, she's in charge of the calendar. Doctors. Appointments. Maintenance. Shopping. Checkbooks. *All-things-organization.*

She shouldn't be checking my inbox, she should be
checking my schedule – telling me where to put things, how
to move them around, when *enough is enough* and how to
scale back from *way too much*.

I feel a constant, uncarriable weight to create opportunities
for the family, for our marriage, for our livelihood. But I'm
not good at *plotting them out*.

Every day, I spend hours thinking and talking to God about
each member of our family. Wedding plans. Vacation
plans. The life I want us to have. I think and pray at the spa,
or late at night when everyone else is sleeping. My best
"work" happens then – alone, and with the Lord. No
interruptions. No phone or computer.

It's a time *protected*.

And I've begun to realize that I need to protect more than
just my time.

My days need to be protected.

My work needs to be protected.

I need to take a break from the constant, self-inflicted
pressure to be everything to everyone. I need to allow other
people's strengths to shine through.

I'm great at formulating ideas, but Jeanette is excellent at
implementation. If *my* thing and *her* thing are ever to

become *our* thing, we need to work as a team and lean into one another's strengths.

Jeanette and my family know me best, and my friends are a close second. I think this kind of complementary approach is necessary for any and every relationship worth investing the time to figure out what that give-and-take looks like.

Here we return to the same question I've been asking for the past three weeks: do we trust one another enough to listen and learn from the people closest to us?

Much of that process is having the humility to acknowledge the need, which isn't particularly comfortable in a world where self-sufficiency is so greatly praised. But we must. The goal of marriage and relationship is not to conform the other into our image and likeness but to combine our everything into *one*.

My Thing + Your Thing = Our Thing

In Levi's letter to his wife, he talks about how he couldn't have possibly married a woman more different than he is and how – for years – he equated *unity* with *uniformity*. I believe he wrote something similar about our relationship in the forward to this book. Here's an excerpt from his letter:

> I could not have married a woman more different than I am. We talk about that sometimes. Ten years ago, both of us thought that we were more alike than we think we are now. And maybe we were. I used to have a tough time with that, honestly. I equated

192

difference with disunity, and even though we have our fair share of shouting matches, I no longer believe that is the case. I think that I had a skewed view of marriage, where *love* was synonymous with *compliance*, and if it didn't translate appropriately, I'd feel threatened instead of gifted with a helper who was strong enough to push back.

Disagreement is not the equivalent of dishonor. It doesn't have to be, anyway.

Marriage is not an ideological unanimity. Does such a thing even exist? And who's conviction will transcend the others? What a sad thing to discover how you thought headship meant "control." The things that I would take back. The subtle manipulation. The quiet degradation. The chauvinistic authority that I would champion as a Pharisee unto the law.

In recent months, I have been learning patience that used to terrify me as passivity. And I grow to understand, little by little, just how patient my bride has been beneath a hand as heavy as two stone tablets that never empowered the reader to live up to their inscriptions.

Jeanette and I have, historically, wished that we would just *become more like one another.* That is – as Levi said above – a massive law to live up to, especially when neither of us were created to be that way, at all. Recently, though, we're starting to see how we might complement one another in a way that has brought more wholeness – more life and joy and intimacy – to our marriage than ever before.

A pioneer and a builder can be an incredible team. Much better than two pioneers who can't implement their daydreams or two builders who don't know what they're building.

That said, to end this mini-series and our On Friends & Family section, I wonder – whether it is in your marriage or in your family of origin or in your friendships – how you might be able to see one another's differences as a positive?

So often (and thus, unfortunately), "the other" is a threat. It doesn't have to be that way, but the log has got to come out of your eye, first. We need to check our blind spots and respect one another.

How can you better listen to and learn from your friends and family? How can you better teach them what you know? How does the *gold* you're able to share with one another, there, get paid forward in ways that benefit the world beyond the borders of those relationships?

What is your one thing?

Why is your one thing?

How can *your thing* and *my thing* become ***our thing?***

P.S. If, at any point throughout the past three weeks in this section, you have found it challenging to nail down the answers to the questions that I've been asking, let me recommend two additional resources that will be helpful both personally and for others in this "inner circle" I've attempted to shine a light on:

howtofascinate.com

As you can likely by now, I'm a fan of personality tests. This one, in contrast to most, will reveal *not* how you might better see yourself, but how you might better understand the way that *others* see you. Think of this as a foundation that supports *"Your One Thing."* I'm willing to bet that it stands to supplement the answers you receive about what, exactly, it is that you do best, and – perhaps – even helps confirm why you'd care to do more of it, in the first place.

The second one is called Human Design. You can head over to https://www.jovianarchive.com/get_your_chart

This is what the Human Design System has to offer. Simply put, if you want to:

Discover how to Improve the quality of your life in a simple yet immensely effective way

Make the right moment-to-moment decisions, resulting in improved relationships and career choices

Manage the challenges that are part of daily life without getting overwhelmed

You have the innate ability to make choices that are in alignment with your authentic nature, and based in your personal Authority; this knowledge will empower you to live a fulfilling life in your unique way.

Human Design offers a map of your unique genetic design, with detailed information on both conscious and unconscious aspects of yourself. Using simple tools, it guides you in discovering your own truth. If you suffer from a lack of self-love or clarity about your purpose and the direction of your life, this system can help.

*Watch Craig expand more on this chapter by scanning the QR code below.

Chapter 17 Sixteen Candles (Money, Work and Rolex Wrist Wrap)

[February 28, 2019 - For Nolan, on his Sixteenth Birthday]

I don't have a bucket list. At least, not anymore. But I never really had one, I don't think, and I never wondered why until recently.

I started off the new year by telling the family that I wanted to challenge myself *not* to buy anything unless I first sold something else. I wanted to try something new. Something I haven't done before.

I have always been able to buy what I want. I started working at Burger King when I was thirteen years old. That lasted about four months. After that, I was selling, not trading baseball cards. That was the hot ticket, and it was through that endeavor that I was able to buy *whatever*. Anything. Everything. (And *if only* I'd have kept all of my vintage Nike gear…man, you'd have had a heyday with that stuff, now.) I owned every tape cassette from every band that I loved to listen to. I attended any and every event that I wanted to go to.

Whatever I didn't buy, my parents did:

- Private junior high and high school

- Tennis camp
- Skateboard camp
- New shoes (Jordans, Vans, Agassi's...all the name brands)
- My first car (brand new)
- College (every penny of it)
- Wedding ($10,000)

The list goes on, but those are the highlights. Knowing what I know now, I can't believe it. Nevertheless, it is what it is. The rest I bought.

For two years – from fourteen to sixteen years old – I made more money than anyone else I knew. I'd attended baseball card shows every weekend and make somewhere between $200 - $1,000 at each one.

The following week, I'd do it again.

I kept the cash in my bedroom closet next to my cards and – one year, for about four months – a single page out of a porno. I remember that, for some reason. Just one page.

I had my own subscription to Sports Illustrated.

I had cable in my room, with a T.V. and sound system.

My dad ran a vending machine business, and our garage was full of every machine that hadn't been placed yet, with all the candy in the world inside. When my friends would come over, all they wanted to do was eat from those vending machines.

I never wanted to eat candy. I never craved it. I never wanted anything to do with it.

I never wanted to work for my dad, either. My business was smarter than my dad's business. At sixteen years old, I was smarter than my dad was at fifty. I knew it, and he did, too.

I wanted to help my dad, but I didn't understand him. He spent his entire life running restaurants for other people, then went bankrupt and lost his own. Why he thought he should run a business after something like that is beyond me.

He bought the vending machine business when I was a teenager.

He said I could take it over, one day.

Like hell.

My dad spent twenty years of his life in the hot Sacramento summer or the cold, Northern California winter, driving a minivan brimming with Doritos, Snickers and exploding Pepsi cans... without ever owning a dolly.

He would park his car, walk out and up to wherever his machines were, and check to see what they needed. He'd take trips back and forth between the two, grabbing handfuls of whatever he could carry up a flight of stairs (or down some hallway) to stock his machines.

Then, he would empty all the change. None of his machines took dollar bills.

Do you understand? My dad got paid in *literal change* for twenty years of his life.

How ridiculous is that?

Eventually, I started helping him. It was my job to fix the machines when they broke. First, though, I'd have to find them. This was before GPS and iPhones, and half the time, I had no idea where they were. When I was able to track them down, I'd find notes taped to their dirty, transparent plastic that read, *"THIS MACHINE SUCKS AND ATE MY MONEY! YOU OWE ME .50 CENTS!"*

I'd have to sort through a mess of keys that my dad gave me to find the one that fit *that particular* machine. In all his life, he never marked a single key for any one of the machines he owned. He just remembered which was which.

Once I found the key that fit, I would disassemble the machine, clean the coil of smashed up Reese's Pieces pieces that had jammed the trigger and replace the parts that I'd learned how to fix.

I hated that job.

I hated it.

My dad insisted on paying me, but I never needed the money, and I never *wanted* the money.

There was never any money in those machines.

I knew his business didn't make any money.

I knew my dad was in trouble.

I knew he couldn't possibly be turning a profit.

And I knew that he could never tell my mom. It would have been too embarrassing – yet *another* failure in my mom's eyes. The loss of yet *another* business. Another job.

And I noticed the credit cards piling up.

And I noticed the increasingly angry *"This Shit Is Broken"* notes on an increasing number of machines that I had to go fix.

And I noticed the increasing number of machines, "homeless" and stacking up inside of our garage.

Eventually, my mom caught on. It got so bad that my dad rented a storage unit for the machines that he could no longer get into stores. He started *paying more money* to house empty machines that he couldn't stand to bring home for my mom to see.

I think I was the only one who really knew how much trouble he was in. I knew it before it failed. I knew it from the moment my uncle wrote my dad the bailout check and told him to start something new, and my mom told him *not* to start with vending machines.

I would try to help, but he wanted none of it.

I remember watching him count and hand-roll his coins into paper wrappers while he drove his van between the machines' locations. He never owned a coin sorter (or counter).

My business was way smarter than his.

Buy baseball cards from kids at school, or people who posted ads in newspapers.

Check.

Be the first in line at Costco when the cards came out (think of it like an in-person *Supreme* drop).

Check.

Mark everything up, and sell the cards to attendees at card conventions (think *Sneaker Con)*.

Check.

Eventually, baseball cards went away, but it was a good ride for two good years.

I got a telemarketing job for two weeks after that (maybe that explains why I still love to troll telemarketers when they call me). Then, I worked at a gas station for two months. That was it, save a job I took in college at a group home, and a brief stint delivering auto-trader newspapers.

I've never worked anywhere else except the church, and now, here at Fireproof Ministries.

I went on a mission trip before my senior year of high school. While away, I felt as though God spoke to me, and made it clear that I was to pursue youth ministry and do for others what Tom (who you know, and was my mentor) did for me when I was growing up.

My grandma was so bummed. She saw my success in business and thought that I should pursue a career there. *"Make lots of money, like your Uncle Bill,"* she'd say.

I didn't listen, and I didn't care.

If I'm honest, I've never cared much about money. At times, I have wanted more of it. I have made some bad choices with it throughout the years, but I have always had an appreciation for it. It can come fast, and it can go even quicker.

I have always known that I can earn it, though.

Call that confidence or call it whatever you want, but I am probably more free with money than I have ever been. I think, at least, I am freer than most people are.

Either way, I have *never* wanted money to own me, control me, scare me, or rule me.

I watch so many of my friends, with more money than I could ever imagine, completely crippled by their terror of it (or, maybe, of losing it).

My dad filed for bankruptcy, and that's an event you can't ever live down. It's a question banks will never stop asking, *"Have you ever filed for bankruptcy?"* It's a *yes* he always had to give.

I guess what I'm getting at is this: they say that, when it comes to kids, more is *caught* than *taught*.

I think I caught a healthy understanding, and I'm thankful for that.

I also think that God really does have a sense of humor, because when I finally did start a company of my own, it was a non-profit ministry organization.

As in one that relies on me asking people for money.

Whereas *making* money has always been easy for me, *asking* for it has never been.

I wanted to work at a church. Then, I wanted to start a ministry that needed to look like a church, so – at twenty-two years old – I decided on a non-profit organization. In hindsight, it didn't have to be that way, but for twenty years now, it has challenged me to rely on the Lord in my weakness, as opposed to relying on myself, and my strength.

We put on a myriad of events. We hosted camps. We traveled and spoke across the country in exchange for speaking fees. We paid ourselves small salaries that first year – and even less the second year when we decided to hire mom – and put every last dollar back into new ideas we had for how we might be able to reach people with the gospel and tell them about Christ.

That was always the goal, and my creative *Craig Brain* (sometimes, I swear, all on its own) spun up new ways to figure out how to raise money for the mission. We started creating products to sell at our speaking events – everything from glow necklaces to inflatable furniture to t-shirts to chain necklaces and Fireproof-branded visors.

By the end of "Craig & Jake" – our first endeavor beneath the Fireproof Ministries umbrella – we were charging five thousand dollars for a speaking gig. I charge five to ten thousand now for an XXXchurch weekend. Maybe that sounds like a lot to you, or perhaps it would seem like a lot to someone else. Every check is made out to Fireproof, and even though we get paid through the ministry, every dollar still goes back there, first.

X3watch – our internet accountability software – came out after I started XXXchurch, in 2004. Covenant Eyes was selling a similar product at the same time that we were giving ours away. It's not all about comparisons, but at one million downloads, X3watch boasted well over the one-

hundred thousand purchases Covenant Eyes was
advertising. At the same time, though – thirteen years later
– we had to offload our brand, and they've made one
hundred million dollars.

One. Hundred. Million. Dollars.

I never really thought about what that might have been like.

If I am honest, my ego couldn't have handled it.

I wouldn't have been able to do the things that I've been
able to do with you and Elise had I been stuck in a big
organization like that. I doubt I'd have ever been able to
coach a single soccer game, let alone ten-plus seasons.

Mom probably wouldn't be around any longer, either.

I wouldn't trade you for all of the money in the world.

I caught a glimpse of making a lot of money a few years
back – in 2016 and 2017. It was a two-year ride – like my
best years with baseball cards as a teenager – but then it
slowed down. It didn't end, but it's not a gold rush any
longer. The market changed. Pogs didn't come out and kill
this one like they did my teenage dreams, but Facebook
sure did get hit by Russia (not to mention our president).
They weren't honest with their users. They'd been selling
everyone's information, and I guess it's no wonder it had
been so easy for us to sell there, in turn, as well.

I've learned a lot these past few years – "money" lessons included. I've been given new opportunities to pursue interests that I've always had but never engaged. I've met new people. I've been able to sit in new rooms and create a few of my own. For the first time in almost twenty years, I have begun to dream anew. It has been exciting and – to be honest, coming into this new year – I felt pretty content to shut almost all of the "old me" down (or, at least, to fire myself).

I am over it, like my Scottie Pippen rookie card.

I started this letter by remembering my New Year's Resolution: I'm not going to buy stuff that I don't need. You read it in my set of goals the night we shared one another's with the rest of the family.

I made that rule because I was bored. I've always been able to buy what I want and thought that perhaps it'd be more challenging to see what I could *keep* instead of spend.

So, this year, I'm flexing a new muscle. It has been an enlightening challenge.

I am beginning to understand what I actually *need* vs. what I *want* to go get. It's a subtle shift, but it has given me a new perspective. It has given me the freedom to pursue other interests – to experiment with what I want to do more than what I'm currently doing for a paycheck – whether or not any compensation is involved at all. *And it has been fun.* I think that's why the early days at Fireproof were so fun, too. It was just Jake and me, and we could use whatever extra money we had to put on some event, book our favorite bands, and tell kids about Jesus.

As I said before, my job in the ministry has always required me to ask others for money, and throughout the years, I've done *a lot* of asking.

People have given our ministry over five million dollars in donations since we started twenty years ago. We don't roll quarters or get paid in change, but your mom has entered every single one of those donations into the computer since then. Every year, we print *Thank You* letters for the people who keep Fireproof alive, and sustainable.

If you want to know the truth: I hate it.

I hate asking for donations. It doesn't come naturally to me. It bucks up against my pride. It requires putting to death my ego. To my increasing levels of dismay, I've got a good amount of ego left to kill.

To *ask* is the epitome of *humbling*.

People you know have given money toward our family and ministry with incredible generosity throughout the years. They've supported us in ways that I don't take lightly. But I always remember, and I still think about paying their gifts back to them.

You overheard me on the phone here recently, asking for money. Next to karaoke and dancing, it's probably the worst thing you've ever watched me do.

That shit is hard. *Really hard.*

I believe in what we do here, so I have always just sucked it up. I've swallowed my pride and gone out and done it. We started this non-profit in 1998. I was only a few years older than you are today, and twenty years later, I'm still asking people for money.

Maybe it's good for me, but I'd still *way* rather create something and sell it than ask for donor support.

I realized that – outside of the ministry – I never *ask.* Or, at least, *very rarely* have I ever asked anyone for anything. Maybe that comes from my dad, but the difference between us is that I actually figured out how to "make it," while he never made it past the *fake it* stage.

I've just never felt right asking something of someone without offering something of my own in return.

Elise's dance competition this last weekend is a perfect example. I invited David Tosti, and I paid twenty bucks for his parking. He told me I didn't have to do that, but I felt bad about him having to fork out money for something that I invited him to. *He shouldn't have to pay to watch my daughter dance.* And – even though he told me that's what friends do – neither should any of the other people who I invited (and whose parking I paid for).

Recently, too, I was thinking about how – within a couple of years of our Super Bowl trip with my dad – I sent one of my best friends, David Deann, his dad, and son to their own version of that *once-in-a-lifetime* dream: the Cubs' World Series. I know that I really do love *giving*, but I've realized something else in the process:

I don't think my issues with "asking" have anything to do with money…I believe that I simply struggle with *receiving*.

Constantly considering how I might give back – whether to a friend or family member or ministry partner – nullifies the gift itself. I'd be bummed, honestly, if others were unable to accept the gifts that I want to give them, but my own feelings of constant indebtedness have left me unable to receive what has been offered to me.

I think it runs in my family. I realized that after I bought my mom a suitcase at Ross the other night. Every time she visits us, she limps off the plane, carrying a suitcase that doesn't wheel anymore. I keep telling her that's Ron Jeremy's schtick (except that – at this point – his suitcase sucks so bad that he simply opted to trade it in for a Whole Foods bag).

Anyway, I bought her a new suitcase. It was fifty-nine bucks.

She had a hard time accepting the gift.

I've got my mom in me, too. You know that because – like the rest of the family – you say I'm hard to buy for. I know I need to work on *receiving*, and I will.

I told you at the beginning that I've been thinking about bucket lists. I even bought a book about them the other day. (It was $4.99, and no, I didn't sell anything before I bought it, so I guess you got me there.)

You and I have worked together to fulfill many of mom's dreams, and we've been crushing it. I don't really have a list, and that's largely because I don't wait to receive what I want from other people. I just go get or experience it for myself. I'd love a Packer Super Bowl with you, but beyond that, I've got nothing to cross off that can be bought with money. Only time will tell whether I've done a good enough job as a father and husband to see those dreams come true.

Anyway, I started thinking about *your* bucket list. You shared it with me a few times now. I haven't looked at it, so I don't know what all has changed (if anything), but I do remember some of what's on it.

You are sixteen years old today.

Sixteen.

I can't believe it.

It's hard to think about sixteen years with you.

You have seen me at my best and at my worst. I wonder what the next sixteen will hold. You'll see me walking your

sister down the aisle. Maybe I'll coach *your son's* soccer
team. Perhaps I'll lose my hair.

I hope you and I can keep sharing shoes.

I hope we can share *so much more* than just shoes.

This year has been fun so far. We're only two months in,
but they've been a good two months for me.

We kicked off 2019 together at Round Table, where I read a
letter to the family and promised to do a better job of
sharing things *as they come*, as opposed to my end-of-the-
year recap that had been my custom up until now. I also
feel like it's time for me to share some of what I've been
learning, and the ways I've been growing, publicly. That all
starts next week with the first episode of *Craig Brain*. If
I'm honest, I am both excited and nervous to share my life
in ways more vulnerable than anything I've released in the
past.

My gift to you is twofold, I suppose. It's me doing what I
said I'd do – sharing my heart as I understand it, myself –
and crossing something off of your list.

I didn't tell mom I was buying this watch for you.

I thought I might be crazy. Mom would tell me I'm insane,
for sure. I thought about it for a while, though (which, in
my fast-paced brain, might've been a solid two or three
days), and decided not only that I *should* buy you this gift,
but that I *want* to.

I have several reasons for wanting to give this to you, but the first is because you want it. You've talked about it. You've shown it to me before. It's on your list.

One day, you'll understand that kind of *want*. It is a father's *want*. I want – and have *always wanted* – to help you chase and obtain the things that you desire. Your lists have never been burdensome. I love watching them expand. I love seeing your diversity, and I love watching your interests – be they monetary, or vocational, aspirational – change and grow as you do the same.

You are *so much fun* for me. Your pursuits – be they design-oriented or otherwise – are inspirational, and it's incredible to see your willingness to chase dreams, work hard, and cross things off of your list.

Your dreams will continue to grow and change as you get older, and you'll likely subtract a few in the process, as well. We joke and say that your life is a bucket list. Sure, maybe so, but I see and believe in the Bible's promise of abundant life for those of us who are in Christ. While that doesn't necessarily mean *materially* or *monetarily*, I – while it is within my ability to do so – wanted to be a part of that abundance by giving you something that just so happens to be a big-ticket item on your list.

Receive it. And hear me – as a man who has been honest with you today – when I say, *"Receive it freely."*

In a couple of years, when you turn eighteen, I will take one more thing off your list for you.

At twenty-one, one more.

It'll be fun to watch you cross a few of your own off during the in-between (and – I hope – help others cross a few off of theirs, too).

Sixteen, eighteen, and twenty-one are significant years, Nolan. At least, they were for me.

When I was sixteen, I knew what I wanted to do with my life.

By eighteen, I had left my parent's house, and I never went back.

At twenty-one, I knew I was marrying your mom.

Let's make these years count, because after twenty-one, there aren't any big-deal birthdays until you hit forty, and that one kinda sucks.

Seems odd to spend your sixteenth in Vegas. It'll be fun, but I want to be here for your twenty-first, too. Mom and I have already talked about being in a good enough relationship to sponsor your twenty-first party in Vegas. If you'll have us, we want to club it up with you and party with your friends. We'll see, I guess.

As for sixteen:

Happy Birthday.

I really enjoy being your father, Nolan.

I love it.

Accept this gift. It's yours.

I hear these keep their value. Matt talks about watches quite a bit. I don't understand them like he does (or, for that matter, like you do) but what I do know is that they were always a point of connection between him and his dad. Let this one be that to you, from me. Give it to your son when he turns sixteen. How cool would that be?

You have been wearing my dad's watch for a while, now. Let's trade. I'll keep his safe while you do the same for this one. When you look at the ice on your wrist, remember that your dad loves you.

At the ripe old age of sixteen, the message that I want you to hear from me is this:

You can do anything you want to do in this life. Keep chasing the passions that others are only able to perceive as pipedreams. Let them call you crazy. *Dream bigger.* Don't settle. Have fun and be smart with your treasures here on earth, remembering that no matter where this life takes you, they will never be as rich as your treasures in heaven.

Love,

Dad

P.S. Whether it's a letter like this or a video, I've shared a few "memorable" moments for your birthday throughout the years. At some point, when the calendar starts anew, I always find myself Googling *"Craig Gross + Nolan Gross Birthday"* and tracking down the link to the letter I wrote and posted when you turned 11 years old.. I want to see if what I wrote still makes sense.

So – in addition to your "new" 2001 watch – I'm gonna get you to read a "vintage" 2012 letter. These things still play, so mess with them!

11 Thoughts For My 11 Year Old

1. *Please stay young.*

2. *Work & Play Hard.*

3. *Be Generous.* None of this stuff is ours.

4. *Elise is Your Best Friend.* Treat Elise like she is the most special person in the world.

5. *Remember to laugh and to cry.* It's okay to laugh (and to laugh out loud). Never get too serious and always remember how fun it is to laugh, and to make others laugh. At the same time, I feel like I have told you not to cry. There is nothing wrong with crying.

6. *Girls. They are fun.* They are complicated, and
they will soon by calling more and more.

7. *Be a leader, not a follower.* Lead people to things
that will bring them life and joy. This is natural for
you. I have seen it in you for your entire life.

8. *Please get to be a size 10.5 in shoes and stop
when you get there so we can always share.*

9. *Stay humble.*

10. *Always take trips with your father.* I can only
remember one overnight trip with my dad until the
time I turned thirty-one. After that, we traveled
everywhere. Nolan, one of our first trips together
was to the Wiggles front row on a flight from
Michigan to Phoenix when you were just three.
Since then, I don't think we can add up all the
places we have gone, but you are never too old for
trips with me. My trips with my dad are some of the
greatest memories I have, and I want ours to
continue, as well.

11. *Get to Know Jesus.* This is more important than
church or fractions or your career. Spend time with
him. He doesn't ask for much, and he is always
there. He won't tweet back at you or FaceTime you,
but you will start to hear his voice. He will help
guide and direct your whole life if you allow him to.
Sit and talk to him and let him know your highs and

lows. Tell him how pissed you were when you got your iPod taken away for two months. *Listen*. You might not hear his voice out loud, but the more you talk to him, sit with, and listen to him, the more I think you will hear. The Bible can seem tough to read when you look at it as a big book, but it is full of Jesus' words and one of the best ways you can get to know him is right there in those pages.

*Watch Craig expand more on this chapter by scanning the QR code below.

Chapter 18 – Dave, What the Hell? (Career, Life and Passion Paralysis)

A brief disclaimer:

After some back-and-forth, Levi and I decided to keep this chapter. It is harsh, to say the least, but after hearing about the way it also resonated with *him*, I was convinced that it might prove valuable for others, as well. This is a private letter I wrote to a friend who was stuck, and I didn't pull any punches (but I did pull his name from the text).

That said – for him, now, and for you, reader – *pay attention to the postscript.*

Dear friend!

I hated your forty-minute *feelings* message.

You asked for my feedback, and I'm going to give it to you. Just remember everything we learned about the Enneagram. This is coming from a *3 – The Achiever –* and I know you're a *4 – The Individualist/Romantic.* I've written responses like this before to people who end up either loving me or hating me for it (it's usually the latter, at least at first), but here it goes…

You are stuck.

You are distracted, you aren't focused, and at the end of the day, you're trying to work for yourself. At the risk of reducing Enneagram characteristics to a box in which to put people, I don't know a single *4* who has been able to run an organization without someone else's help.

Music is a hobby.

Or at least, it's not a job until someone is paying you to make it, play it, and tour on it. No one is paying you to create or tour your music anymore.

Right now, you have to focus. You have two kids, a soon-to-be wife (so, maybe more kids on the way) and the number one thing you need to make all that happen is...

Money.

Yes.

And I know that stings, but I'm not trying to be a feeler right now. I'm not trying to appeal to your emotions. I'm trying to pound a fact into your brain.

Remember learning about Maslow's *Hierarchy of Needs* in high school? It's the pyramid, whose foundation is "Basic Needs," followed by "Psychological" and "Self-Fulfillment" needs?

You want to be fulfilled, but there is very little fulfillment when you're still stuck in and scrambling for even the most basic of needs – when you're always worrying about whether or not you have enough to eat food and put a roof over your family's head. And I know you want to be creative, too, but creativity doesn't flow well from anxiety while you're out Ubering people around, wondering whether tonight's going to be a good enough night to make rent on time.

Right now, you're broke, and your music is a hobby.

But broke people don't have hobbies – they have two or three jobs. Broke people don't do dinner parties – they're at work, *working* on getting *un*broke.

Find a job.

I don't care about whether or not it's a nine-to-five behind a desk in a cubicle, or whether you work remotely from home. *Just get to work.* You're distracted, and the hard truth of the matter is that you need to take some of the dreams that you have, and the creative, *this-could-be-so-cool* distractions, and put them in a "later" jar for the time being.

You don't have to throw them out forever, but you won't ever get to any of them if you aren't able to provide for your most basic needs, first. If you keep treating all of your fantasies like a golden ticket, they only haunt (and eventually crush) you.

Put all of the new product ideas and shows and albums and experiences into your *later* folder and file them away until you actually have a means of seeing them realized, and a stable enough foundation to function from. You need a platform to make all of those dreams come true, and right now, you simply don't have one, let alone the money to build a new stage from scratch.

This sucks to hear, but you're out of the game. You've been out of it for too long to leverage your old audience, and starting over isn't an option. It'd be like if Nolan quit acting for forty years, then when back to his agent and told her, "I'm ready to be successful now."

Good luck.

Now's not the time for you to create a bunch of stuff that really only flows well out of excess. Now's the time that you realize you're unhappily functioning out of a deficit, and:

You.

Need.

To.

Get.

A.

Job.

Stop trying to build your own projects and help someone else build theirs. It's not like you'll *never* be able to make your own, but your contributions to other people's successes (already established enough to *pay you* for your participation) will create the opportunities that you need to garner attention and get noticed.

For starters: Don't say *"yes"* to anything if there aren't dollar bills attached to it, or you *know* – without a shadow of a doubt – that whoever you're working with is someone capable of generating money for you.

"NO" NEEDS TO REPLACE YOUR "YES."

When you say *"yes"* to everything you feel, you might end up working on the things that you love, but then the things you need to survive suffer. And how long can you really be in love with things that don't contribute to your actual survival? You'll end up hating what you loved, and spoiling all of those passions that used to bring you joy.

I know you love to be in front of people - that's fine. You're a people person. It's a strength, and you're good at it – in fact, when you're in a good headspace, you're *the best* at it. But that doesn't mean you're destined for a life behind a microphone as the vocalist of a band successful enough to provide for you (let alone your family, let alone whoever else is in the band, let alone their families).

Don't come at me with that ethereal, *the universe has no deadlines* nonsense. Either that or figure out how to become a philosopher.

There *are* deadlines.

Rent *is* due.

Tuition *is* expensive.

Power companies *will* turn your electricity off.

People *are* evicted from their homes.

We all agree that the world *could* or *should* be something different, but this is what it is, and living in your head, outside of this reality, is paralyzing you. And I know the comparisons you make there – whether to me, or to whoever – is ceaselessly frustrating, but that's not helpful either.

The only reason I can take on extracurricular projects is that I've had a job for eighteen years that I've been showing up for every day. And I've had a lot of help along the way. Business partnerships. People who fill my weaknesses with their strengths and help build whatever it is that we're creating, collaboratively.

You know how to grind. You did it while you were with the band, and you did it after you traded your band for a camera. Your work is excellent – it's worth getting paid for – but your business model sucks.

I know how to start, run, and scale businesses. I think I know how to spot talent, and I think I know how to help those talented people get off their feet in ways that they'd never be able to on their own.

I am often playing the role of *visionary*, but I excel in implementing. You are an *incredible* visionary, but you haven't been able to implement your visions.

The way I see it, you only have two options when it comes to making your photography something that moves beyond "hobby," as well, and becomes a viable business.

1. Get signed on with a big company, show up, and shoot. They'll handle all of the business management and get you bookings, and you can simply show up and do what you're best at.
2. Reestablish your own company, but bring on a partner at a 50/50 split. Bring on someone who knows how to implement, push forward, and scale. It doesn't matter if this person knows how to shoot photos – that's your job – but he or she needs to see your talent, and grow your business with you.

Personally, I like Option #1 for you because I know that, deep down, you don't want to do photos – you want to do other things. I think photography could become your second job (maybe even a *hobby* job) someday, and you could use it for fun (or for diapers).

Make this decision first. Chart the path depending upon which one you chose, and *do not* go back to any studio, anywhere – until you do.

If you choose something completely unrelated to your photography, I say you should get a job with someone in the health food industry, or the coffee space, or in yoga, or at a creative or ad agency or event company.

Whatever you do – the crux remains the same – *don't build it yourself.* Not right now. And don't do it "on the side" to "help" someone. Get hired by someone who can pay you. It's not about how much they can pay you. If you need 100k per year so survive with a wife and kids in Los Angeles, and they can only pay you 60k, then give them 60k's worth of work while you prove to them that you're worth more, and make the extra 40k elsewhere until they believe it.

Call everyone you know. Find companies and leads in the area you want to be in, and go crush it.

You're chasing a high instead of chasing a job.

You want to be a spotlight solo on stage, but you need to share that stage with others, and play a background melody, somewhere.

I know you love music. Yes, you could get a break in music, but the chances are slim to none, and it is not going to come while your music is so attached to pain and frustration that you don't know what to say, anyway.

Get in a better place, so you know what to say. Let it go. Give music your free time instead of treating it as an occupation. Besides, not to sound as though I'm manipulating Him, but the Lord seems to love fulfilling our desires the moment we lay them down. Who knows what He'll do in your life if and when you're able to unclench your fists, and lay them flat before His feet.

Someone will hire you. When they do, don't gripe about employment – it's a good thing. Besides, you can always treat it as a means to an end, and you still have Your fiancé to help create a structure for you, personally. Give her permission to tell you, *"No, don't do that... turn right here. Stop going left. Stop making u-turns."*

Use the differences between you to balance one another out. Defer to her strengths, and vice versa. Become a kick-ass team together. And right now? Let her drive and push you out the door and into *action*.

Create filters for yourself. If you have an idea or receive an offer or invitation from someone else, ask yourself:

- Is this a distraction?
- What will doing this take me away from?
- Do I have time to do this right now?
- Is this a *"hell yes"* or a "no?"
- WWJD? ;-)
- Am I in a financially secure enough place to do this or do I need to be working on what's making me money?
- Can this wait?
- Do I love this?

Here's another thing: you're more than capable of working wherever you want, and doing whatever you want. That said, financially, you might very well have the option of making money doing whatever that is, or of making *more* money doing something that might not be as personally fulfilling.

Say you could make 50K and love it, or make 100K and…*not enjoy it*. I do not believe that everyone should pursue the starving artist's life of love. Are your feelings worth a 50K pay cut? I don't think so, because 100K would free you to do what you love – and keep it that way – outside of work, as opposed to taking on a second job to make up the difference.

If I were you, and you were Tom Hanks in the movie *BIG,* I would:

- Fold my photography business and pursue something else or bring my business to an agency, and provide them with excellent contract work for hire, at "X" amount.
- Either way, I would then go get a stable job that you know you can do well, and that will pay you the most.
- If I had to choose between multiple job options at a higher pay rate, I would do so in this order:
    - Best flexibility.
    - Best pay.
    - Best passion.

During these shifts and changes, I would say no to everything else besides what I need from you (and will pay you for). Get all of this dialed in, and use whatever extra time you have to pour into your kids, and Danielle.

It took me three years to finish college, three more to pay off my debt, and twelve years until I made decent money. I worked hard, and I worked consistently. It gave me the chance to build a few great things, and it now gives me the leverage and time to pursue new opportunities with other businesses and other people.

Call it a snowball effect.

Somehow, by the grace of God, I have also managed to keep my marriage and my family in order. Without them, no amount of personal fulfillment would transform into "success" the failure that my efforts would have actually become.

I want to help you. I assume this all sounds harsh and abrasive, but I believe in you, and if you want my help, I'd love to connect you to some of the people who I believe can help make these things happen.

I know you watch American Idol or America's Got Talent, or one of those shows. Do you ever cry when all three judges give someone a *"No?"*

Well, I just gave your dreams a big fat, *"NO."*

But it's only temporary, and every single one of those auditions ends with the judges encouraging their contestants to "come back next year."

Get this stuff in order, and I promise you: *there will be a "next year."*

Craig

Postscript: In the year-or-so that has passed since I wrote this letter to my friend, much has changed. In what I can only call some sort of divine irony, he *is* hard at work on a job… *helping my son pursue a career… in music* (among other creative – and financially viable – endeavors).

This isn't the kind of letter that you can write to just anyone, but it is the kind of letter that you can write to a friend of twenty-something years. It is the kind of letter that you can write to a friend who trusts you (and vice versa).

And he's had much to teach me since then, as well. I've heard Levi say that wisdom is the collision of pendulums swinging, and leveled out in the middle. I think we've done that for one another throughout the years, and are walking forward with mutually beneficial wisdom to offer both through and because of our differences.

I know a good kick in the balls is needed, sometimes. I also know that "a soft word turns away wrath." This is the former, but I've also learned a lot about the latter, and I'm thankful for the help he's given me in that regard.

To my friend – and you know who you are – thanks for every *"Craig, What The Hell?"* you've given back to me. I need it every bit as much as you said you needed this, and I look forward to what the future holds beyond the paralysis we've both been working through.

*Watch Craig expand more on this chapter by scanning the QR code below.

Chapter 19 – Quarterbacks & Coaches (You Do You, Boo)

"I don't know, Craig…I don't know what's happening. I don't know what's changing. But I know that something is. *And it's big, and I see it…"*

My friend and – aside from my wife – longest-standing partner in work and ministry, Michelle Russell, sent me a message not long ago. Apparently, the changes she's seen in me throughout the past few years and – perhaps especially – more significantly realized in the recent few months' worth of releasing these episodes, have been significant enough to raise her eyebrows.

Maybe she's not the only one who sees it.

Maybe she's not the only one asking, *"What's next?"*

Let me back up.

I want to talk about sports.

I love football. Maybe you've heard of it? God knows my editor hasn't, so I guess he'll have a field day (pun intended) with this one.

I've been to more games than I can count, and I've written about many of the best of them here, salted throughout this season of *Craig Brain*. Super Bowls with my dad. Packer games with my son, Nolan. What I can't attend in-person, I make up for in the fantasy league. (Nolan's beat me a couple of times, which is annoying, but hey… *"raise your child up in the way he should go…"*)

The average age of a professional NFL player is 26.6 years old. I don't want to sound like the walking dead, here, but as a forty-two year old man, *twenty-six-year-old-me* may as well have been Gumby, or some claymation character from MTV's Celebrity Deathmatch who could twist and contort himself in ways that allowed for the kind of pummeling that the present (my friends might say *rickety)* me can no longer imagine…

Which is how I got to thinking about Tom Brady.

By some absurd miracle, the forty-one year old New England Patriots quarterback has taken his team to the Super Bowl *eleven times* (more than any other team), boasts *six wins* (more than any other quarterback), and plans to continue jerseying up through his mid-to-late forties, hoping to bump George Blanda out of his *number one* spot as the oldest NFL player in history.

Two years ago, a commentator from CBS asked Brady how much longer he hoped to play the game.

"Five to seven years."

I hope he makes it (and that's coming from a cheesehead), but I also know that – regardless of *when* – the end will come, as all things do.

You can't play football forever.

A couple of weeks ago, Ron Jeremy and I flew to the University of Kentucky to argue about porn with one another. We've been hosting *The Great Porn Debate* together since 2008. This time, my friend and co-worker, Carl Thomas, joined us there in Lexington, and asked me a question:

"Where do you see yourself in five years?"

After all of this time – after all of these years spent assuming that I'd be playing quarterback for XXXchurch until… *forever* – I couldn't answer him, but I do know that if this ministry is a field, it's time for me to step off and over to the sideline.

I've played this position since 2002, now. I know who to pass the ball to, and how to throw it well. I know how to call the audible. I know how to orchestrate the team. I'm not comparing myself to one of the greatest quarterbacks of all time, but I do know that – like Brady with the Patriots – there's something special about playing on the same team for an entire career. A trust that forms. We're about the same age, and I *do* know that – whatever life you're living – there's a wisdom that comes with each decade invested on our respective field.

There's also a reason that most pro players' average age lies in their mid-twenties. One's body only allows for so much thrashing. One can only take so many concussions. One cannot demand thin air for extra stamina that no longer lies inherent within his bones.

I've been running up and down this field at a sprinter's pace for twenty years, and I'm coming up on empty.

It's time for me to step off the field.

Perhaps the trail of breadcrumbs left throughout each of the lessons I've learned in these journals I've been writing is more glaringly front-facing than I realized up until now:

I cannot do it all.

I don't know what lies in Tom Brady's future, but I do know that I am moving from quarterback to coach. Humility is one of wisdom's hardest-taught lessons, but I know that there are stronger players out there, hungrier for the ball.

When Carl asked me about my five-year plan, I knew, like a gavel struck the block: *I don't want to play this role anymore.*

So there it is.

Michelle called it: *something's changing.* And for me, it's huge.

It's bittersweet.

I don't want to disappear, but I can't play this position anymore. I always thought I'd play quarterback forever.

Maybe my jersey will still say that, sometimes, but as of now, I'm transitioning out of the *player* role on this team.

Over the course of the past few years, I have been learning new skills and working in new ways. Frankly, it's a long story, but if I were to summarize it…

In my opinion, one of the best projects we at XXXchurch ever released was called *My Pilgrimage.* What is visible and front facing – the book and video series and every related resource – is amazing, but the work behind it all began years before it ever materialized into a full on ministry program.

Seth and David Taylor were the main authors on that project, and before I ever agreed to publish any of it, I wanted to dive into their perspective, myself. I wanted to see where they were coming from, as – though not entirely out of left field – their proposals about *how* to approach pornography addiction were more nuanced than some of the work we'd released in all of our years prior.

During that learning and vetting process, one of the experiences we had together took place in Alaska (which is why we eventually started including our "Alaska Pilgrimages" for the men in our final program). It was 2013 and – though I'll spare you the intricacies here – I felt as though that trip led to some major breakthroughs in my health, life, and future.

I heard two things, clear as day:

1. Go, as planned, to the opening day of the new 49ers stadium. Even though your dad died. Even though it will be hard to go without him…*go*. Don't avoid the pain – run toward it, however difficult it may be. When the schedule came out, their season opener was against the Chicago Bears. I smiled and called one of my best friends – David Dean – who is a die hard Bears fan, and he came with me. It was a special night, and I'll never forget it.

2. Step away from XXXchurch.com.

The first *"Go & Do"* was difficult for me, but I did it.

The second made zero sense whatsoever and, given my personality (and at this point I think I can say *ego*), I assumed that meant "leave immediately." I knew stepping away *then and there* wasn't possible.

As I write this today, six years have passed. It's June 2019, and I have never forgotten about that process, or the words I heard through it. Still, though, Levi was the only person I ever told about that sense of direction shifting.

I kept quiet.

I *did* start working on another project, though. One that existed separate from the ministry. I worked with an online influencer who I happened to be friends with, and I really enjoyed it. It was the first time in my adult life that I worked behind the scenes, as opposed to being the front-facing, talking head of everything. The expertise I had to offer really did end up making a difference. We were able to scale his business, and we were able to start offering that scalability to others, too.

I have never struggled with confidence. I suppose I don't think that I need more of it, but since this thing is called "Craig Brain," maybe you'll understand that I simply needed a purpose to run *toward*, as opposed to simply running *from* something else. So, I thought, *maybe it's this current venture?*

As it turns out, it wasn't, but it did help me clarify a few realities that were only ever cloudy in my mind. It helped me realize that a whole different path – an entirely new trajectory – could be possible, even at my age. So, while Michelle says something is changing, let me clarify that this change has happened at a snail's pace.

I don't like quitters, and there is a part of me that has never allowed myself to even *think* about walking away, because doing so makes me feel like one. Mike Foster, my friend who started XXXchurch with me, left after two years in the game. He told me that he believed I could take it further, and entrusted me with that responsibility. If I'm honest, I harbored ill feelings toward Mike for a long time. A *really* long time. Because he quit. I get now why he couldn't do this for longer than he gave it. Me walking away now – or jumping into a new role – is *not* me quitting.

I'm not losing.

I'm not running *from* but rather *toward* new ideas that I'm excited about. *Toward* whatever's next.

Six years removed from that day in Alaska, I've got a bit more clarity on what *next* means, and I believe that this step – this chapter, this announcement – will only further act as a means toward that end.

I am finally following *not just* my brain, but my heart and my heart is telling me that it is time.

Moving forward, if and when I lead a huddle, it won't be for XXXchurch.

All of that said, *none of this* means I don't care any longer. And it doesn't mean you won't still see me on the sidelines, coaching my team. With any luck, maybe I'll even be something like a Belichick (even though, gosh – as a Packer fan – I *hate* that guy)...

But it *does mean* that – particularly for those of you who have followed this ministry closely throughout the years – you're going to begin to see some changes take place as I transition from *QB* to *Coach*.

So much of this season – whether of *Craig Brain*, or life in general – can be summarized by "lessons in self-awareness." Or maybe: self-realization. I've changed. The process (maybe something like puberty) has been some tornado of awkward and painful and new and exhilarating.

I'm still growing. I'm still finding my sweet spots. I'm still developing new passions.

I'm coming to the realization that – as a ripe old blue-haired *dadager* – I can't time-in for quite as long, or play quite as hard, and have begun to save up some of my remaining field-time for whatever's coming next.

I'm switching sports here, but Steve Kerr was Michael Jordan's right-hand man with the Chicago Bulls for years. He wasn't ever the superstar, but Jordan trusted him, and at this point – as coach for the Golden State Warriors – he's gone on to break his own player records for most wins in a NBA season.

I hope I can be that kind of coach. I hope that the future of XXXchurch is brighter than it's ever been. I hope that I can be some kind of Belichick or Kerr to a Brady or Jordan, and that ours will be a legacy defined by having introduced freedom to generations of men and women and families whose lives have been completely transformed by the gospel's power to break every chain and redeem every year that pornography and sexual addiction – like a locust – has stolen.

As *coach* to the team that I founded and love, then, I want to make sure that our next *QB* has the arm for the job, the passion for the work, and the love for the people that XXXchurch will continue to seek and serve.

As we move further in the direction of finalizing this transition, I'm sure that the ins and outs will be more fully realized on a public scale. I'm not writing this, today, for the sake of getting into the weeds about each and every detail, but at the very least, I wanted to move out of my brain and into my heart.

To announce the shifts.

To let you know that – as my 18 years in this position come to a close – I want to "end" well, and *we* want to set this ministry up for another 18+ successful years.

How to end this one? How to conclude a chapter on a season that's just beginning? I suppose this will be a story that continues on, and will likely weave its way in and out of whatever stands to follow. Until then…

Thank you for allowing me, my wife and our family the privilege of functioning in this role for so many years. This life has harbored everything from utter joy to seasons of deep despair and back again, but every high and low – every valley and mountain top – has, from this vantage point, made for gorgeous terrain, beautiful to have traveled through. I am honored to have participated in what I can only call *re*creation for so long, and I am excited about what the next chapter holds for this team, for the next *QB* and for myself.

Yours truly,

Coach

P.S. On Friday, I plan to announce the next QB of XXXchurch.com. We'll do so on that website and through those channels, as Craig Brain won't be the place for what is sure to be an ongoing conversation about this role, specifically. If you are interested in how this transition unfolds, please follow along there, I look forward to introducing you all when the time comes.

*Watch Craig expand more on this chapter by scanning the QR code below.

Chapter 20 – Stepping Out (And Trust Falls)

"People who have a problem with flying…don't. What they have is a problem with their lack of control."

A flight attendant told me that recently. I used up every last frequent flyer mile I had to purchase a Delta One suite so that my daughter and I could fly it home from Washington D.C., following her 8th grade trip because that is CREATING FUN.

I hate flying. I do *a lot* of it, but air travel has always freaked me out. Paying the big bucks for a lounge experience at 38,000 feet helped at first, but then we hit turbulence, and all the points in the world couldn't buy it away.

Meanwhile, Elise is sitting next to me, eating a cookie and smiling without a care in the world.

I want to be like a child.

Let me rewind.

A couple of weeks ago, I surprised my friend, Matt Shatto, with a ticket to an event called The Lock Inn at the Oxbow Hotel in Downtown Eau Claire, Wisconsin. Each quarter, one of my favorite artists – Justin Vernon of Bon Iver, together with his bandmate Sean Carey – puts on a unique performance, "paired" with food and drink and an overnight stay at the hotel.

There are only thirty packages available for each of these limited experiences. I've been once before, so *this time* – especially now that my daughter is winning dance competitions throughout Southern California as choreographed to Bon Iver's song, *Creeks* – I knew that I had to find a way to talk to Justin.

I had to make a conversation happen.

Naturally, then, I snuck and hid inside a walk-in freezer, feeling pretty creepy, and asked Matt to play lookout for me so that I could catch Justin before he left for the evening. It worked. I got to give him a thank you letter with the letter I gave to Elise that included a link to her solo dance. We talked briefly about his upcoming performance with TU Dance in D.C the following week, which I'd also be attending.

During our conversation, Matt asked Justin a question: *"How do you do it?"*

What he meant (I think) was, "How do you create? How do you make the music you do? How did you get to where you are? How do you make this kind of life work? How can you explain this in a way that makes actionable sense to me?"

Justin responded with something to the degree of, *"I'm thirty-seven years old, man. Don't ask me that. You think I know?"*

And then – with that artistic-ethereal-thing, albeit slightly more grounded – *"Trust."*

Trust.

Matt hated that answer.

I can't say it sits naturally with me, either, but it's been stuck in my brain ever since.

Trust.

Let me rewind.

Before either trip – to Wisconsin or to D.C. – I took a group of Hillsong youth leaders to the spa around the corner from my house. I recently hired one of the LA campus youth pastors to work for me full-time as a project manager and assistant, and we've been trying to figure out a way to support and pour back into the staff there.

The leaders are young – early twenties, maybe – and we were having a conversation about *God's will.* I realized anew how deeply ingrained the idea of a *life calling* is in a young person's mind, and particularly in the church.

It's not that I don't believe *calling* exists – after all, I remember the Lord specifically leading me to youth ministry, myself, after graduation – but I sometimes wonder if our paranoia about whether or not *we've found it* is, well...founded.

Everyone, sweating in the sauna that day, sat so convinced that there are specific, life-altering decisions to be made, and they are either *inside* or *outside* of God's will, and that His will is somehow knowable (or, at least, discoverable*)*.

But also: mysterious…

And also: (at least potentially) at conflict with the actual desires of a person's heart.

Which begs the question (and stokes the fear): *What if I make the wrong decision?*

How does that *not* lead to paralysis?

Meanwhile, I'm sitting there as a 42-year-old man thinking,

"Do you have kids?

Are you married?

Do you have a dog?

'No' to all three?

Get out there and do what you want to do!!!"

When I left my job at a church to start Fireproof Ministries as a twenty-two-year-old, I specifically remember thinking, "I can get this job back if I need to." At this stage in life, I'm answering "yes" to all three questions – married, with kids, *and* a dog that I swore I'd never own – but I just received the final edits on a statement announcing my departure from quarterbacking the ministry I began when I was these kids' age.

At this point, it's *way harder* to think about doing something else *now* than it was back then. And yet, both as a young man and here again at the start of something new, I am forced to practice *trust*.

I don't want to be reckless, but I don't think life's as regimented as we grow up believing it is. Or, at least, it's not as locked in as I thought that it was, and I don't think it's as locked in as my spa day friends think it is, either. (And no, for anyone wondering and before I get into trouble, I *did not* pass out special brownies to the Hillsong youth leaders for our day in the jacuzzi.)

I'm not sure God always gives us clear and audible *yes* or *no* answers to specific, directional questions we have about which path to take before we simply step foot on one of them and begin walking.

Is *trust* really *that* if we're already in control of the outcome?

Why don't we trust the process?

And will past evidences of the grace of God ever be enough to console our restless anxieties about the present moment (let alone the future)?

To come full circle: *I want to be like a child.*

Children don't have much control over anything. Therefore, children don't have much choice in the matter: they *must trust* (and shame on anyone who takes advantage of that innocence). Assuming they have healthy and loving caretakers, I doubt they *think* much of whether or not they *should trust*, either...they just do.

It reminds me of the Apostle Peter, who didn't stop to ask Jesus if he could have Aquaman's superpowers to be crystal clear about his ability to run on the water before he did it. He just *did it,* and the sinking began when he abandoned the moment for second-guessing his actions in the presence of the One who upheld him in the first place.

When I asked our flight attendant if she ever feared turbulence the way that I always have, she responded, "No. My husband is a pilot, and I've been flying for thirty-six years, now. People who have a problem with flying...*don't.* They have a problem with their lack of control." She decided long ago to relinquish control and trust the process.

So, I laid down in my weird airplane bed and thought, *"Why shouldn't I?"*

I thought, "This airplane is going to land the same way that Justin Vernon's songs do. The same way they *did land* last week in Wisconsin when a largely unplanned jam-session became an awesome experience for an audience with an opportunity to watch his *trust* in action.

Perhaps it's not meant to be explainable. Perhaps – however frustrating or scary to Matt or to me or to a twenty-something searching for direction (or to you, reader) – the "answer" is *let go*.

Let go, frankly, seems synonymous mainly with faith amid a trust-fall, like closing your eyes, crossing your arms and falling backwards off of the picnic table in the schoolyard, believing your friends will make good on their word to catch you.

I've sought (and, mostly, *been in)* control for my whole life, and most of the decisions I've made have been *stepping into* something that I am still in control of.

Right now, though, I'm in a season of *stepping out*, and if I'm honest – I don't have a clear picture, like I normally do, of what exactly that means.

What I do know is that it's not the same as stepping *down*. For that matter, it might not be stepping *up*, either.

I think, rather, that stepping *out* might also be a kind of *stepping aside* – aside of my comfort, my control, my *self*.

Whether it's trusting that stepping out of XXXchurch is the right move, or whether it's trusting that this newfound vulnerability is worth putting out into the world. Or believing that paying forward what I'm learning might matter to someone – that it's going to land, that it's going to help, that it's going to be worthwhile – I know that I'm learning anew what it means to "take steps of faith," as it were.

It feels similar to the way it did when I stepped "out" of the traditional church role I was in twenty-some years ago – and although I can empathize with my friends who want certainty in similar positions – I know now that the sweet spot is the fall, itself:

I don't have to have it all figured out, and I don't really know how the story unfolds, but I'm trusting the process.

*Watch Craig expand on this chapter by scanning the QR code below.

Chapter 21 – Christian Cannabis

A brief disclaimer: I wasn't sure whether or not this "announcement" fits here, after the *trust* chapter. At this point in our series, it's old news, anyhow. But the more I thought about it, the more it made sense because of *how* and *when* I launched Christian Cannabis. It didn't fit chronologically – as far as my podcast schedule goes – to announce a new venture before talking about my transition out of an old one. Now it does. In the end, the decision to launch on Easter Weekend – 4/20/19 – came out of the idea of *trusting*. I felt it in my gut, and in my spirit, and though it didn't *all* make *complete* sense…it was time.

Before – Holy Saturday, April 19, 2019

When I was a kid, Easter never had anything to do with a bunny, eggs, or ugly, pastel color-palettes.

In our house, Easter was a celebration of Jesus' resurrection from the grave. On that Sunday, we'd get dressed up for church. Later, we'd replace our regular Sunday-afternoon routine at the Sizzler salad bar with a delicious, home-cooked meal.

As a kid, I didn't care much for church. When I was in high school, I took a job selling baseball cards at weekend conventions, mainly for the sake of getting out of Sunday morning services. Nevertheless, by the time I graduated with my diploma, I felt called to pursue a bachelor's degree in church ministry. I took a job as a youth pastor straight out of the gate.

I am, officially, an ordained minister available for weddings and funerals. I have spoken at over one-thousand churches across the country throughout my years in ministry, and I know that Easter is the Super Bowl of "Christandom." Some churches even rent out stadiums to fit all the people attending their celebration services. I remember taking my kids to Anaheim Stadium one year for Easter – not to see a baseball game, but to see Rick Warren preach after the Jonas Brothers sang their songs.

Last week, Coachella announced that they were adding Kanye West to their second-week lineup. Not for a headlining spot, but for a 9 AM Sunday morning service.

What?!

How do you even get out of bed for that after Tame Impala plays their Saturday night set? How many people will wake up for it? Main stage? Side stage? Where do you house the service? Personally, I love that *Kanye* – and not his celebrity pastors – is leading the charge with his music this year. What will it be like? Will ninety-thousand people go to an Easter-morning church service at Coachella?

The following day, I was driving my son, Nolan, to an audition in Los Angeles. The weed billboards alongside the highway are many and growing (no pun intended). Cannabis is, simply, the new normal.

I started to think about the billboards people pass on their way to Coachella. Nolan wondered whether there might be any left for my idea.

There weren't. Everything was sold out.

On land.

Then I remembered the sky.

In 2002, I made an announcement by flying a banner overhead. Seventeen years later, we've got skywriting. When we called about availability, the woman on the phone said that all time slots were sold out.

Minus one.

An afternoon slot on April 20th.

Wait a minute…*this year's Easter falls on a 4/20 weekend?*

I looked at Nolan and thought, "Wow, that's fifteen days from now…what do we need to make it happen? What still needs to happen? Is this the right time to introduce this conversation to the world that I have known for so long…?"

I called five people, including my wife, and the response was four-to-one in favor of booking the spot. It seemed pretty convincing compared to the past eleven months of dreaming, exploring, and building some of these ideas out with friends and agencies.

I didn't write new content. I didn't add pages or start freaking out about how I don't have enough information on the website. I simply removed the password-protected barrier and made it live.

For the sake of context, I bought the web domain eight months ago thinking that I would build out a content-driven website and gather a team of experts who could write, host podcasts, and begin a new conversation among fellow Christians surrounding this taboo substance that is quickly gaining legal traction throughout the United States.

I enjoy a good splash. I like using what is loud to lead to better conversations behind the noise.

In that way, I love the name *Christian Cannabis.*

But I'll be honest: it's a love/hate relationship.

On the flipside, just the word "Christian" – when paired with anything other than a person (and even then, sometimes) – is usually awful. We've got an unfortunate knack for poor ripoffs. I guess I've got my work cut out for me if I'm going to prove that this is something other than the B-movie version of things that I hate as much as the next guy.

Cannabis is, decidedly, *not "Christian."* Just like all other non-human things.

But this name is simple and straightforward – as would I like to be. So, here you have it.

I am setting out to create a conversation that targets Christians, so why not call it like it is? For many of us who would use that word to describe ourselves, this will be a new conversation. Or, at the very least, a new *public* discussion.

I think, though, that many Christian cannabis users will come out of the woodwork.

Others, justifiably so, will say, *"Nope, not for me."*

I'm open to all of it.

I'm excited for all of it.

I know that some will hate me for it, and I know that others will thank God that someone finally said something.

I know that there will be both *constructive* and *destructive* criticism.

Whoever you are, and whatever you think, I'd love to open up a public dialogue.

This is a conversation. May all of us feel free to talk. May we also have the humility to incline our ears to listen.

Welcome in.

Yesterday, I spent the day at Coachella, watching some of my favorite bands play music.

Today, I celebrated Easter Sunday at a 9AM "church service" led by Kanye West.

What is life, again?

Kanye called it a *"Very Christian Spiritual Experience."* There wasn't any preaching, and it was certainly different than what you might've seen on TBN this Sunday, but honestly? It was refreshing and new. Definitely the most unique Easter experience I've ever had.

People showed up for it. Thousands and thousands of people showed up for it.

Maybe you saw it online. Perhaps you're wondering what this is all about.

Well, I did something on this 4/20 Easter Weekend, too.

http://christiancannabis.com/announcement/

It was a stunt.

It was a splash.

It was a disruption.

It was an experiment.

Most of all, it was the start of a conversation.

A new one.

Call me crazy, but that little green cross pointed my eyes toward the real Cross, and I finally saw it.

My life has drastically changed since that day.

We can joke about it. Sure, some things move slower for me now, but that does not say I'm asleep on the couch with pizza crumbs all over my stomach.

What I mean by "slowing down" is that the to-do list no longer dominates my entire life. What I mean by "slowing down" is that I am no longer absent from the very people I'm sitting in a room with.

What I mean by "slowing down" is that I have become a better husband, father, friend, and boss.

What does it mean to you? I am not sure yet.

I'm not sure what this becomes. The last thing I did – which also launched at a festival – is still going strong after 18+ years.

There are other things I want to do. I am 43 years *young*. Sure, turning 40 felt like life was half-over, but I still believe the best is yet to come. I hear that often, but I don't know many people who really believe it. I do. I am living and walking in that belief.

In an upcoming episode of Craig Brain, I write about Quarterbacks and Coaches, Brady and Belichick. In it, I announce my departure from the field…but this isn't the reason.

I am not moving from the *Pastor of Porn* to the *Pastor of Pot*.

The episode will come when it comes, but for the time being, let's just say that I had felt called to start moving in a new direction ever since 2013 when I experienced a profound encounter with the Lord that began to set my life on a new trajectory.

Usually, I move extremely fast. It's been six years since that day – an eternity in my world – so I guess you can say I've taken my time with this one.

I'm not retiring. Neither is Brady, apparently, but unlike him, I'm moving more toward trading the field for the sidelines.

I have other sports to play, and other teams to coach.

Some endeavors are non-profits, and others are regular-ole businesses. Some ideas are safe, and others are risky. Just because this one launched first doesn't mean there aren't more to come. New projects and initiatives take time.

I've poured a lot of myself into this project, and many others have done the same for me. When it comes to "Christian Cannabis," the time, thought, energy, prayer and long, in-depth conversations with friends, pastors, mentors and many others are too many to count.

I remember the first, honest conversation I ever had about marijuana with my friend, Krissee. I felt like I was hiding in the closet, whispering to her from behind a pile of clothes.

People love to weigh in on those who come out of their closets (whatever their hidden "secret" might be). Bring out your scales, I guess. Here we go…

My closet is different than yours.

I don't expect you to wear, understand, appreciate, or connect with every piece of clothing in my closet. In fact – if you know me well – you know my closet makes no sense to anyone but me. My clothes are bold, outrageous, and loud. Also, I own a lot of sweats.

I used to hide cannabis mints in my closet. Now that my whole family (and the rest of the world) knows, the lockbox next to my shoes is full, but nothing is hidden.

The other thing the people who know me well understand is that I love hacks and shortcuts. My understanding of cannabis has been neither. This has taken me a long time. I'm finally ready to talk about it, and I'm inviting you to do the same.

What if Christians were to begin understanding how something like cannabis could be used in beneficial ways to support their lives?

What if we were to entertain the idea that legality is not the equivalent of licentiousness, and neither must we demonize and condemn every single thing that we don't quite understand?

What if – rather than trading our feelings for platitudes and "should be's" – we were to begin to understand them better?

What if cannabis proved to enhance mental clarity, diminish anxiety, and lend itself toward physical healing and integrative wellness?

What if cannabis proved to dissolve the self that is constantly getting in the way, enabling one to better prioritize others, and the qualities and relationships that make for a full and vibrant life?

That has been, in part, my experience…all from a plant.

Which brings us back to the present.

Introducing:

ChristianCannabis.com

Join the conversation

I welcome it.

Craig

*Watch Craig expand on this chapter by scanning the QR code below.

Chapter 22 – The Babysitter Club (How to Be a Responsible Adult)

Dear Children,

You'll never believe this, but recently, I had an idea (okay, I had four hundred ideas, but here's one):

The Babysitter Club.

It's an E-course on how grown-ass men and women – particularly contractors, clients, and rock stars – can *finally* learn how to be as responsible as one might (wrongly) assume they would be after all of the years accumulated between the birth canal and their fully-adult selves.

It includes such *hit* lessons as:

- Step One: Set an Alarm
- Step Two: Wake Up
- Step Three: At Least *Try* to *Pretend* That You Have a Job to Do
- Step Four: At Least *Try* to *Pretend* That You Know How to Use a Calendar
- Step Four: Clock Yourself In
- Step Five: Open Your Email

Okay, so I didn't actually create *The Babysitter Club*, and sure, it's a facetious list. But like an acquaintance of mine, Propaganda, says…

"Sarcasm is really the only time people tell the truth."

I've written about coaching quite a few times during this season so far – whether it was my pursuit of an official (and eventually, forfeit) certification at a firm for *My One Thing* or the announcement that I'd be moving into more of an "executive coach's" role at XXXchurch. The reality, though, is that I've been coaching people, albeit unofficially, for years now.

As a dad, one of the best roles I've ever played was as a coach for my kids' soccer leagues. Throughout ten consecutive seasons, I coached teams that both of my children were on (and even led three of them as undefeated, *thank you very much*). I'm the guy who printed "Undefeated Champion" T-shirts before we played our final game. Some people find that abrasive. I say it's confidence.

(In reality, I admit, it's probably *both*. Nevertheless, I mean… we *did* make the win, so…)

As a professional, though, the majority of my coaching has developed naturally out of the relationships I've built with subcontractors who have helped me and my teams bring our goals to life, and *particularly* with artists.

I won't lie: I have a love/hate relationship with most creatives (and, to be fair, given the fact that most people who create don't like to be called "creatives," I'm sure the sentiment goes both ways).

Most of the time, it's like pulling teeth to get an artist's work delivered on time. But it's not *just* the artist – it's the *work-for-yourself* crowd. It's the *I'll get to it when I get to it* mentality. The "fluid workspace" which is much less a nontraditional parameter for most people than it is a complete lack of any boundaries, whatsoever.

Many of the creatives (humor the noun) who *have done* or *are doing* consistent work for me, though, enjoy having me as a client. I finally realized why, and it circles around to the same epiphanous realization I keep coming back to: I'm also their coach. They like working with me because I push them, drive them, remind them, keep them on task and – often – deal with the day-to-day logistics that they hate (but need).

That's all well and good – and I *am* a more natural-born leader who isn't as bogged down by logistics – but often *(and all of my guys know this, so don't damn me as passive-aggressive)*, it can be exhausting.

Babysitting is a tiresome chore, and I'm continually trying to figure out how to impart some of my strengths as a self-starter to others who have very little of that trait as intrinsic to their own personality. Simultaneously – lest one assume that I view myself as only and ever the *teacher* – I've learned much about the benefits that patience brings to a final product.

Nevertheless, deadlines are deadlines, so whether they're past due or agreeably stretched, the main question I have is:

How do you work for yourself?

A layer beneath: *How do you do* **deep work** *for yourself?*

It's not like I haven't had to answer the same question. Ever since I sold baseball cards as a fourteen-year-old, each of my jobs has been an entrepreneurial endeavor. I value working for myself, as do most of my clients, but self-employment necessitates a certain level of discipline that must often be built – like one might build a muscle – if it is to be a strong enough foundation to hold up a life.

And when I say *"hold up a life,"* I really do mean *a life* – not just a paycheck. Many a self-employed person deposits substantial numbers but does *very little* beyond the work it takes to accumulate them.

We've got to think *lifestyle over revenue*. I learned that lesson from a wealthy man who is richer in relationships than his bank statements will ever account for, and I agree with him.

We all traded our parents' *Nine-to-Five* for what we thought was freedom, but in reality: half of us are working *24/7* with no boundaries or breaks, and the other half *feels* like they're working just as much – always *"on"* and mentally exhausted – without ever accomplishing anything for lack of personal boundaries or working systems.

Without parameters, *every* thing bleeds into the next, until *all* things become *no* things.

Without boundaries, you might be *there*, but everyone knows you're not *present*.

Without figuring out how to get your work under control, your work will always control *you*.

I've spent a lot of years talking about how difficult it is to rewire neural pathways in the brain. When it comes to addiction, *change* is as difficult in work as it is in porn as it is in eating habits as it is in whatever other rut you might've been digging for the past however-many years.

If I'm not intentional about creating a schedule, locking it into a calendar and then *sticking to it*, what should have been an eight-hour workday will double to sixteen before I even realized it happened. I can almost guarantee you, though: it will not have equated to another full day's worth of accomplishments. Instead, it will become a frenzied and anxiety-inducing afternoon/evening, full of short-tempered impatience toward myself and my family, before I have to do it all over again.

Maybe you know what I'm talking about.

I've had to get extremely practical when it comes to creating a schedule, and I've had to ask for help. Recently, I hired a personal assistant. I gave my wife control of my calendar, and then I started using Calendly to schedule meetings where time slots remained available so that – instead of arbitrary work meetings interrupting family dinner – I can *both* plan for their start *and* look forward to their end.

I'll say this, as well: many a self-employed person experiences compounding misery atop his or her already-unkempt calendar due to the vague-yet-constant feelings of urgency that our world's unrelenting interconnectedness impresses (or, *oppresses)* upon them.

Here, too, putting in the *work* to develop a *working schedule* is helpful. If you've already allotted time – an hour, perhaps – for catching up on whatever you might miss throughout the day, then you don't need to worry about following every tangential beep and notification tempting to pull you away from work at hand. Chances are, *you're not missing anything*. But if, in fact, you are, then you can come back to it, and schedule it in when you've got the time to focus on *only that thing*, rather than succumbing to the overwhelming lie that *all things* must be happening *all at once.*

Also, to reiterate a favorite and familiar lesson: *turn your damn phone off.* Silence your notifications. *Do Not Disturb* is your best friend. It's no wonder we're all so scatterbrained, and so late on our deliverables, while incessantly bombarded with distraction. A few years ago, a study on "digital distraction" came out of UC Irvine, concluding that it takes a person about twenty-five minutes, on average, to return to her original task after having attention diverted by some dinging device.

Finally – and especially because so many of the people I work with and I want to grow and scale our endeavors – there is a massive difference between working *in* something and working *on* something.

In the beginning, especially, almost everyone has to spend time in the weeds. Eventually, though, we need an overhead view to get a clear perspective of all that we've been tangled up in. At some point, it might be time to delegate tasks that would have otherwise swallowed up your time to continue developing your vision.

My question for you – *grown-ass-adult* that you are – is: whether or not you've got a job that affords you the privilege of choosing your employer… *are you capable of being a reliable employee?*

Can you hit a deadline (without having to be chased down)?

Can you be counted upon to reach a goal?

Are you disciplined enough to create your own?

Do you need some sort of junior-level assistant who might be able to take on the grunt work that's bogging you down so that you can scale your business?

Do you need to give your wife your calendar?

Do you need to bust out a dictionary and check out what a calendar *is?*

It *is* possible to be a responsible adult. To set an alarm and get out of bed before you've hit snooze for a full hour.

I joke about *The Babysitter Club* for "contractors, clients, and rock stars" because they're/we're often the ones who know the *least* about creating healthy rhythms in and from which to function. Frankly, no matter how put together or enviable those folks might look on Instagram, they're often the *most* disorganized and *least* satisfied with the chaos of life, yet with little to no clue about how to change their circumstances, or get out of the ruts that have become Grand Canyons.

Levi likes to tease and call me *"dad."* Well, son, let me run with that analogy (since I've spent plenty of time babysitting you, too)…

It might've been easy to piss into your diapers for so many years, but it was also uncomfortable, and unless someone helped you out, or you pulled them off, yourself, you'd have just walked around in your own private urine pool all day long.

Potty training sucks, but once you learn how to aim, you're free from what used to be a trap of your own making.

Taking responsibility is kind of like that. You're happier, and I'm done changing diapers.

- Step One: Set an Alarm
- Step Two: Wake Up
- Step Three: At Least *Try* to *Pretend* That You Have a Job to Do
- Step Four: At Least *Try* to *Pretend* That You Know How to Use a Calendar

- Step Four: Clock Yourself In
- Step Five: Open Your Email

And don't forget to clock out. Your mind needs it, and so does your family (and so – for that matter – does whoever you call *"boss"* for the sake of the fresh, creative mind he hired you for).

It'll take some *work* to *work better*, but dammit ya little baby, it's possible and worth it.

With Love,
A Grown Up

P.S. David Allen has a pretty amazing book on productivity, task, and work-life management called *Getting Things Done*. In reality, it's more a methodology than anything else. Its subtitle is, *"The Art of Stress-Free Productivity,"* and he provides pragmatic offerings for *how* one might go about organizing *not just* a day, but a *brain*, into orderly and actionable steps so that you can uh…*get things done.*

*Watch Craig expand on this chapter by scanning the QR code below.

Chapter 23 – Alex Cooper Was Right (School Sucks)

I wrote a poem today. It goes like this:

> *School sucks,*
>
> *seven-plus hours stuck in a classroom is a waste of time,*
>
> *grades don't matter,*
>
> *a degree doesn't equal a job, and*
>
> *I hope my kids don't go to college.*
>
> *The end.*

There's nothing quite like a soft, even-keeled set of opinions to really get the people going.

I mean it, though. Our education system is broken, and with over *one trillion dollars* in U.S. College debt, I think it's a waste of time and money.

Of course, God decided it'd be fun to give me a daughter who is <u>a Number One on the Enneagram</u> – the Perfectionist – who *wants* to go to college because *it's the right thing to do*.

She's a black-and-white-thinking rule-follower, and I'm a black-and-white-blending rule-breaker.

We'll see. I guess I've got my work cut out for me. Maybe this will become an argumentative essay that I can stack atop her diploma and gift her on graduation day (not that it'll work – Ones can't be reasoned with.)

Five years ago, I published a blog titled, *"Don't Give a Sh*t About Grades."* It went over about as well as one might expect with an audience who gives *tons of shits* about grades. Still, I stand by it.

Straight A's don't equal *smart kids.*

That's *not* to say that you should raise stupid kids. I mean they're *already* stupid, right? LOL OMG. Kids just pop out of their moms and don't know anything! Kids are dumb as rocks!

I'm joking. And I digress.

The point is: *the game has changed.*

Well, *most* of the game. Education seems to be the only thing stubbornly clinging to the past while the rest of the world – especially given the rapid advancement of technology – progresses.

I went to grade-school and maintained a solid *B* throughout. I worked just hard enough to pass, but couldn't be bothered to strive for perfection, especially come high-school, when mindless homework and standardized testing paled in comparison to the profitable business I'd already begun selling baseball cards on the weekends, and the work I did with my dad (I wrote all about both of those jobs already, here).

When I went to college (yes, *I went)*, my whole mentality revolved around a single question:

"How can I get that stupid piece of paper in the shortest amount of time?"

The system didn't make it easy (which is both the problem and the point).

I went to Hope International University in Fullerton, California – *not* because it was a great school, but because they were a *Southern California school* offering a degree in Church Ministry (without the annoyance of a curfew that most Christian universities impose…after all, the devil is a night owl).

Still, they put me on academic probation, limiting me to four classes per semester, which meant that I didn't stand a chance at graduating within four years (but they sure stood to make more money).

Most people don't.

The average student – whether due to taking the wrong classes, or switching majors, or too many hungover mornings – takes about four-and-a-half years to finish college. Only fifty-six percent of the students who enter America's colleges and universities graduate within six years, and only twenty-nine percent of students who enter two-year programs complete their degrees within three years.

And these are old stats.

I remember writing briefly about this for the first time shortly after Obama was sworn into office. Clinton endorsed his new student loan policy by saying that *"it will change the course for all Americans."*

If what he meant by that was, *"This plan is crap, it will keep you in debt, but you'll get to avoid adulthood and responsibility while you do it!"* then…sure…it changed the course for all Americans.

Here's the deal: if my daughter wants to go to college, I'll help her do it. But she won't come out of it with the debt that most people do.

You'll never believe it, but I've got a few thoughts for both parents *and* students about how to avoid a lifetime spent paying back college loans, as well…

1. Start saving money for your kids. Right now. <u>Start a 529 Plan</u> and put whatever *extra* you can afford into it. Pennies, even. Whatever. Just start.

2. Teach your kids about money by encouraging them to participate in the investment. My wife paid for

everything. She worked at Burger King, Costco, a pizza place, a preschool and the school library before *and* during college. The whole, *"you can't work while you're in school"* mentality is garbage.

3. Four-year universities are expensive, and so is moving away to go to one. Out of state tuition is outrageous. Enroll in a local junior college. If you *have* to move away, enroll at whatever the "cheap" college is, there, and start knocking out your general-ed classes. Do you want to spend $30 or $3,000 for your guitar lessons? Pick and choose or take online, transferable courses.

4. Full-time tuition costs the same whether you're taking 12 credit hours or 18, *so take 18*. That's six classes per semester. I remember sitting in my dorm room following the news about my probation and realizing that I needed 124 credit hours to graduate and was only given twelve to start. That's when basic math matters. I sat there, on my bed, until I had a plan that'd put my degree in-hand in three years after being on probation for the first year.

    I enrolled for *"J Sessions"* – week-long classes between semesters that'd help me knock out three credit hours in seven days. Perfect. I also enrolled in summer school. It sucked, but it was cheap. I had to average eighteen credit hours, take *J Sessions*, spend two summers in class, and cram my last semester full of twenty-two units.

It worked.

Yes, the extra classes cost money, but not nearly as much as an additional school year. Maybe I sound crazy, but I helped my friend plot out the same path, and he did it, too. You just have to stick to a plan.

5. College degrees are growing *both* less and less critical *and* more and more expensive. A degree (as I wrote in my powerful, introductory poem) does not equal a job. If you can swing it, jump into an internship, or look for part-time work in your field of interest. Gain experience, create connections. Textbook knowledge isn't enough.

6. If you have no clue what you want to do, don't go. Don't spend the kind of money just because you think you have to. Take a year off, go on a mission, or figure yourself out first.

That's *if* you go to college at all. Take it or leave it, I guess. All I have is experiences and opinions– and my feelings won't be hurt if you don't like either. I have used *very little* of my expensive degree, and I am putting my own kids through a customized and expedited school program. I am simultaneously giving them work-life experiences at a young age, as I don't see traditional education churning out students who are anywhere near prepared for the real world (let alone focused on what actually matters in it).

I think, perhaps especially as parents, we have to ask *why?*

Why aren't these systems evolving? Why are students still forced to take classes on subjects that they couldn't possibly care less about? Why do we still treat bubbles correctly shaded in with No. 02 lead pencils on sheets like ballots as though they are any indication of a person's actual intelligence or ability?

Levi recently shared with me that his wife, Brandi, has been struggling to pass a fitness-coach certification program she's currently enrolled in. Brandi has dealt with learning disabilities throughout her scholastic life and - despite being one of the *most qualified* coaches regarding the actual hands-on implementation of her knowledge in a class setting - is now threatened with the loss of her credentials due to a circle wrongly blackened on a test intentionally designed to ask unclear questions.

Why?

You've got the thumbs up on expertise, but you can't get the job (or the piece of paper) because you got confused about a question that has nothing to do with what you're interested in?

Why?

Prereqs and standardizations make for machine-men with machine-minds (I know Charlie Chaplin's *Dictator* speech wasn't about the SATs, but I love that wording).

In <u>an article published by The Guardian</u>, George Monbiot comments,

"In the future, if you want a job, you must be as unlike a machine as possible: creative, critical, and socially skilled. So why are children being taught to behave like machines?"

The author goes on to say that children – when allowed to apply their natural creativity and curiosity – *love* to learn. I can attest, and so can my kids. My thoughts aren't at all about whether or not we should be teaching the next generation (of course we should), but about *how*.

Ultimately, we send our kids to institutions that we don't necessarily even believe in because it's easier than spending time with them or working toward creating a solution.

I'm not blameless, here, but I have learned to move past my assumptions.

My daughter – for instance – always wanted to be homeschooled, but Jeanette and I didn't think we'd be able to give her the kind of experience necessary to appropriately foster and fuel her interests. At the same time, *"normal school"* was driving her insane. She became obsessed with straight *A's*, perfect attendance, and whatever other checklists her teachers used to judge her usefulness as a cog in the wheel. Anxiety dominated her education.

At the same time, my son was burnt out on the system (not to mention: well beyond it), so as a father who hates the "school rules" as much as anyone, I started to question all of them.

How do we know we can't give Elise the experience she needs if we pull her out of the traditional public school system?

Is there a way for Nolan to be done with school completely?

And just what does school *have* to look like in the first place?

My wife and I decided to become the answer to our own questions.

We created the *Gross Life Prep Academy*. After all, if you're not happy with the system, merely complaining about it isn't going to make much of a difference. You've got to create your own system (or, at least, add to the one you're dissatisfied with).

We said *yes* to Elise's homeschool request. Education, for her, is no longer bogged down by whether or not she made it to her desk before the bell rang. Now, it looks like our last trip to Washington D.C. to see TU Dance and Bon Iver perform together. It seems like a life experience that is actually connected to her dreams and interests – much more like a trade school (and, therefore, much more beneficial for and applicable to her *actual* field of study).

Nolan, following his ninth-grade year, tested out of school altogether. He was done before he turned sixteen. The kid can stand up to any graduating senior with the knowledge and expertise he has acquired as a young man. He can't speak Spanish, but he can speak Adobe. He has been learning how to write music and play the piano. He can speak Photoshop. He directed a commercial for Nike and he just directed his second video for Hillsong LA, and the jobs aren't slowing down.

I want to be a good teacher, and if my kids don't want to go sit in a room for seven-plus hours a day, my lesson *will not be*, "Well, you have to, because that's just what people do." I'd like to give them something more than an imprisoning mentality that'll continue to rob them of their true potential at 35 when they're still going through the motions because it's still *just what people do*.

None of this should be read as though I consider education unimportant.

Neither am I communicating that the parent/child roles should be reversed, or that sometimes you just have to suck it up and learn things you'd rather not.

But I am saying that our traditional systems are absurd.

I'm still teaching my kids every day, and they're both students now as much as they ever were in a traditional class setting.

As parents, we can't *not* teach our kids. For that matter, we can't help but be teachers. They're going to learn from us either way and what kind of environment are we going to create that moves them in the direction of preparedness for life ahead?

Are we willing to be involved? Are we ready to be a part of helping create something better?

Craig

P.S. I know that this reflection won't satisfy everyone, largely because that's all it is - a reflection. Diagnostic in its own right, but necessarily reductionistic. I didn't set out to write a thesis. Obviously, there is plenty more to discuss. I understand privilege and the lack thereof when it comes to this topic of education reform.

Nevertheless...in a world where all the information it holds is a click away, I wonder if it might be appropriate to ask what it means to be educated, qualified or *ready* for the life ahead. I'd argue that the majority of what our kids are taught as "important" doesn't make the cut. To quote thirteen-year-old Logan LaPlante who, years ago, spoke at a TEDx conference in <u>a presentation titled *Hackschooling Makes Me Happy*</u>, *"What if we were to base education on the study of being happy and healthy? Why is that* not *considered education?"* With over ten million hits in the years since, I know I'm not the only parent asking how we can do better with the time allotted us, together with our children.

*Watch Craig expand on this chapter by scanning the QR code below.

Chapter 24 – Talent Shows

I've always hated talent shows, and I've always thought that we should probably be calling them something more appropriate, like:

Not-So-Talented-Shows.

Like, "Hey, would you like to come watch me be *not-so-talented* on stage tonight?"

That was before my newfound interest in dance. I'm now two weeks past the letter I wrote to my daughter before her solo competition performance when she stole the show with her choreograph to Bon Iver's *Creeks*, and at this point, I'm learning to observe "the talent show" through a different lens.

The old pair of glasses I'd watch these performances through was my "waste of time" glasses. It's harsh, I suppose, but it's true.

These days, though, I'm feeling more neutral. Supportive, even.

I'm learning to tell the difference between a *talent showpiece* and a *performance* piece.

The former, one would *pay* to enter. The latter, one would *get paid* to win. Or, simply, to be seen.

As a naturally competitive person, I think I've always been more attracted to the performance piece – the final product, as it were. But I'm realizing more and more just how essential the talent show is in the process.

The performance pieces *"win"* the talent shows, and move beyond them. But the *move beyond* wouldn't be possible without the practice that events like the talent shows afford their contestants.

There is no winner without a contest to compete in.

And also (mind-blowing a realization as this has been): *not everyone enters to win.*

Maybe that's why I always hated sitting through *not-so-talented-shows*, too. Maybe my expectations were too high for a group of kids who either weren't really so talented as to warrant a performance garnering that description, or – perhaps – I was just bored with what I deemed their lack of drive to win (as though everyone is as motivated by a medal as I seem to be).

But as with many aspects of life these days, I'm learning to enjoy the means as much as the end.

Today, Old Man Gross is saying that – while I have, historically, had a hard time watching talent shows – I understand the need for them. From my recent vantage point, I see their purpose as *at least* twofold…

On the one hand, they serve the kids. The kids who want to win, and the kids who just want to enter for the sake of performing something, but don't need to, want to and/or expect to podium at evening's end.

On the other hand – and I think this is the realization that has recently occurred to me – talent shows are also for the parents. Those of us who see potential in our kids and want to allow them to hop on stage and rid themselves of the fear of it.

Who knows…perhaps fear becomes love, or passion, or calling…?

Kind of like it has for my daughter, Elise.

Or for my son, Nolan, who just recorded his first professional, studio-produced song. He's been singing since he could talk. Every old video that we have seems to find him behind a microphone, whether he's singing an old Justin Bieber song to open up for one of my events, or standing in our old living room holding a plastic Fisher-Price mic. Those are talent shows, and here he is moving beyond them, but not without the gift that they've been, propelling him toward whatever he's becoming.

I think the whole idea is applicable beyond our kids' stages, too.

Maybe it's the difference between a hobby and a profession, but just because the former isn't synonymous with one's occupation doesn't mean it shouldn't be engaged in. Do you love it? Do you love the talent show? The community? The camaraderie? The fun? Do you love it solely for what it is, regardless of what you stand to get out of it?

That's wonderful.

In the past, I'd have likely said to remove it from your life, but at this point, I recognize that I've also entered into talent shows of my own. Dipping toes into the water atop stages I'm not sure I could've *"won"* to know that some entries are worth it just because contesting is what I want to do, and that is enough.

Maybe your "talent show set" evolves into something more, and you see an opportunity to step out of the *hobby* circuit and onto a more professional stage. I don't know. But neither will you unless you try.

As for my part, I finally realize that you can't have one without the other. It's a simple lesson, and in the simplest of terms:

You can't have the professional performance without the practice that makes it such. At the very same time, you don't have to move into the realm of "professional" for your performance to matter.

The talent show is a necessary part of the process, and not merely some tedious chore to move past as quickly as possible.

For that matter, if you love the stage your standing on right now – if it brings you life and joy and fulfillment – maybe you never move past it at all.

Enjoy it for what it is, *now*, and not *only* for what it might become.

Do what you do.

Love what you love.

I'm learning to do the same.

*Watch Craig expand on this chapter by scanning the QR code below.

Chapter 25 – Just Say No (To "No")

[Started December 22, 2017]

Dr. Samuel West is a Swedish psychologist whose research focuses on "innovation and what organizations can do to promote a climate of exploration and experimentation."

In 2017, he founded the Museum of Failure, which showcases over one-hundred failed products and services from companies all over the world. Since then, his museum has gained notoriety, traveling across land and sea to cities throughout the globe – including Downtown LA, which is where I treated myself to a birthday gift and perused the collection for the first time.

As a forty-two-year-old entrepreneur, I was encouraged by the display. Maybe that sounds strange – to leave *motivated* by a museum showcasing failure – but I think that's part of the point. It's a testament to creativity. It's a story about *trying*. These products and services were created by people and companies who refused to take *no* for an answer.

And sure, sometimes saying yes when the rest of the world is saying *no* results in failure, but – if the companies represented in the Museum of Failure are any proof – *failure is rarely the end.*

Apple products like the "Newton," which was supposed to be a digital notepad that could also send faxes.

Heinz's purple and green ketchup.

Coca-Cola's coffee soda, "Blak."

Colgate's beef lasagna.

If anything, failure is an educator or a stepping stone.

Which brings me to a failure of my own…

I believe that I know how to be a good friend. I've never struggled to make friends, and the nature of my work throughout the years has allowed me to meet new people regularly. Whether that's through a product, company or idea of my own creation that I used as an opportunity to collaborate with others, or mere luck that brings us together, I love joining other people's journeys – especially those who I see potential in – and exploring what our futures might look like.

I also believe that I know how to *deepen* the friendships I have. I pursue people and help them develop and grow. A friend of mine, Tom Ramsey, did that for me when I was a teenager, and I know how unique a relationship ours was. Most people don't have a mentor like Tom to help them through.

I know my wife didn't.

The other night, Jeanette told me that she struggles to make friends. She doesn't know how to put herself out into the world, or what she would do with herself if she tried.

She asked me *how* I did it.

I laid awake long after she fell asleep. I didn't sleep at all
that night, actually. It occurred to me, as a thought carried
on the sound of her breathing, that in all of our years of
marriage – and for all of the friendships she's seen me build
and maintain – never once had she asked me about how to
make a friend.

The following day, through tears, I told Jeanette how
painful that long night had been after having come to the
realization that *I have failed* to impart something that I
know how to do so well to my wife. How had none of it
passed through me to her? How had the two of us *not*
become one in this way?

I began to wonder at how powerful a thing it might be if we
were able to walk in the strength and confidence of one
another's giftings, and not *only* our own.

And then I thought about our kids – 50% of both of us. It is
no wonder that Nolan and Elise are so unafraid when it
comes to gracing the stages they stand on. At the same
time, it is no wonder they *are* so afraid of the unknown, and
all of the rejection that threatens to meet each of us there.

This is, of course, *not* to say that Jeanette is only bringing
fear to the half she contributes. It was merely a realization
that – in light of the context – perhaps I see *failure* as less
threatening, and am, therefore, less inclined *not* to try, or to
believe that something *can't* be done (or – at the very least –
attempted).

Failure is an opportunity to learn, and here – glaringly in front of me – is mine.

I want to impart the *yes* in me.

I've spent a lot of life telling everyone what I'm *against*. I want to spend the rest of it telling everyone what I'm *for*.

I want Jeanette to know that *yes*, – despite every *no* in her head – she should risk the vulnerability it takes to pursue genuine friendships because it is worth being known (and also: *yes*, she is worth knowing).

I want my son, Nolan, to say *yes*, to his dreams of fronting a band despite every *no* the world gives him. Despite his friend's mom telling him that, "It's a nice hobby, son, but no, it can't be done." I've never been more excited to give him a *yes* instead. Pursue it. Make a career out of it.

I want to help him do it for him, but I also want to help him do it for her.

We need to quiet the voices that keep telling us, *no*. The critics who keep saying, "*You can't*." The elders whose ways are tired and worn out.

I want my daughter, Elise, to say *yes* to dreaming, to dancing, even in the face of the lies that tell her, "No, you're not good enough, popular enough, *fill-in-the-blank-enough*," because – damn it – she *is* enough.

Elise and I, specifically, have been talking quite a bit recently about what her "yes" would mean when it comes to her passion for dancing. We've connected more since I finally took an interest in better understanding her heart and her love for the craft. When we went to see Bon Iver's performance with TU Dance in Washington D.C., one of the head choreographers there – Tony – told her that, "If you want to do this one day, you're going to need to move beyond the competitive circuit, and into performance, itself."

That day is coming. Elise is winning competitions now and can create a troupe of her own. I know because I can help her. We sat up for two hours that night, dreaming together about what and who would make the perfect dance group. She could build and launch it now, at thirteen years old, from her own home, and by the time she's old enough to run a studio or lead a troupe, she'd have over ten years worth of experience under her belt, with every connection needed to make her dream come true…

And then, amongst the excitement, the fears start creeping in. "*But dad, those kinds of opportunities only happen for famous people…*"

How often do we dream without ever even trying to chase after our desires, quenched by insecurities that keep us from giving ourselves the permission to start?

I did my best to silence every *no* with a *yes*.
To look past the fears that arose, and the *what ifs*?

To replace *can't* with *can* try.

At the end of the day, I know that the best I can do is model
the *yes*. I know how to argue, but ultimately, the freedom to
try isn't imparted through the winning of a debate about
what's possible, but through somehow receiving the courage
to *step into it*.

The courage to *risk it*. In spite of the unknown. In spite of
the fear.

In many ways, *Craig Brain*, itself, is the purest example of
that risk, for me. Leaving my role at XXXchurch. Starting
something new. It's an awful lot more difficult at forty-three
than it was at twenty-two, but it's a part of me, and I don't
want to forfeit what's next for fear.

It's impossible – especially in our social-media-saturated
culture, where *everyone* weighs in with an opinion on
everything – to avoid critique. It contributes to the paralysis
that's already difficult enough to avoid when navigating
personal relationships (let alone trying to save face before
the entire world) and traps us into believing that we have to
receive permission before we can move.

You don't. It's okay to color outside of the lines. Not
everyone needs to be on board. It's okay to pursue
something unconventional. It's okay to invent. Maybe even
to create something that ends up in the Museum of Failure,
but at least you will have done it.

Yes might not be the equivalent of *success*, but you will never know unless you try.

In my mastermind groups, we have portions of our meetings together dedicated to what is called a *Hot Seat*. If you're in it, then the rest of the group spends the session focusing on your particular questions, problem areas and/or issues you're facing. The group provides insight and feedback, harnessing their wisdom and strength to help counter your weaknesses. During this time, the person in the hot seat is allowed to clarify anything the group deems necessary, but…

…he, or she is not allowed to say no.

One can only take the suggestions received and try.

I've got the *try* in me. I've got the *yes* where my family and friends keep hearing *no*, and I want us all to sing a new song together. Some of that means slowing down to a pace that others can match. Some of it means asking others to speed up.

A friend of mine recently told me, *"Things just work out differently for you than they do for me, Craig."*

In truth, she wasn't wrong, but I told her the secret:

You don't stop at the first no.

You're willing to challenge, patiently but persistently, and write a new story of your own (as opposed to merely playing a role in someone else's).

I think, too, it means you're willing to show up *first*.

And here again: *first is scary*.

First is riskiest.

It's also the most rewarding.

First – even for a company like Apple – means that your "Newton" pad might end up in a failure museum because the technology isn't yet up to par with the vision. But also, first meant a thousand songs in your pocket. First revolutionized not only computer technology, but it also changed what a "phone" is, the way the entire music industry worked, and the world as a whole.

The combination of *first* and *yes* meant Elon Musk could persistently challenge the *no* when a team of MIT researchers told him that, actually, it is possible to both launch *and* successfully land a rocket.

Tony Hsieh did shoes-by-mail with Zappos when others told him it'd be impossible.

Hell, *Donald Trump* is the president of the United States. Let that one sink in.

Eighteen-hole courses are being replaced by Top Golf. Netflix outed Blockbuster. iTunes flipped the record industry entirely upside down. Amazon started as an online bookseller and has gone on to champion every other big box store in the world. Uber provided a better alternative to taxis. I'd even go so far as to say that Jesus did this same type of work in place of the religion that preceded him.

These people are disruptors. They don't take *no* or *can't* for an answer. At least, not a permanent one.

I tend to function as similarly, and I don't plan on stopping now. XXXchurch was *The #1 Christian Porn Site*, and although I've always joked about how that's easy when there's not a *number two,* taking a risk on just the *name* of that ministry, let alone everything it entailed, was risky. It was scary. But I'm convinced the first-ness, and the twenty years' worth of persisting despite every *no!* we receive, is also what has made it a successful and worthwhile endeavor.

I want to say *no* to *no,* and I want to encourage my friends and family and *you* to do the same.

Yes is for leaders and changemakers. It's for rule-breakers more often than it is for rule-followers. It's for people bored with the routine and the status quo. It's for those of us who see a better way of doing things – sometimes, even when we're not quite sure what that better way is…but also fully aware that we won't unless we take a step toward it.

I am a dad, a husband, a business owner, a ministry leader, a friend, a [fill in the blank]. There's always a role to fill, but whoever I am, I want to make sure that the people I come into contact with – my family, those I love and meet along the way – catch something of a *yes* from me. I hear my wife, daughter, son, friends tell me that they can't...

But we *can*.

Stop listening to the *no*.

What do you mean you can't?

If not you, then who?

*Watch Craig expand on this chapter by scanning the QR code below.

Chapter 26 - An Instagram Husband (In the Amazon)

In 2018, Amazon released <u>an advertisement for AWS</u>—
their online cloud platform. In their commercial, a narrator
lists several ideas, tech, and entertainment that Amazon
didn't dream up- Yelp, Netflix, The Mars Dune Buggy,
Airbnb, and Samsung-all recognizable examples of forward
progress and innovation.

The advertisement ends, though, with a "reveal" wherein
the service boasts that-though *they* weren't the dreamers,
per se-they are the "only cloud with the experience,
opportunities, and know-how to make [their client's
dreams] happen."

To my knowledge, AWS had never released a public,
commercial advertisement like that, and it was as though
Amazon's first televised introduction to the world about
their back-end web services said, "You don't know this, but
we're running the world. *We power everything you love.*"

All of that to say, for every front-facing thing that *we* love,
there is *a lot* of work going on behind-the-scenes. And it is
the back-end support that makes what we end up seeing as
valuable, possible.

I've done a ton of front-facing work. Part of the reason, I
think, is because I am willing to take the heat that I enjoy
creating. When we launched our ministry in 2002,
combining the letters "XXX" with the word "church" was a
dicey move. Seventeen years later, people still refer to me
as *the XXXchurch guy.*

But there is *no way* our ministry would have lasted, let alone grown for 17 years without a countless number of people working with me behind the scenes…my wife Jeanette not the least of them.

In recent years, although I've remained "the face" of XXXchurch, I have had the opportunity to play more out-of-sight positions, as well, whether in a coaching role supporting other ministries and/or businesses, or helping entrepreneurs launch their ideas, or as a mastermind creator, etc.

It's in the mastermind/group facilitator role that I was first thrown into the world of social media influencers. I had been working with one of these "influencers"– Jefferson Bethke (you might recognize that name thanks to his viral YouTube poem, *Why I Hate Religion, But Love Jesus*, which now boasts over 33 million plays)–for close to four years by the time we put together a room of our own. We've worked on many online projects together–from digital products to physical book sales–and even launched a publishing company in hopes of working with other like-minded artists and solopreneurs.

The company, however, was just the two of us, and we weren't able to scale it the way we wanted to. By the time it began to plateau, I had been a part of Jeff Walker's Platinum Plus Mastermind Group, launched my own Collide Mastermind for small-business leaders, CEOs, and friends who I wanted to help, and decided to propose a shift in focus for our company:

What if, instead of publishing books for influencers who are spread out and disconnected from one another (and us...and the rest of the world), we were to bring them all into a small community wherein they could meet, learn from and build actual, real-life *relationships?*

Thus, we launched the <u>Influencer Inner Circle</u> and defined the purpose of the group as a means toward going far, *together*.

It's a weird world, to be sure.

These people might be loosely connected by faith and social influence (I'd call it more of an awareness of one another's existence, or a vague association based–at best–on a follower count).

These people "know" *everyone*, but they don't *know* anyone.

The "top" as perceived by a half-million social-media followers, for all of its front-facing glitz and glam, can be–without relational intentionality–a lonely world. Many people wield enormous power and impact online, but their neighbors have absolutely no idea what it is that they really do. We wanted to create a room into which these influencers could come and feel understood, share secrets, build relationships, listen to and learn from experts, and create lifelong connections.

As it turns out, the majority of our attendees are couples, and they're all trying to figure out how to function together beneath the enormity of the influence they hold. Also, though not true of each couple, the majority of the "status-holders" are women. The wife is the popular one in the relationship.

Which bring me to the fascinating role of The Instagram Husband.

Four years ago, <u>The Mystery Hour released an ever-popular parody video titled *Instagram Husband*</u>, filmed as a fake public service announcement to all the "human selfie sticks behind every cute girl on Instagram." It's hilarious. It went viral, and a quick look at the YouTube comments a mingled mass of typewritten joy, utter disgust, and some sarcastic combination of both—will give you an idea of the love/hate relationship that people have with the state of our society today…

> *"Thank you for bringing awareness to this terrible condition millions suffer from.□ "*

> *"Honestly, I find this video more disturbing than funny. I know it's a joke, but it's actually very true. It's sad how wrapped up our society is in social media. Whatever happened to doing or eating something for the sake of enjoying it? Not for you to post it so you can gain more followers or likes...sad."*

> *"I found myself laughing so much. Then crying.□ "*

There are millions more to wade through. The gist of the video makes a mockery of this lifestyle, and though it's certainly *not* for everyone, the truth is that in the age of social media, people really do make a significant living by posting pictures on the internet. It *is* a viable business model.

In January 2019, The Atlantic added to the narrative with an article titled *The Instagram-Husband Revolution*, claiming that "the men behind the camera are ready to step into the spotlight," and that "while men used to be seen as begrudging participants, more so-called Instagram husbands are embracing the term and becoming an integral part of their partner's business."

There are plenty of these men/husbands in our Influencer Inner Circle. Their wives are brimming over with online popularity, and they're trying to figure out what to do with it. Do they leave their jobs to help a growing (albeit volatile) business that seems to have fallen in their lap, or stay in something more stable? What about their career goals? What about their dreams?

One of the couples interviewed in The Atlantic's article is in our group–Dani Austin and Jordan Ramirez. Dani is a fashion blogger, and her husband acknowledged the difficulty: "I was raised in a generation like, *Here's what the atomic household looks like. You're supposed to go out and be a banker, doctor."*

What I see happening through our mastermind group, the relationships there, and the insights formed as a direct result of having now worked with many of these couples is that the ones who are *really* crushing it are the ones who have decided to take that proverbial step of faith and team up together.

I've been in the internet/online space for a *long time*. XXXchurch had hits before social reach even mattered, and way back then, my wife and I teamed up together to learn how to generate awareness for the things we believed to be necessary.

For me, then, this social-influencer group is one of the most fun things I've ever been a part of.

In our day and age, social reach is *everything*.

If you have it, you can do *anything*.

But that *doesn't* mean you have the wherewithal to steward it wisely or foster it well.

I'm not the guy with a gazillion followers. I don't have that reach, personally, but–while I don't believe it is arrogance speaking, here–I do understand that world, and I thrive in these spaces. I have the skill set to complement the work that folks like Dani, Jordan, and the Bethke's are doing. It is fun to share knowledge with others who not only need it but want it. Here's a large part of *why:*

People get popular (or–if not popular–discover some measure of success) doing what they love to do. But growth, success and/or popularity involve maintenance, and it doesn't take long before you're stuck in the weeds, where working on "maintaining" your passion replaces all that you were passionate about in the first place.

I've had to do my fair share of learning about all of this, as well. I've come to discover that I enjoy strategizing with and talking to people, not sitting in my tiny bathroom-office and building funnels for them. I like helping people figure out how to thrive in what they actually love. That's what *I'm* passionate about. That's what I love. And no, that'll likely never wholly extinguish days (or seasons) that we hate, but the point is that mutually-beneficial, complementary and/or appropriately delegated roles spur us along toward a life that isn't bogged down by a dead-end cloud of dismay at what it has become.

The point is that we are better together.

I'll be honest with you: as a mostly front-facing guy for most of my life, taking on roles as "behind-the-scenes" guy – what I am tempted to think of as the "back seat" – has been a humbling experience. Sometimes, I find myself in bouts of self-pity thinking, *"What about me?"*

I also think that – right or wrong, good or bad – many men in a male-dominant world sometimes struggle with entering into a more "support-based" role for (improperly thought of as "second-to") their wives.

But I legitimately believe that it is better to give than to receive.

I wrote one of the guys in our group recently and asked him:

What if *you,* being an "Instagram Husband" and supporting your wife's endeavors ends up better positioning the both of you for success over the long-haul…maybe even for future generations on down the line? What if you took the knowledge you have gained from your work experience in the business world – your management capabilities, your corporate job, your brand development, your marketing know-how – and all of the knowledge that is currently at your disposal in order to partner together for the sake of your marriage, family, and kids?

The goal is never revenue, but a lifestyle. That being the case, what does it matter who takes the shot? So your wife scores the goal… and you made the assist. *Perfect.*

And who has any idea what the future holds?

Jeff Walker was a stay-at-home dad for years while his wife went out and worked for their bread. Everyone thought that he was a failure. He had $400 worth of disposable income *for the entire year,* and he used half of it to buy a Tony Robbins DVD, which taught him enough to start an income-generating-newsletter that has since evolved into a twelve-million-dollar *per year* business.

Being "jobless" wasn't ideal back then, but in hindsight, *not having one* gave him the ability to devour what he needed to learn. That season has since become as close to priceless as he and his family can imagine.

Maybe *you're* in something like that season, now (even though you're *far* from jobless). Perhaps you feel like handing over the reins somehow makes *you* a failure.

It doesn't, and support goes both ways.

To bring it all full-circle, you have the chance to be the AWS for your wife's dreams – to participate in powering everything that she loves. To help create the systems that are necessary for her work to flourish. Maybe her weeds are your passions, and vice versa and collaboration means neither of you ends up with Goat's head thistles sticking into your skin.

When all is said and done, I think that if you have the opportunity to work together and support one another–her for you or you for her–you should take it.

Beyond all of that, in the end–if you absolutely *need* the affirmation–your wife isn't going to say *"I"* anyway…

She's going to say, *"we."*

*Watch Craig expand on this chapter by scanning the QR code below.

Chapter 27 – Wear One Hat (Give the Rest to Tech)

I wanted to close out this *Work & Workmanship* section with something a bit more pragmatic– less "self-reflective journal entry" and more "practical thoughts on getting ideas launched and work accomplished."

As mentioned previously, I work with a ton of *solopreneurs*–people who set up and run businesses on their own. Perhaps they eventually scale to include new employees, or maybe theirs is a model that allows for an ongoing "one-man-show." Either way, most of these creative/business types are full of so many ideas that the limitless possibilities before them usually aren't as freeing as they are paralyzing.

Here, I find myself in a bit of a conundrum. I honestly believe that anything is possible, and I love it when I have the opportunity to instill that belief in others. On the same token, though, I have to acknowledge that the "American Dream" narrative has left a huge number of people disillusioned by the letdown that life can be when reality seems intent on pummeling dreams into submission.

"Anything is possible" isn't the same as saying that all of our wildest dreams will come true, but I do think that–in our attempts to go for gold–there is more help afforded *all* of us than *any* of us realize, especially at this point in history.

Enter *technology*.

I can't help but laugh-that whole buildup just makes me think of *LaFawnduh's Song* in the movie Napoleon Dynamite:

> *We met in a chat room*
> *Now our love can fully bloom*
> *Sure, the World Wide Web is great*
> *But you, you make me 'salivate'*
>
> *Yes, I love technology*
> *But not as much as you, you see*
> *But I still love technology*
> *Always and forever*

The moral of the story is this: if technology can help Kip find true love, maybe it can help us out in our business endeavors, too. (I consider this one of my stronger analogies to date.)

In today's world, a person's barrier to entry-for doing *anything*-is tech. Unless you own a cash-only storefront and have zero interest in advertising (which, in that case, might I suggest you close up shop now?), *you need tech.*

Too many people consider tech a problem *in the way of* their dreams as opposed to *an opportunity* to make them possible.

Too many people are *held back* by technology when it should be a tool used *to propel* them forward.

I don't consider myself a tech-savvy person, but I've had to figure enough of it out throughout my career to know that none of what I've accomplished in business or ministry would have been possible without it. Our ideas only extend so far as people can engage with them, and tech provides the visibility necessary for that engagement.

Most people don't know how to free up storage on or locate their phone, declutter their cloud, or back up their contacts. How, then, are we to set up a functional business whereby technology is capable of accomplishing the heavy lifting that would otherwise stop us dead in our tracks before we even have the chance to begin?

Last year, I launched betterandbetter.co – a "One-stop-shop for every resource to build, scale, and grow any online product or internet-based idea you have." The premise – as inspired by marketing guru Seth Godin's challenge – is this: *your idea "doesn't count 'till it ships."*

Better&Better isn't an agency so much as it is a team of experts versed in all of the tech necessary to get people's ideas off of the ground. To get them shipped. To make them count. We have designers, illustrators, photographers, videographers, editors, copywriters, web programmers, app developers, site builders, engineers, project directors, ad buyers, account managers, marketing professionals, content creators…you name it.

This isn't a pitch (although, obviously, we'd welcome your inquiries) as much as it is an example of *all* the things necessary to successfully launch an idea into the world. It takes quite a bit more to assemble than most people realize when they consider "making a Squarespace landing page" as though that alone will be enough to garner visibility.

So, yes, the above list of fifteen different areas of expertise necessary for launch is daunting. Overwhelming. And it's not even comprehensive. The point, though – whether one uses our services or goes searching through UpWork or Fiverr or whatever – is that *help exists*, and that's enough to gift oneself with a bit of fresh air when otherwise suffocating beneath the ever-increasing to-do list.

I've talked quite a bit about masterminds lately. I hope I'm not beating a dead horse, but much of my learning has come through my involvement in them – like a postgraduate course, or some form of ongoing education. One of these groups is almost entirely dedicated to scaling your business through tech, and I walked away from our last meeting astounded by the number of people in the room with little to no idea about *what* tech to use, let alone *how* to use it. And I'll be honest, it's not a cheap room to sit in, especially if you're not going to learn how to wield the tools you're paying for (or, at the very least, build connections and hire the work out to a third party).

People come with ideas and never launch them. They don't understand how. They're overwhelmed by or ignorant of the tech needed to bring their goals into fruition. They're a one-man or one-woman show with little-to-no budget for outsourcing work, and they're too overwhelmed by the learning curve to get it done themselves. They think that boosting Facebook posts is the same thing as running

Facebook ads. They don't understand automation, or the
way that tech might allow them to work smarter (or, even,
entirely on their behalf). Little by little, they overload their
job description until they've forgotten what their vision was
in the first place, or why they ever thought that pursuing
their dreams once held such a sense of enticement.

To help, then, I simply wanted to write a bit about a few of
the tools that I/we use regularly. If this section ends up
being nothing more than a list of suggestions that you
overlook, so be it–but that's a lot of what the folks who
have yet to ship their ideas are doing, as well…

Reading about is a far cry from *implementing,* and I know
that sometimes putting one's education into action feels (or
legitimately *is*) risky. The unknown is always scary. It
sounds too…*what?* Daunting? Expensive? New and
fandangled? I get that, but I also know from experience that
you won't get far without it.

Perhaps it's reductionistic to suggest that any of us can ever
get down to wearing *just one* hat, but I do know that ample
opportunity exists to offload many of them in exchange for
the tech at our disposal. That said, whether what I suggest
below suits your needs, or simply sparks the inspiration to
seek out whatever might, here are some of my favorite tech
tools–a combination of my own creations and those of the
folks we've used–including the *what* and *why* of each.

> **Basecamp.** *Basecamp combines all the tools teams*
> *need to get work done in a single, streamlined*
> *package. With everything in one place, your team*

*will know what to do, where things stand, and where
to find things they need.*

I use Basecamp for everything that I do. I know that
Slack seems to get all of the popularity as the new
"collaboration hub," and that's totally fine. Use
Slack if it suits you, but Basecamps suits me, and
the platform there keeps all of our tasks–personal,
business, and ministry-related, in order.

Visit Basecamp.

Kajabi. *Kajabi is an all-in-one platform that makes
it easy to create online courses, launch marketing
campaigns, build landing pages, and design the
perfect website.*

I've used Kajabi for everything we've launched
throughout the past five years–particularly when it
comes to video resources, which we've developed
for ourselves and others. Stronger Marriages,
XXXchurch, My Pilgrimage, Recover.org, and more
all use Kajabi as the host for our E-course products.

Visit Kajabi.

Wishlist. *WishList Member is the premier solution
for delivering digital content on a WordPress site.*

Wishlist–like Kajabi–is another option for membership-based hosting/solutions. As WordPress continues to be the primary go-to for website-building, this is an excellent solution if you want to integrate a new membership idea into what you might already have on their platform (as opposed to sending them to a separate URL).

Visit Wishlist.

Sit On My Gift. *Do you wonder if you have a special gift, talent, or superpower that no one else has? Not sure what that is? Let us help you.*

This is an idea that my friend Matt and I developed. Most people who venture out on their own end up playing the roles of CEO, manager, content creator, bookkeeper, blog- writer, marketing director, and a thousand other titles. One day, Matt called and asked, "Craig, what is the *one thing* you do better than anyone else?" I answered him, then paid the question forward to some of the people who know me best, and they confirmed my conclusion. I then asked them to do the same. We used that experiment as a basis to develop a free tool whereby friends and family can help provide you with extreme *clarity* and *confidence* about what it is that you should be spending your time on, and what you should leave behind. I've used and encouraged the process ever since, and you can read all about it, in detail, in

Visit <u>Sit On My Gift</u>.

Dropbox. *Dropbox is a modern workspace designed to reduce busy work so you can focus on the things that matter.*

Dropbox has been a lifesaver for my team and me when it comes to cloud-based storage. I've even linked my computer screenshots to autosave to my account so that I never lose a thought. Think of it as an online hard drive where you can both store and share what is valuable to you, as well as create documents and collaborate with others whose eyes you need on a project.

Visit <u>Dropbox</u>.

Facebook Agencies. *We have strong relationships with three different Facebook Paid Ad Agencies, and if you want to know who might be an excellent fit for you, <u>please email me</u>.*

Facebook–like it or not–dominates the market, and remains the best bang for your buck when it comes to paid advertising that actually converts. As previously mentioned, though, "boosting" a comment isn't the same thing as running Facebook

Ads. The real deal is a more intricate process, but nothing we've done would have been possible without diving into it with the help of our expert friends who know the game.

Email Me.

Better&Better. *Better&Better is your one-stop-shop for every resource to build, scale, and grow any online product or internet-based idea you have.*

We are a team of experts, professionally versed in every possible skill that you and your organization requires to support your online efforts, and get your ideas off the ground. Put simply: *If you're online, we can help you.*

Visit Better&Better.

Creating Fun. *Fast is fun when it comes to product launches, getting your dreams shipped, and creating a conversation.*

If you want to bring your product to market or if you have an internet-idea, we can get it out to the world. If you are paralyzed by the possibilities, we can identify which option to pursue. If you are two days or two years out we can help, but we work best launching projects to the world in 30 days or less.

<u>Visit Creating Fun</u>.

As you might imagine, there are thousands more to choose from, and the tech you need will vary according to the projects you're undertaking, and the ideas you're attempting to bring to life.

Maybe you need to email marketing. <u>MailChimp</u> is a great platform for it, especially if you're just getting started.

Or perhaps you need a more comprehensive and customizable way to send your audiences along various sales paths according to their interactions with the content you're sending them. <u>Infusionsoft</u> is literally *the number one* software for it.

I've written a good amount about membership sites, and perhaps you're interested in how to build that kind of business. <u>Stu McLaren's *Tribe* workshop</u> is a great place to start learning.

There are countless suggestions that I could give you, and they're all at your fingertips. This is the stuff that fires me up, so if you need any help in the process, <u>feel free to drop me a line</u>, as well.

At the end of the day, my main goal in concluding the *Work & Workmanship* section of Craig Brain this way is to encourage you that the resources you need *exist*. Throughout the past three months, I've shared so much about my processes, changes, failures, successes, and all of the ups and downs that coincide with a life lived the way my family and I have chosen to. None of it would have been possible without utilizing the tools at my/our disposal.

It won't all come together perfectly. You can expect to fail, but that means you can expect to learn from your failures. There will be plenty of *trial by error,* but don't get so overwhelmed by what you don't know or can't handle that it keeps you taking that first step.

In the end, I suppose my final encouragement is, simply, this:

start.

*Watch Craig expand on this chapter by scanning the QR code below.

Chapter 28 – The Opposite Sex (A Lesson Learned During a Private Massage in a Hotel Bedroom)

At this point in the blog series/podcast/book, most of you will be familiar with my story about spa day. I love the spa. Picture Buddy the Elf singing, *"I'm in love, I'm in love, and I don't care who knows it!"*

[It's good when you can crack yourself up. The mental image of *me* jumping up and down in the middle of a sauna, bubbling over with joy, feels hilarious.]

Not long ago, my wife and I took a vacation-weekend to Vegas. Between a brief stint living in the valley and all of our trips to porn conventions with XXXchurch throughout the years, we've got a pretty good lay of the land. Despite all of the seediness associated with the city, there's nowhere quite like the strip when it comes to exuberance and hospitality and there's nowhere that I can think of with quite the spa scene.

Yes. I said it. It's ridiculous, and I don't care.

"Spa scene."

Hotel properties, in my opinion, have the best spas, and especially in tourist-trap cities like Vegas. Jeanette and I enjoy the Aria and the Palazzo, and of course, the Cosmo was where my "official" *Spa Day* encounter with the Lord took place a few years back.

Spas are cheap in resort towns, too. Even if you're not staying at the place, thirty bucks is usually enough to get you access to a whole day's worth of relaxation if you've got the time for it.

Anyway, this time around, Jeanette and I decided to try out a new place. We each scheduled appointments for a massage and a facial at the resort we were already at, but when we arrived, the desk clerk informed us that they'd accidentally overbooked their beds. They had a space for Jeanette but asked me if I would be willing to take my session in our hotel room, instead.

I obliged. The next thing I know, my wife's off in her spa-world, and I'm stripped down to nothing but a pair of boxers and a bathrobe, following an attractive young woman back across the hotel grounds to a room that *isn't mine*. I felt uncomfortable and all-too-aware of myself and my surroundings, massage table ready and music playing lightly into an unfamiliar atmosphere, intruded upon by some mostly-naked guy who is most definitely giving off "the appearance of evil" (old platitudes die hard).

The woman asked me what should be her primary area of focus for the hour we had together. In the past, I've received massages from both men and women, but I've never gotten one in some random resort-room like this, and neither have I ever had an attraction to the woman working on me…

"Upper body, please."

"No lower body?"

"No, thank you. Only upper body."

Better to be safe than sorry.

And then…

[suspense]

…nothing bad happened.

She started talking to me and asked if I get massages often. I told her about my membership back home, and about how my daughter and I like to drive around Orange County, looking for fifteen-to-sixty-minute spots at all the cheap places around town. Elise loves them, and she's down to do it all. We've tried Thai massages and Swedish massages. There's a foot place she loves, too.

Most of those spots don't have any sense of atmosphere whatsoever, but we have fun *daddy/daughter dates* together, and they get the job done. The other day, we visited a place that only had one room, and whoever happened to be there for an appointment was lumped into the same space together with the rest of us. Honestly, it's fun, sitting there next to Elise. We both carry the same kind of tension in our upper bodies, and there's a type of connection experienced in working it out together. At this point, some of the therapists even know us by name.

When I told her that Elise has also been giving *(and charging our family for)* massages since she was a little girl, my therapist laughed and responded that she had done the same at a young age, which then evolved into a full-time profession for the past ten years. It reminded me of the *talent-show-contestant-becomes-a-professional* idea, especially when I think back on my daughter's makeshift mobile massage and foot station that she used to "service" our family and friends as a little girl.

She wondered aloud about whether or not Elise might be interested in pursuing a career in this type of work, and though I can't answer that definitively, I realized as she spoke about her own experience that I could see my daughter excelling as a massage therapist.

Who knows? I digress.

The point of *all of this* is that *nothing bad happened* between an attractive woman and me during the massage that day. It's almost as if one can find another human attractive and not destroy an entire life. Who knew?

And I don't want to be a fool, here (maybe you've already decided it's too late for that). Maybe there's a better analogy for getting at what I'm getting at than that of my private (albeit accidental) hotel-room massage experience with an attractive woman.

But the whole thing got my mind racing about the overarching narratives I've always heard (and taught, for that matter) about what interactions are and are not appropriate between men and women. Whether it's books like "I Kissed Dating Goodbye," directions given for men to "bounce their eyes" away from the opposite sex, or–I think–even my work at XXXchurch throughout the years, I wonder if some of the foregone conclusions I and my fellow tribesmen have come to have had the potential to be less helpful than we intended. (I mean, <u>Josh Harris straight up apologized for and discontinued his publication</u> for the way he came to believe it instilled more fear than love in his readers).

I'm not, in any way, questioning the need for appropriate boundaries. I'm just interested in whether our attempts to err on the side of caution have, instead, instilled so much fear into others that human interaction is reduced to a question of right or wrong. Be aware of personal weaknesses, for sure, but don't be so scared that you can't have a conversation with another person simply because you find him or her attractive.

And also, don't try to shift the blame away from *your personal* weakness by casting it onto *someone else's* appearance. *They* are not *your* responsibility.

In 2017, Mike Pence was blasted for observing *The Billy Graham Rule*, which is some of what I'm talking about, here: this idea of (what others have criticized as) fear-based gender boundaries. Granted, not everyone observes these boundaries out of fear, and I'm not in any way suggesting that folks do away with parameters altogether, no matter what their motive. (I certainly didn't plan on my experience that day, and I'm not setting up another appointment like it.) Brittany Shoot wrote <u>a great article in The Washington Post</u> that followed the media-storm Pence experienced, and I valued her thoughts on women-*elevating* (as opposed to women-*blaming*) observances such as these.

Nevertheless…it is interesting: the "fear of all who are not your spouse" mentality. As though men are *only* lust-hounds and women *only* Jezebel-temptresses.

Levi – the guy who is editing and helping me write some of these chapters – is married to his wife, Brandi. They both feel kind of like my kids, and they're two of the only people I know who spend time with the opposite sex, without one another. From what I've experienced in the Christian world, that kind of "behavior" is highly suspect and often coupled with questions like, *"Well…what if you end up having sex with that person?"*

As if the next step after "being in the presence of someone who is not your spouse" is somehow "immediately committing adultery."

But Levi trusts Brandi, and vice versa. I trust Jeanette and vice versa. That doesn't mean we've abandoned all reserve. Sometimes, though, it might mean that there's a real allowance for *friendships beyond our own* to be real-life possibilities!

I've lost too many friends to their marriages. The ones who – as soon as they've said, *"I do"* – are suddenly not allowed to maintain relationships with the people they were close to mere seconds prior. It's frustrating, and though I don't believe it needs to be that way, I know where it comes from.

With the mind I've had for so long, it's hard to be in a situation like the one I was in that day without jumping straight to those worst-case-scenario conclusions, too. I suppose it's fine to practice self-awareness, but at this point, some of that feels more like extra-Biblical conditioning, and I'm almost ashamed of assuming the worst of either of us.

Anyway – and, I know, this is going to be a huge point of contention for some people – *I recently allowed my male friend to talk to my female wife.*

Dave Tosti and I were hanging out one day, and he started to tell me about what he'd say to Jeanette if given permission. Nothing crazy, just some insight and encouragement. And I'm sitting there, thinking, "What do you mean, *'If given permission?'*"

I'm the guy who's going to send you an email or call, or badger you with voice-messages, or show up unannounced at your doorstep. If I've got something to say to you, I'll create the opportunity and ask for forgiveness over permission. I'm very rarely afraid to speak something out into the open whether it lands well or not.

Dave has been a friend of my family for twenty years. He doesn't need permission to speak with Jeanette.

So, I called Jeanette then and there and invited her to join us for dinner. When she arrived, I told her that Dave had some thoughts he'd like to share with her.

That was a *great* conversation.

I, husband to Jeanette, sat listening to one of my best friends talk to her in a way *so different* than the way that I do. I realized that Jeanette has been listening to *one guy* – me – for twenty years. Here, through tears, magic happened through David that allowed for her to open up and be known in a way I hadn't seen before. To call the evening *special* is an understatement at best.

A few weeks later, Dave helped Jeanette again (and, I suppose, me in the process). Jeanette's mom had been hospitalized and – because this is the best explanation there is – a ton of *crazy, God-ordained stuff* kept happening in conjunction with her admittance, but I wasn't communicating well with Jeanette that evening.

I wasn't home, either. I was with Dave, who overheard our conversation, and asked to speak with her, himself.

I'm not going to lie: I made them talk on speakerphone, recorded the entire twelve-minute conversation on David's phone and airdropped it to myself afterward. I didn't do that because I didn't trust them, but because I came to realize I trusted them so much that I wanted to learn from the experience. Dave had a different approach than I did, and he was able to get through to Jeanette when I couldn't. While I love that, I don't want to spend the rest of my marriage telling Jeanette to call Dave. I want to be able to learn how I can do better.

If you've been following along for enough time now, you know how competitive I am. This sounds stupid, but I'll say it because it's fine to say silly things sometimes:

After that phone call, I told Dave, "You know, I've heard my wife break down in tears twice now after talking to you. Imagine what it's going to be like when she does that more often with me than with you…*HASHTAG WINNING!"*

[Laughing emoji whatever face.]

And we have had some of those moments since. I haven't learned it all. I'm not beyond the "talent show" phase yet, but I'm learning and growing. I'm able to say, "You know what? My friend knows how to do that better than I do. He's not me, but I trust him with you, and you with him. And I'm learning from him, too, because I'm not the only man that there is to learn from."

Just like that woman from whom I was afraid to receive a massage taught *me* much of *this*.

Speaking of whom, I ended up telling that gal, "It would be fun for you to work on my daughter."

I know that, unfortunately, people will continue to use and abuse one another. They'll ruin relationships. They'll take advantage of power and authority. Proximity. Anything.

I know that. I hate it.

But it's not to say that's the *only* thing that will *ever* happen and sometimes, I just think that we react poorly by swinging all the way in the opposite direction, using the worst of those stories to instill fear, or enact unrealistic policies – at work, at church, at home, whatever.

For example, my friend works at a church, and I had to pick her up for a meeting a while back. I've known her forever, and she's practically a sister to me, but she's not allowed to be seen getting into a vehicle with me (without a third party) thanks to worst-case scenario assumptions about motive and intent.

At best, that feels at least equally as unhealthy a position to defer to as its all-things-go opposite.

At worst, "sin seizes the opportunity afforded by the commandment," and produces even more of a desire for the off-limits than there would have been without such a law in the first place.

I hope this makes sense. In the end, I suppose, what I'm trying to say is, "Not all things demonized are demons, and perhaps there's even some good to be had in reconsidering the ways (or, at the very least: the *whys* behind the ways) we choose to interact with one another."

Be self-aware, sure, and flee when - like Joseph in response to Potiphar's wife - you're self-aware enough to know that fleeing is required of you.

But perhaps the umbrella of terror that I've witnessed should be a bit lower on the list of motivators for why we can't stand in the same room together – or learn from one another – without defaulting to the depraved.

For me, that meant, *"Only upper body, today, thank you."*

And I learned a good deal from it.

*Watch Craig expand on this chapter by scanning the QR code below.

Chapter 29 – Tics (& Trials & Parenting Through Pain)

In 2014, I wrote the following email to a woman at the Tourette Association of America.

To Whom It May Concern,

First, though I am writing this letter to you today, I would ask that you do not share the following story publicly. At least for the time being.

Last week, I wrote a friend of mine – a renowned storyteller and videographer – with the idea that my wife Jeanette and I have been considering:

sharing our son's story.

And, inevitably, our story. As parents, painful as it is to admit, we didn't do this right. You'll see what I mean in the ensuing pages.

In conclusion to this story, I have attached a brief write up as penned by Nolan, detailing his experience. The combination of our narratives should give you a clear picture of what the past few years have been like.

We haven't shared this story with anyone. Given Nolan's current acting and modeling career, we've been cautious. We don't want to ruin his shot at growth within the industry he loves. How, then, can we share our experience in such a way that it doesn't come across as crippling, but rather: empowering? At this point in our journey, it is finally becoming the latter, but the road has been long and lonely. Only a few people know about what I'm here to share, which I would assume is similar to many of the stories you hear.

What follows is the letter I sent to my friend, and I am forwarding it to you, here, as well, for your consideration.

I have been married to my wife, Jeanette, for 18 years. We have a son, Nolan, who is 13 years old, and a daughter, Elise, who is 11. We live in Pasadena, California.

My wife and I couldn't be more different from one another. Sharing this story will be a challenge for her, but it will also be richer thanks to the emotion and sensitivity she brings to the table.

Our son, Nolan, is destined for greatness. We believe that. He is a natural-born leader. He's fearless. He loves performance and has never shied away from the stage (more like: he has *always* gravitated toward it). He loves people.

Aware of the lack of musical talent in the Gross family, Jeanette and I decided to steer Nolan in the direction of acting over and above the pursuit of music. He thrived. At seven years old, he had a Hollywood Agent and was cast in back-to-back Super Bowl commercials for Hyundai and

Cadillac. He got involved in acting classes and went out for auditions weekly. His hard work, even then, led to guest roles on big-name shows like American Horror Story, CSI, Masters of Sex, and more.

At the age of nine, he auditioned for a supporting role in Darren Aronofsky's movie *Noah*. The directors cast him as "Young Ham" – a role shared with Logan Lerman – opposite Russell Crowe and Jennifer Conley. That summer, he spent upwards of three months on set between Long Island, New York, and Iceland.

The following summer, he went on to shoot *Terminator Genisys* in New Orleans, Louisiana.

Roughly eighteen months ago now, Nolan signed on with a manager named Nils Larsen, in Beverly Hills. Larsen represents some of the biggest, most "up and coming" young talent in Hollywood. Nolan is the "least famous" actor on his roster, but Larsen saw something in my son, and he began his 12th year on planet Earth with all of the momenta anyone could want or hope for.

And then, Nolan nearly lost it all.

When I think back to the earliest days of Nolan's career as a performer (or, at least, as far as I can remember), I can recall my son's "habits." Or, so we called them. These "habits" would come out of nowhere, hang around for months at a time, and then disappear as replaced by something new and unexplainable:

- The "Justin Bieber" hair flick
- One hand down the back of his pants, itching
- Incessant eyebrow-raising
- Quick, constant eye-blinking
- Lip-biting
- Moving his neck like a giraffe
- Ceaseless sniffling

Perhaps each of the odd habits sounds harmless enough, but Nolan would be stuck on them for ages. His sniffling, for instance, began with a cold, but then lasted three months beyond it. Every day. All-day long.

We would yell, *"Nolan, stop sniffling!"*

"Nolan, do you even know what you are doing?"

"Nolan, get a tissue!"

"Nolan...*STOOOOOOOOOPPPPPPPPPPP."*

When it came to hair-flipping, we'd tell him, "Nolan, we are cutting your hair if you don't stop."

When it came to scratching himself, we say, "Nolan, what's wrong with you? You don't have an itch."

We assumed, because of the way that Nolan would only practice one of these odd (and increasingly irritating) habits at a time, that that's all they were: *habits*. Bad habits that could be undone.

But *why?*

We never knew. We assumed that no one else knew, either, or paid attention to any of the things that were ever before us at home. But we were growing increasingly frustrated with Nolan, and – although nothing had yet begun to interfere with his acting career – I was becoming increasingly afraid that these habits would start to impede his upward momentum.

It did.

Immediately after signing with this manager and experiencing the craziest pilot season ever, I began to connect the dots. The habits moved to his face, and they were hard to hide. At that point, not only were we upset at him for his "lack of self-control" in everyday life…now he had his driven, competitive dad on his back, driving him around to auditions and attempting to coach him about how to suppress these habits during auditions.

Nolan would come out of the room and instead of asking him how he did, or if he had fun, or if he felt confident- would ask, *"Did you watch your face? Did you do any of your habits on camera?"*

Of course, Nolan would tell me, *"No."* But then, he would also tell me *"no"* when he was right in front of me, doing it. He'd say to me *"no"* even though I'd just witnessed it seconds prior.

Jeanette and I grew more and more concerned until – finally – we took Nolan to Kaiser for a medical check-up.

The doctor informed us that these "odd habits" were not habits at all. They were *"tics."*

Unfortunately, he didn't give us much information beyond the name-change. He recommended that Nolan begin to see a counselor and – though I understand therapy is a beneficial aspect of many people's lives – I admit that I took it poorly. There my wife and I sat – great parents (so we like to consider ourselves) – watching as our son sits in a room without us, talking to someone we don't know about whether or not he is sad, or depressed, or considers his *tics* a result of either.

Eventually, we found someone who would allow us to be present in the room during his sessions with Nolan. He used redirection techniques to teach Nolan how – when he would have otherwise experienced a facial tic – to focus instead on something he could do off-camera like squeezing his fists or clenching his toes. We thought this might work.

At the time, we couldn't (or didn't want to) tell anyone about what Nolan was dealing with. Jeanette began to worry about his social experience at school. Kids are mean- what if they make fun of him? I grew increasingly afraid that Nolan would never work again. He hadn't been receiving many callbacks as of late, and I assumed this was the reason.

Last summer, when Terminator Genisys released, Nolan's

facial tics were particularly dominant. He was scheduled for multiple Red Carpet interviews, and I remember being so worried about whether his "inconsistencies" would be visible on camera, or threaten his career. There are certain interviews we can't watch for how noticeable they are. Nolan would get angry that he *ticked* on camera and – to my shame – so would I. Our displeasure began to corrode at his confidence, and the fearlessness that I always loved in him waned.

Shortly after that, I called Nolan's acting coach and said, "I have to ask you about something we've been dealing with for quite some time. Nolan has been doing some…well…*things* with his face…"

Before I could finish, she said, "Craig, I instruct Nolan face-to-face. I've seen it. I've never said anything to either of you about it, but yes: I've seen it."

I asked, "Do you think it is hurting him? Is it keeping him from getting roles?"

She responded, honestly, "I don't know for sure, but he should be fine if he can hide them."

Hide them.

Our $200+ redirection sessions with Nolan's therapist were giving him tools to use, but he was only able to do so when he *realized* that he was ticking, and most of the time…he *didn't*.

Nolan doesn't know when his tics are happening.

In my mind, I know that. I can nod in assent to the reality of his uncontrollable situation, but I still grow impatient. His tics still bother me. I still yell at him even though I *know* that he has no idea what he's doing. I feel like I'm losing it.

One day, I Googled "Tourette Syndrome."

Jeanette freaked out. She got angry. Embarrassed. Afraid. She swore up and down that Tourette's is for people who – like Cartman's stereotype in Comedy Central's *South Park* – cuss and yell uncontrollably.

Not Nolan.

Not Nolan.

I read the following:

What Is Tourette Syndrome?

Tourette syndrome is a condition that affects a person's central nervous system and causes tics (movements or sounds that a person can't control and that are repeated over and over).

There are two kinds of tics — motor tics and vocal tics. Motor tics are twitches or movements a person makes but can't control. Vocal tics are sounds a person makes but can't control. To have Tourette syndrome, a person must have at least two motor tics and one vocal tic. The person has to have the tics every day or off and on for over a year — and they have to start before the person turns eighteen.

Tics are kind of like hiccups. You don't plan them, and you don't want them. You can try tricks to make the hiccups stop, like drinking water upside down, but you can't just decide to stop hiccuping. Hiccups that last too long can even start to hurt and feel uncomfortable. Tics can be like that, also.

I kept reading. I stayed up most of the night. I watched a Netflix documentary and, in the morning, asked Jeanette to do the same. We both cried, and through tears, finally admitted what had become undeniable: Nolan has Tourette's.

Definitely Nolan.

The problem with the documentary, though, is that it only detailed *super extreme* cases of Tourette's. Like that South Park episode. Like the movies, or the stories that are so difficult to stomach that they almost appear embellished. I can't imagine it. Nolan wasn't yelling cuss words, but what if he started to?

Our worry overwhelmed us. We made Nolan watch the documentary, too – a true parenting fail if ever there was one. "Hey, Nolan, come watch the worst of what you might become. Enjoy." *What the hell were we thinking?*

Still, we kept it quiet. We only spoke about it between the three of us. We were afraid of how *sickly* the word "Tourette's" sounded. It rang too difficult to admit.

I tried to channel our new information into my efforts to become a better parent, but if I'm honest, Nolan's tics continued to annoy me. Because of that, it was easy for me to harp on him even when I knew he didn't deserve it. I'd get angry at the tics and take my anger out on him. Then, I'd wallow in anger toward myself, with no one to turn to in the silence and secrecy we created surrounding his condition.

Since Nolan signed on with his new manager, he has auditioned for over eighty roles on both television and film and booked *two* jobs. I can't blame it all on tics. Half the time, casting directors don't know what they are looking for. But I know that the tics have stripped away at Nolan's confidence, and that has been difficult to watch.

While all of this was happening, Nolan's print and modeling career took off. He booked jobs for Target, Disneyland, Nescafe, Nike, and Nordstrom. Last month, Nolan did a photoshoot with <u>Kristina Pimenova</u> – the world's youngest supermodel. The campaign isn't out yet, but the point is: Nolan can book *print* because it doesn't matter what he does with his face. The photographers are always able to capture a great shot.

Because of his success in the print world, Jeanette suggested that Nolan take a break from acting until the tics subside, or disappear altogether. I refused her proposal, saying that these *things* Nolan can't help aren't going to take away his shot at a legitimate acting career. I said, "We're not taking a break…let's just figure out how to keep hiding."

So we did. And how? We went to see a Botox specialist as recommended and paid for by Kaiser. Botox was first licensed for a less than glamorous purpose than that for which it is now known: to treat muscle spasms around the eyes. What doctors soon realized was that it also cuts movement and motion, which is why it's such a joke when you see people on TV whose faces look plastic.

That said, though, the firming up of the skin also allows for a covering up of facial tics.

When you get cosmetic botox, they (whoever *they* are) charge you by the *unit*, and there is no shortage of these toxins injected into a person's face. My son's face. I held Nolan's hand a few short days before the *Terminator Genisys* Red Carpet as the specialist injected his *whole face* with Botox.

He cried. He thought that he was going to pass out and asked, *"Dad… do I ever have to do that again?"*

Botox takes about two weeks to go into effect, so the whole procedure made no difference whatsoever at the *Terminator* premier. Of course, though, *I* was convinced that no one could tell because no one said anything about it. It's like when you have your zipper down. No one wants to be *that guy* who tells the person his zipper is down, but everyone is looking at it. Perhaps the saddest part about our story is that, after having concluded that hiding is hard, and doing no good for anyone, we continued forward anyway, convincing ourselves that we were doing a great job.

Nolan has continued to receive the Botox shots, which he goes in for every three months. The doctor always jokes with him, saying, "You're an actor, so we can't give you *too much* of this; otherwise you won't be able to smile!" Amazingly, they *have* helped him hide his tics from the camera, and even if a new one arises – depending upon how wide the injection area – the new muscles have a difficult time picking up the slack. Additionally, most kids grow out of their tics by the time they hit puberty, and as of yesterday, Nolan's doctor says that appears to be the case for him, as well. He hopes that he won't have to see Nolan again.

As parents…we were so excited.

For those parents whose kids have an even more debilitating syndrome, our whole story will probably seem like it's no big deal. I understand that, and I'm not trying to compete. The reason I am writing this, though, is because I believe – given our experience – that Tourette's Syndrome has the potential to be more embarrassing than many others.

It might not kill you, but the hiding will.

The tension developed and pain caused in your relationship with your child might.

I'm furious at myself right now, as I type some of these very words to you, because – though it all makes sense to me today – none of it made sense to me for five years and the last two of which have been an utter nightmare.

Ten days ago, Nolan and I went to an LA Galaxy playoff game. Tim Howard – the USA National goalkeeper – was on the opposing team. He is the greatest USA goalkeeper of all time. Nolan *loves* soccer, and halfway through the game he said, "Dad, Tim Howard has Tourette Syndrome, and *he's a beast!"*

We laughed.

I don't know of anyone else who has talked much about this. Jeanette and I certainly haven't heard from other parents about what to (or not to) do. I do know that Nolan hasn't ever talked to another kid his age about it, and at this point in our journey, we all think it's time to change that.

These days, Jeanette and I see kids like Nolan *everywhere*. It is easy to spot.

Between my work, life, marriage, and – despite all of the failures I've detailed above – attempts at good parenting, I am busy beyond belief. I don't need a cause to champion, but I wanted to reach out to you today because I think there is a story here. A story that would speak to parents, or their children, or a world that only views Tourette's through the lens of its worst symptoms when so many more than they exist.

I don't know what else to do about it other than to share our story, trials, mistakes, and cover-ups.

Personally, if you agree that our story might be helpful to others, I think we could capture a powerful and resonant video that helps get the word out. That will likely be only the beginning, but I know – for as fearless as my son is – he'd be willing to talk about it. And as hard as it may be for my wife, she'd open up if it meant another family - or other parents - didn't have to go through what we did.

Earlier this evening, I asked Nolan to write his story down for me. I didn't tell him why, or that I'd spend the next few hours doing the same. I just wanted to see his take on what this journey has been like for him.

To complete the narrative, here it is for you to read, as well.

> Genetics: a unit of heredity that is transferred from a parent to child.
>
> I don't know if my parents had tics or habits, or if anyone in my family ever had them, but I always wondered if this was because of them.
>
> I always thought that having tics and habits was a bad thing. Now that I think about it, though, they have shown me a different side of myself than I have never seen before.
>
> Dealing with habits and tics taught me that when I am faced with a difficult situation, I have to find

different ways around the problem. When the solution doesn't show itself, I have to keep persevering.

I don't remember anything before my first habit: hair flipping. I would do it all the time. My excuse was that my hair was always in my face (even though, when I would flip my hair, it would go back to the same place every time). There wasn't ever any reason for flipping my hair in the first place. I was growing out of the habit, and when I cut my hair, it ended completely.

I would always roll my eyes, too. I hated this one (well, I hated all of them, but this one might have been the worst). It burned my eyes, and I had no idea why I was doing it.

One night, I started crying in my bed and thought to myself, *"Am I going to be doing these tics and these habits for the rest of my life?"*

I hated that thought because it meant that people might notice. They might say something. They might make fun of me.

I did an interview on the *Terminator* Red Carpet. I just watched it back, and the first thing I saw was my nose twitch. It just kept twitching. Then my neck tic started. It saddened me to see myself do that because it was on camera and other people could see it, too. If a kid at school had said something, I wouldn't have given a crap, but because it was on the internet, it made me mad.

I've always bitten my nails, too. I don't *think* that nail-biting is a tic, but it has been a habit for a while now. When I first became a hand model, I had to put this stuff on my hands so that I wouldn't bite my nails. It tasted horrible, but it didn't stop me. It's like someone who keeps going back to the thing that hurt them because they can't stop.

When I moved to LA to pursue acting, I didn't know that I had a mild case of what I now know is called Tourette's, but I knew that I had been dealing with these things for a few months.

My tics progressively got worse. I remember my parents always talking to me about them and how I had to stop doing them. At the time, though, I wasn't fully aware of when I was doing them. I would always feel bad when my parents would tell me to stop my tics, but I don't think that they realized I couldn't control them most of the time.

I still wanted to be an actor, and I knew that this was going to be something hard for me to overcome. I had to figure out how to make these things go away.

The two tics that I have been dealing with for the longest time are:

1. I move my eyebrows up and down and then
    flicker my eyes. I know, it sounds really
    weird. At least I'm not barking.

2. I pull the muscle on the side of my neck
    while I tilt my head. It's not like it feels nice,
    but it's something I can't stop.

The reason I said *"at least I'm not barking"* is
because my dad showed me this documentary about
a few kids with very severe cases of Tourette's.
While I was watching them, I kept thinking about
how thankful I am that my situation did not escalate
as theirs did. Inside, I felt awful for them because I
knew that I had something like them.

I started to see this guy who would give me
techniques on how to control my tics when I had to.
When I first began "therapy" (which I wouldn't
even call it that), I remember feeling uncomfortable
because I didn't want anyone to know about any of
the things that were going on with me, even though
my parents said that he couldn't say anything. The
man would ask me how I was doing, and then he
would talk to me about my tics. How could I work
on them? How could I make them go away? At first,
his techniques were working well. I thought that
they would work for a long time, but that wasn't the
case. Even though they were good, they weren't
working for me when I needed them. I stopped
going to him because it wasn't helping and if
something isn't working, fix it.

The last path that my parents and I thought that we could take was getting Botox. It wasn't because I had wrinkles. It was because I wanted to stop the muscles from "ticking." The first time I got Botox, I thought that I was going to faint because they put so much in. They put it in my neck, my forehead, and close to my jaw. I left worried that I would have to get that much Botox every time. When I kept going, though, the pain of the needles in my neck started to fade away.

This last time that I went in, the doctor said he noticed that it was getting harder for me to pull my neck out so that they could put the Botox in, which also meant that it would be harder for me to do the tics. I looked at my mom and thought, *finally*. For the first time in this five-year experience, there was a sign of relief. I wasn't going to be doing these tics for the rest of my life!

So, this started as a sad story about not knowing how long these tics would go on. But it ends with conquering tics and finding ways to kill the opponent (which, in this case, are the tics).

The best news that I have heard in this whole process came through eight simple words, *"I might never have to see you again."*

That meant I might not ever have to get Botox again, and that I finally (almost) overcame something that I had been dealing with.

I've always thought that if I ever get around to this, I would reach out to you. On top of that, finding out Nolan was almost out of the woods on all of this seemed like great timing.

Thanks for considering it,

Craig Gross

At this point in our journey, it is 2019, and we're five years removed from the letter above. It wasn't the right time, but I do think that the time is still coming.

Nolan is a young man now, and at sixteen – though we suppressed it in the past – his love for music continues to grow. So does his resolve to speak boldly about things that we should never have kept hidden.

As Levi wrote into his forward at the start of this process, sometimes the things a person best champions for others are also those that he struggles most with, personally. I am aware of the disconnect between my beliefs about transparency and the way that we closeted the realities our family was dealing with during this time. As I wrote above, there's plenty to be upset with myself about, but what else do I do now then share our stories, trials, mistakes, cover-ups, and conclusions, especially now that Nolan has decided to do the same?

I think that honesty breeds a sense of empowerment. Just recently, he has begun to find his voice as a lyricist, even going so far as to spend studio-time vocalizing his experience through the power of song. Personally – and I know I'm biased because I'm the dad (and also, the dad experiencing a sense of redemption for the years "the locusts" stole) – I think there's huge potential for my son's story to be heard by many a person who needs it in this world. Maybe more. We're in the process of figuring out how best to release it now. When the time comes, I'm sure I'll participate in spreading the news.

Until then…

*Watch Craig expand on this chapter by scanning the QR code below.

Chapter 30 – I Only Have Eyes for You (& Your Penis)

"Are you okay? You seem preoccupied...?"

Jeanette knows me, so *of course,* if she's asking about whether or not I am preoccupied, the answer is *yes*. I tried to ignore her question, though. To avoid a lie, I reciprocated it with one of my own. She didn't press me on it, and I didn't offer up the truth.

Three months ago, I took Jeanette out for breakfast. As is often the case, I spent the evening prior with a racing mind, wide awake long after the rest of my family had fallen asleep. During that time, I wrote down three qualities that I love about my wife – things that she excels at – with the hope of encouraging her the following morning.

One of my specific goals was to encourage Jeanette that the investments she had been making in her health were not in vain. She works *incredibly hard* at keeping in shape, eating correctly, and maintaining a general sense of well-being.

Throughout the years, Jeanette has suffered a list of discouraging medical conditions that often cause her to be overwhelmed by what she is (or is not) eating. Each issue comes with a different recommended diet, so which condition should she be "eating for" today?

That morning, Jeanette told me that she wanted to try intermittent fasting, which a friend of hers had recommended, given the fact that she needed to work on lowering her cholesterol. Jeanette is one of the most highly disciplined people I know, so why not? For her, a new meal schedule would be a breeze.

Fast-forward to the present. Jeanette has been diligent about her eating. Tireless in her attempts to lower cholesterol, specifically. A few days ago, she had a doctor's appointment, where she received a slew of test results that gave us a picture of her progress. I called after she left the office, excited to hear the results.

Nothing had changed. Her cholesterol was at the exact same level as it had been three months ago, on the day she started.

A couple of nights later, when we found the time to talk more, I asked Jeanette a few questions about her weight. Though it hadn't done anything to improve her cholesterol levels, I wondered about how intermittent fasting had been affecting the scale, and whether it was helping her goals, there.

As an aside (or maybe this is the main point), I should recommend treading lightly when it comes to weight questions with your wife because no matter what, you're screwed in these waters.

If you have to ask, it means *you don't know*. And how could you possibly not know? If your wife lost weight, and you didn't notice-why? And if your wife gained weight and you didn't notice, you're suspect *(you liar)*. She certainly noticed. Are you avoiding acknowledging the reality head-on in exchange for a passive question by which you hope she'll admit the truth that you clearly see?

It's like trying to answer the question of whether or not "these jeans make me look fat." If you respond *"no"* too quickly, you're lying, and the answer is *"yes."* If you answer *"no"* too slowly, it also means *"yes."*

Jeanette avoided my question. And it bummed me out. Which is ironic, considering it's what I did to her at the start of all of this. Nevertheless, it did, but I didn't know *why* her avoidance was affecting me so negatively. It made me worried that perhaps her test results were direr than she was letting on. I love Jeanette, and I want her to be around for a long time. I wasn't trying to hurt her with my question about her weight – I was trying to understand.

Which brings me to the crux of this chapter: I'm not always convinced – no matter how long a couple has been together – that men and women *do understand* one another.

Where is the disconnect? Did I offend because I didn't ask the right questions, or did I offend because my question about weight triggered something inside of my wife, who is constantly comparing herself to other women? To *their* physique. To *their* beauty.

Today, I have to write a blog post for XXXchurch about "the visual nature of men" and "the mind of the woman" (me - who can't even get inside my wife's brain). Sometimes, I feel like the best I have to work with is presumption. But that's what I'm doing right now, and I can't help but pull from my recent conversation with Jeanette. I suppose this will be as specifically for her as it is for anyone following our work with the ministry.

When I have an idea, I usually write it down or record it immediately for fear of forgetting and losing it later. More often than not, it spews out like word-vomit, and I have to forward the message along to someone else who can help me organize my thoughts. This time is no different. I sent a series of four, rambling voice memos to my friend and co-worker, Carl Thomas, who responded with a concise summary of what he thought I was trying to say:

1. A man has a difficult time explaining the visual nature of his brain to a woman without it hurting her feelings (despite how he phrases the conversation).
2. A woman is often comparing herself to the images that capture her husband's brain all day long.

That's all good and well, and I'll get there, but I'm still preoccupied with *my* dilemma.

Did my weight question sting because it made Jeanette feel as though she wasn't measuring up to some other hypothetical woman I might have been comparing her to?

Beyond our situation, what we've learned through our work at XXXchurch is that wives, in general, have a difficult time believing that they live up to the women their husbands see every day – on the street, on a billboard, watching porn. The comparisons eat away at a woman's confidence because at the end of the day, *she* wants to be

the subject of her husband's visual fantasy, and it crushes
her to see him looking elsewhere for what she is designed
to give.

And then Carl offered up a *horrendous, awful,* and *not-quite-comparable* analogy, which I'm going to use anyway
because it is as funny as it is horrifying, and *might* help me
get the point across.

"A husband," he said, "has no idea what is going on inside
of his wife's brain when she sees him with eyes gawking at
someone other than her. Just like a wife has no idea what is
going through her husband's brain when he sees some
woman walk by or an image on a screen."

For Carl's scenario to work, though, one has to pretend that
a woman's brain works the same as a man's when it comes
to visual stimulation. He continued:

"Imagine I am walking around the mall with my wife,
Katie. Everything is normal except that nothing is normal,
because all of the men (myself included) are pantless.
We're all completely naked from the waist down. Now,
Craig, you know me – I'm a pretty confident guy. But with
my pants off, I immediately start to compare myself to
everyone else. In my mind, I'm losing it. I'm wondering:
am I big enough? Does my wife think I'm big enough? In
this world, instead of me being the one trying to avoid
Victoria's Secret store to my left, my wife is pretending
she's not entirely taken by all of these other men's genitalia.
She doesn't take out her camera, but I know she's taking a

good look at everything that I don't have to offer her (and there are some *massively* large penises out there, Craig).

So then, later that day, Katie starts up some casual conversation with me after dinner.

'Hey! Have you ever thought about the size of your penis? Like, don't get me wrong – I love it and everything, but I'm just wondering if you have thought about trying to make it bigger?

I mean, you're not small, Carl.

I am not saying *that*, Carl.

I didn't even notice all the penises at the mall today, Carl.

I only have eyes for your penis, Carl.'"

Uh.

Okay.

I laughed and immediately thought of the blog title, *"What If America Was as Fascinated by the Penis as We Are With Boobs and Butts?"* And look, I get it – the analogy is dumb, and it breaks down immediately because penises are disgusting (however, the hilarity of what fun "cleavage" clothing might be available to men in that scenario has me losing it).

How would that make Carl feel, though? Pretty thankful for jeans.

We live in a world where the woman's body is on display far more than the man's body. The point of that scenario, however dumb, was to get husbands to consider what it might be like in their wives' minds when they're doing the same thing – comparing, contrasting, measuring up and against their spouse.

What kind of insecurity does that create?

What kind of insecurity did I create in my wife, who is a part of this world? Who is already concerned about her health *without* her husband asking tactless questions about her weight, who *is also measuring herself* up and against other women. Either "just because" or under the assumption that I am doing the same?

I was so bummed the other night. All I could focus on was trying to solve the problem: why didn't Jeanette feel comfortable enough to confide in me? And is there anything that I need to learn from this situation that would be helpful to pay forward to others once I do?

After sitting with it, feeling it and allowing the weight to press down upon me, I came to this conclusion:

I don't do a good enough job of encouraging Jeanette or telling her that she is beautiful.

However disconnected or discombobulated the collision of these stories may seem, they have led me here, to a list that I made for myself – and am now paying forward to you, reader – about how I can better understand and/or do a better job of navigating difficult conversations with my wife, as opposed to skirting around them, or feeling as though concerns are being avoided.

The change must begin with *me*.

1. Tell your wife that she is beautiful. *Often*.

2. Encourage your wife when you see her working hard at things (for example: working out, eating right, dressing up).

3. Do #1 and #2 in front of your kids (and others, as well).

4. Expect your wife to be hurt by you, angry at you or insecure about your love if you don't practice #1, #2 and #3 and especially if you continue to do #5.

5. Don't humiliate your wife by looking at porn or gawking at a woman. My friend Shaunti said this, and it ever since she did, it has been before me.

6. Looking once means your alive. Looking twice says you dissed your wife.

7. Join your wife in some sort of activity together (gym, bike, skateboarding, whatever).

8. Your wife's level of security in your love is a key predictor regarding her passion and confidence in physical intimacy with you (another Shaunti win).

9. Keep up on yourself, as well (i.e., don't let yourself, or your physical and mental health, go).

Beyond that, while I'm well aware of *not* being a woman, here are a few numbers that wives might consider adding to their list, as well:

1. Your husband thinks you are the most beautiful woman in the world (even if he doesn't say it enough).

2. Remember that it is not your fault that men are wired to notice a good figure in tight clothing.

3. Everything in our society is fighting against him, luring his eyes and his brain. That doesn't make him a victim (and he is still responsible for his actions), but if possible, make an attempt at appreciating or empathizing with his efforts to fight against the temptation that is ever before him.

4. If you happen to catch his roving eye, gently express the intimidation it makes you feel, rather than blasting him with a derogatory cut about his caveman practices.

5. Openly engage in conversations about these experiences and be open to trying new things (sex with the lights on is much more relaxed after this conversation).

A brief disclaimer about *Point #1* on the woman's list above. Recently, I read a great response to a question (<u>on Quora of all places</u>) that seems to align itself well here regarding whether or not a wife should *believe* her husband when he reinforces her "unrivaled beauty."

After all, plenty of adulterers have told their wives that they "don't have eyes for anyone but her."

So, a woman posed the question, *"Does my husband believe that I am the most beautiful woman in the world?"*

In short, the response was this:

Yes, because beauty is more than physique. It is more than sexy. Does that mean there aren't more attractive women in the world? No. You likely aren't at the top of the proverbial food chain (and neither – I'm willing to bet – is your husband). Objectively speaking, and especially if you are only looking at and comparing yourself to *one facet* of beauty, you *aren't* the most beautiful woman in the world. But as the woman who encompasses more than "sexy" for your husband – the woman who's personality, connection, romance, emotion, desire, chemistry, and multifaceted uniqueness attract him to you – then yes, *you are the most beautiful woman in the world.*

And Jeanette is undoubtedly *mine*.

I think I'll let her know.

*Watch Craig expand on this chapter by scanning the QR code below.

Chapter 31 – Sexpectations (Get Some)

Years ago, Jeanette and I partnered with some friends of ours to create StrongerMarriages.com – a resource dedicated to *strengthening* and sustaining lifelong marriage relationships.

After many years at XXXchurch, a ministry dedicated to serving men and women whose marriages are falling apart, I wanted to be a part of a conversation that spoke more to *preventing* fallout before we have to start talking about *recovering* from it.

As a means to that end, we had to talk about sex. Openly, honestly, vulnerably, and bluntly. We created a married-couples' resource titled *Best Sex Life Now*, and dove straight into the deep end, beginning with our own stories and convictions.

Sex and strong, healthy marriages seem to be connected at the hip (pun intended). We've never heard of a "great marriage with horrible sex," or "great sex in a horrible marriage." Jeanette and I believe that couples need to learn how to have frank conversations about sex with one another and that until they're able to, the overall health of their marriage will be stunted. From what we've seen, this is especially true in "Christian" contexts where sex is treated as taboo, and shame and secrecy thrive. As people who claim to be followers of the God who created such an incredible gift, I can't even come close to describing just how frustrating that reality is.

They say that you can either complain about the way a thing is, or try to change it. So, my wife and I decided that we were going to model the frankness we longed for by talking about our own sex life.

I've spent the majority of my career in a ministry dedicated to destroying taboos. Whether it's books like <u>Questions You Can't Ask Your Mama About Sex</u> or Live Q&As assigned specifically to "nitty-gritty sexuality" at churches for the past fifteen years-we are every bit as much about *encouraging* more (and better) sex as we are about *discouraging* pornography use.

There's a lot to tackle, and unfortunately, I think that approaching a conversation like this head-on can come across as abrasive to people who usually skirt around essential discussions. I remember a day when Levi told me he'd received a text from one of his friends about our "boldness." He shared our workshop with a couple in his church community group, and they responded with discomfort instead of leaning into the very topics that they needed help with.

Personally? I don't think we're *bold*. I think we've seen how beneficial it is to make what *should* be a *normal conversation* into, well, a normal conversation.

All that to say: let me tell you about our sex life and five of the best lessons we've learned about the bedroom.

I'll start here: I was a virgin when I married Jeanette. She wasn't. Given the "purity-ring" idealism I'd been raised with and the resulting expectations about the way life "should happen," I almost allowed that reality to ruin our dating relationship before we said *I do*. How many people are in the same boat, struggling with what *should* be in the face of *reality*? Are you going to talk about it? Are you going to sweep it under the rug? Are you going to separate in disgust or open yourself up to understanding and forgiveness, and move forward?

Now that we are married, we try to keep intimacy at the forefront of our relationship by remembering that:

1. **Sex is fun.** Jeanette says that of *all the things* we should be working on in our marriage, our sex life takes the highest priority. I'm more than happy to agree with her. She jokes that if sex is difficult to talk about with me, it's because as soon as I hear the word, I want to stop talking and start doing.

   We believe that married sex should be the best sex. I'd even go so far as to say that married sex *as Christians* should be the best sex because we claim to worship the God who made it and told us to enjoy it.

   My friend and infamous porn-star, Ron Jeremy, says that after having sex with more than 5,000 women during his career, he can't image how monotonous monogamy must be. Sex with *one woman* for an entire lifetime?

But that's what I've experienced with Jeanette, and our sex is only getting better. Even physiologically, we know that investing (and what a fun investment it is!) in our physical intimacy decreases our stress levels, makes us laugh more, and has helped us view life with way more positivity and fullness than when we're lazy about our relationship.

Don't be awkward about it. If you're too afraid to start talking, how are you ever going to start acting?

I can't say it loudly enough: *THERE. IS. NO. SHAME. IN. SEX.* I know that many of us were raised believing the exact opposite. A one-off "talk" with your dad or mom awkwardly staring at the ground and saying "don't watch porn or masturbate, and don't have sex until you're married" doesn't precisely scream *open* and *healthy* conversation, but you don't have to follow suit. We talk with, about, and around our kids about sex all the time. They're well aware that it's a natural and *enjoyable* part of life. One of the most exciting results of our work in this space has been hearing about how other parents have begun to do the same. I'm convinced that fighting against shame in adulthood begins with killing it in childhood, and we're trying to reframe the narrative of sex as "gross" with sex as "good."

2. **Set *Do's* and *Don'ts* in bed.** If you're anything like us (or, I think, *human*), then you've probably been asking some form of "*what can we do?*" since well before marriage.

For most Christian adolescents, it begins with something like, "How close can we get to having sex without *technically* having sex?"

To be clear, I'm not saying that's the *right* question to be asking…I'm just saying kids ask it.

Once you're married, though, the question shifts: *"Well…what are we allowed to do now? Is anything off-limits? Should some things be off-limits?"*

Even though I've grown to enjoy talking about the things I'm *for* above the things that I'm *against*, I'll start with what you'd expect to come first from *the XXXchurch guy*:

Don't bring porn (or other people) into the bedroom.

Chances are, if you can relate to the vast majority of men and women who have wrestled with pornography in your past, you're already bringing enough baggage to the table, personally, without continuing to allow it a foothold in your relationship. Despite how "progressive" people think I might be when it comes to other subjects of conversation that I've chosen to tackle through this project, I'm conservative when it comes to a Biblical perspective on pornography. It creates unrealistic expectations and doesn't contribute to purity in any way whatsoever. (For example, anal sex is all the rage among porn consumers, but most people don't realize that it's likely not as common a position in real life as it is on screen for actors and actresses. They get paid double to engage in it for the sake of viewership and analytics).

God calls us to *flee* from sexual immorality. Luckily, he's also given you an attractive, naked man or woman to escape to. Invest in the *real, physical person* next to (or above or below) you.

As far as sex positions and experimentation, Jeanette and I defer to the rule-in marriage, mutuality is critical. If you're both down for it, go for it. Scripture says that all things are permissible, but not all things are beneficial. Be conscientious of one another. That said if you want to get creative, do it! If you're into role play, play away. If you're into oral, give and receive it. If you want to get crazy with lingerie, enjoy. Whatever two married people respectfully decide is beneficial, *is*. (And by the way, hotel sex is amazing. You're out of the norm, and you don't have to worry about the dirty laundry.)

I love this passage from 1 Corinthians as a general outline for marital intimacy:

"It's good for a man to have a wife, and for a woman to have a husband. Sexual drives are strong, but marriage is strong enough to contain them and provide for a balanced and fulfilling sexual life in a

world of sexual disorder. The marriage bed must be a place of mutuality – the husband seeking to satisfy his wife, the wife seeking to satisfy her husband. Marriage is not a place to "stand up for your rights." Marriage is a decision to serve the other, whether in bed or out. Abstaining from sex is permissible for a period of time if you both agree to it, and if it's for the purposes of prayer and fasting—but only for such times. Then come back together again. Satan has an ingenious way of tempting us when we least expect it..."

3. **Understand *why* you're not connecting in bed.** The number one question we've received from people related to sex in marriage is: *why doesn't my spouse want to have it?*

    Jeanette has had some excellent feedback for husbands who are frustrated by their wives' lack of interest, and I'm going to pay it forward here:

    - **She's had a bad experience with sex in the past that she's never worked through.** Some friends of ours had sex on their wedding night, and it ended up being a traumatic experience for the wife because it triggered her memory of having been molested in the past. After that, her husband tried to avoid putting her through that pain again. However well-intentioned, though, their "abstinence" meant his needs weren't met, and eventually he sought fulfillment elsewhere. Instead of finding yourself in a similar situation, you need to lead your wife by encouraging her to pursue counseling or a woman's pastor who will be able to help her work through prior abuse. It very well might take years to work through her pain, but failing to be proactive about healing will only allow the past to continue destroying the present (and – eventually – the future).

- **She doesn't enjoy it, or isn't having an orgasm.** Listen to your wife and what *she* wants. Maybe she needs touch and physical affection throughout the day, and not only right before you're looking to *get some*. During sex, she may think she enjoys a position, but then come to find out that a different one leads her to orgasm. Just ask what she might want to try and make sure she orgasisms before you do.

- **She's too tired.** This one, *especially* after you've had kids, is real. You may have to get on her schedule for a while; sex is fun even if it's at 6 pm after the babies are in bed. Also, you can help build sex into her schedule by clearing other to-dos out of it. Help out around the house. Take care of the kids. Do what you can to relieve some of her obligations to make sure she feels able to have and be present during sex without the weight of all else that remains to be done.

- **Her walls are up.** Woman can't seem to compartmentalize conflict (before I get in trouble, remember that these are my wife's – *a woman's* – words, not mine). If you get in a fight before you head off to work, she's stuck thinking about it all day. Husbands tend to go to work and forget about whatever happened until they walk back through the door that evening. Meanwhile, women are at home trying to fight their emotions about what was said and how much it hurts. Make sure she knows everything is okay before you leave (and assure her that you will work things out when you get home).

- **She's insecure about her body.** If your wife hasn't had babies yet, get ready for this: her body is going to change, and it will never be the same again. Weight goes up and down during different seasons of her life. Please, encourage her by telling her she's beautiful. Tell her that you love her just the way she is. We always want to be beautiful in our husband's eyes. If you can, offer to go on walks (or to the gym) and eat healthy together, it's easier to stay in shape and eat right if you are helping the situation instead of tempting her by taking her to McDonald's every day.

When it comes to the men, while we certainly do deal with issues related to body image and insecurity, as well, I will break down some of our sexual hangups more bluntly:

- **No man wants to have sex with his mom.** I know this is harsh, but it's true. If we begin to feel like our wives are treating us more like mothers than friends or lovers, it's a huge turn-off. Women, we long for respect. Men, that also means we have to act in a way that makes us worthy of it. If you're not respectable, then, of course, you won't be treated with the admiration you desire.

- **He doesn't feel wanted.**

- **He's dealing with medical issues or depression.**

- **You pay more attention to Facebook or Instagram than him.**

- **He's getting it somewhere else.**

No more excuses! Start working on overcoming these issues and creating a more fulfilling sexual relationship. To reiterate what God himself has to say about it, *"Marriage is strong enough to…provide for a balanced and fulfilling sexual life in a world of sexual disorder."*

4. **Set clear [s]expectations.** Setting clear expectations with one another is so important to a healthy and thriving sex life. In marriage, two separate individuals say "yes" to becoming one. That oneness might happen – physically – in a moment, but it doesn't last for long without discussing the expectations that both of you have brought in to your marriage bed. Porn, as I mentioned earlier, creates a slew of *unrealistic* expectations that could very well crush spouses unable to (or uncomfortable with) living up to the fantasies it has created. Regardless of whether anyone is bringing a negative sexual history into the marriage, there are still worthwhile questions to ask about how to build a life together.

   For example: how many times a week will you have sex?

   We tend to go on autopilot after the honeymoon phase wears off. We give one another our best at the beginning of the relationship, but eventually, our enthusiasm falls to the wayside. Work together to make communication about sex a priority in your marriage. Transparency and honesty always lead to intimacy, and intimacy – among other things – helps reduce the chance of either spouse giving into temptation that exists outside of the marriage.

5. **Don't do what your parents did.** *Maybe* this final point doesn't apply to everyone, but we've heard far

more horror stories than we have positive examples of parents killing the *Birds & Bees* conversation.

It's worth saying that if you don't want to become your mom or dad, then you've got make an intentional change in the way you discuss *all of this* with your kids. It's not going to happen unless you're purposeful about it, because what other experiences do you have to pull from than your own awkward and uninformed one-off "conversation" (in reality, they probably just talked *at* you) with your folks at some point during puberty?

Jeanette offered something that I think is super true and insightful: *the easier it becomes for you to talk to one another about sex, the easier it will become for you to talk to your kids about it, as well.*

To the parents out there: start talking to your kids about sex sooner than later, and make it an ongoing conversation. The more you're able to transform "the talk" into "a bunch of talks," the more natural and more normal it will be, and the less unnecessary, awkward silence will rule the home. As you uncover you and your spouse's values, share them with your kids. Who would you rather have them learn from – you, or all that you're already afraid of "out in the world?"

To close this chapter, I want to give you a little bit of homework. It's called *The Conversation Challenge*. And yes, you guessed it – the conversation you'll be challenged to have is about sex.

You know those magazines you pass by in grocery store checkout aisles with headlines that read, "How To Get Hot & Heavy In The Bedroom," "Have Better Sex Than Ever," and "Six Tricks To Make Her…"

Whatever.

Well…I made my own version. Sort of. But instead of giving away answers, I wanted to ask questions.

I don't care about what some author says about how my wife and I can have a better sex life, I care more about what *my* wife says about how we can have a better sex life.

Today, I'm inviting you and your spouse to <u>take *The Conversation Challenge* here</u>, at ReclaimingSex.org. (Don't worry – you don't have to pay for it or anything.) There are no wrong answers – all Jeanette, and I would ask is for you to be honest.

Here's to your best sex life, now.

Craig

*Watch Craig expand on this chapter by scanning the QR code below.

Chapter 32 – My Vows (& Our Victories)

One night, my wife and I were talking about what we should do for our twentieth wedding anniversary. We decided it'd be fun (and far *funnier*) to throw a massive celebration for our nineteenth, instead. Who the hell throws a random nineteenth wedding anniversary party?

We had a blast. We invited all of our closest friends to meet us for a few days in Las Vegas, Nevada, told them we'd be hosting a costume contest, and offered the winner $1,000 in one-dollar bills, which we presented to them at dinner, crumpled up inside of an old briefcase.

Goth couples showed up in all black with heads shaved and pentagrams drawn onto their chests, visible beneath Hot Topic fishnet long-sleeves. Donald and Melania Trump impersonators filed into the party bus. A husband and wife in Bad Grandpa costumes hobbled around on walkers borrowed from a nearby nursing home. A rich white guy and his mail-order bride held hands at dinner-a Ron Jeremy impersonator hobbled around the strip, sporting Crocs.

Jeanette and I wore our original wedding clothes-down to Jeanette getting her hair and acrylic nails done the same way.

Before the evening's end, we renewed our vows atop a stage in a parking lot filled with tiny homes where Tony Hsieh and a group of Zappos executives live, including my friend Krissee, who hosted us there.

What follows are the words I spoke to Jeanette and our guests that night (before we headed back down to Old Vegas, and Grandma and Grandpa started clubbing in their MegaMax diapers).

August 7, 2017

Jeanette,

I've recited these vows to you twice now.

The first time, I didn't understand them. I didn't know how much they meant. This time, they make a bit more sense.

I could never have imagined how quickly the years between then and now would pass us by.
Nineteen years.

Nineteen years.

Ten different homes. Eight different cities. Three different states.

Funny enough, we've begun to dream about moving *again.* This time? To the beach. We say it will be our last move, but who knows? The memories and miles traveled, and all of the life we've lived has only been possible thanks to your willingness to go along with every crazy step we've taken together.

We tell our kids that friends will let them down, and family is everything. I'm so glad that we have one another. I'm thankful for the memories we've made, and for the memories, we will make with the rest of life that we still get to experience together.

Thank you for being by my side for nineteen years, and for the nineteen that are to come, and beyond.

Thank you for your unwavering support and selflessness.

I haven't always lead you and our family well, but you have always supported me *100%* – in *all of this* – and for that I say: thank you.

Your discipline is inspiring, and I love it about you. I tend to cheat, but you stick to anything and everything you commit to, and you don't cut corners.

I am grateful that even though we often have opposing ideas about how to resolve our differences – even though my approach is sometimes the polar opposite of yours – we still get through it. We always come out on the other side.

I rewatched our wedding video and listened to Arty tell me that *everything is my fault.*

During the ceremony, he said, "Craig, if Jeanette burns down the kitchen, it is still your fault."

I think – because he cracked it like a joke – we must not have thought he was serious.

We've had our fair share of issues, fights, and differences throughout our nineteen years together. Of those 6,935 days, I've spent probably thirty nights out on the couch, and one night in a hotel room when we needed to get away from one another. I wish I would have listened, all those years ago, to that joke. Maybe we could have fought less, and I could have saved us some sexless nights, but this is my promise to you for the years ahead:

I won't hold you at arm's length, waiting for an apology. I won't waste time deferring blame, or insisting on what was *your fault*.

I will set anger aside and work toward a resolution, and I will begin those conversations with what *I* have done wrong.

That is my vow to you.

I have some funny stories about you, Jeanette – many just from our most recent vacation. Like how you somehow – immediately – got drunk upon checking into our hotel at 3:30 on a Wednesday afternoon while the kids stood there wondering what happened to mom. Or dancing with the Norwegians on our cruise. Or another night (not drunk), where you gave the kids headphones and told them to dig their faces into their devices and keep their heads down because you want to have sex. Somehow, we both finished, too.

Maybe that's too much information for all of the guests listening to me talk right now?

Speaking of...now onto our friends.

We had a party when we celebrated our tenth anniversary. We told all our friends to do the same. Many of their marriages didn't make it to ten – let alone another ten on top of that – and only one couple threw a party.

To those of you *young ones* here tonight: throw a party at ten and celebrate the win.

Hell, celebrate the win each year.

I find that we, as a culture, don't celebrate the wins anymore.

Your business just did a million dollars. *Celebrate it!*

You had the best month of your career at work. *Celebrate it!*

You got sober. *Celebrate it!*

You have your health. *Celebrate it!*

Take time to celebrate. Do something special. Make a big deal about it. Stop and appreciate the work it took to get there. Talk about how you did it. Talk about what you want to do next.

I've had the lyrics to a song I love stuck in my head all week:

"There is nothing I've got when I die that I keep."

Perspective isn't about celebrating all the new things you can acquire. Perspective is about celebrating the memories you've made with one another. Not on social media. Not on text.

With each other. With your family and with your friends.

Thank you for celebrating this *nineteen-year win* with me, Jeanette.

And to our friends: we hope this evening gives you a peek into who we are – as people and as partners.

We'll be looking for invitations to all of your stupid-ass parties soon, and we hope they trump this one. (And even if you don't throw a party, *remember to celebrate the wins –* no matter how big or small they are).

*Watch Craig expand on this chapter by scanning the QR code below.

Chapter 33 – How We Love (On Identifying & Breaking Patterns)

June 15, 2019

Every adult, to one degree or another, functions from negative patterns that were ingrained in them during childhood. To break free from those patterns – to establish new, healthy ways of *being* – we first need to identify what they are.

In other words: we're diving headfirst into the deep end.

If you've made it this far into the *Craig Brain* journey with me, then you've likely gathered how much of an investment I make in self-discovery. Personality tests. The DISC. The Enneagram. Myers-Briggs. Kolbe. Etc.

I love *tools*. I've dedicated much of my life to learning how to wield the ones I've managed to get my hands on and to create usable tools for others to use, as well.

What I don't love nearly as much as tools are *talks*, so when Jeanette told me that she wanted to visit a marriage counselor together, my agreement was begrudging at best. As an "achiever" on the Enneagram, I tend to equate the need for therapy with failure. *"You're doing something wrong."* I know it's not true, and I would never tell it to anyone else, but it is still – unfortunately – the lens through which I tend to view my need for help.

That said, when the counselor told Jeanette and me that she'd recommend *twelve weeks'* worth of therapy – like a chiropractor or something – I was annoyed. And then what? We take three months to evaluate whether you're the right guide for us? We didn't even know if we *liked* this lady yet.

What I did know was that I liked her less when she ended the first session by saying, "come back next week, and I'll give you the *tools* you'll need to work through this."

I thought, *"like hell,"* and asked for the tools right then and there.

That's how we discovered Kay and Milan Yerkovich's incredible resource, How We Love.

The Yerkovichs are a married, seventy-something-year-old couple who happen to live not far from us in Orange County, California. Both are licensed counselors with decades of experience – Milan as a part of New Life Ministries, and Kay with a master's degree in counseling – specifically related to couples' attachment therapy.

Over the years and in their marriage, the Yerkovich's developed a typing system that they call "Love Styles." It's not the same thing as a "love language." Instead, Love Styles are better thought of as wounds.

You take <u>a five-minute test</u> which will then give you one-or-more of five possible "love style" results.

To call How We Love a "personality test" isn't quite right. The point of *this* resource is more to help people identify and heal from the negative patterns in their lives than to tell them about a box they're stuck in. To borrow from Levi's post about the same, if the Enneagram helped Jeanette and I understand *how* we are, then How We Love helped us unlock *why*.

We took the test. I discovered that I am a <u>Vacillator</u>, and Jeanette is an <u>Avoider</u>. After that, we paid $1 for an hour-long audio conversation between the two authors, wherein they broke down the "core patterns" and hangups that married couples, specific to our results, face.

It was the best buck I've ever spent.

It was as though we'd given them a key to our bedroom. Like they'd somehow gotten inside of our heads and spied on two decades' worth of arguments between us. Their diagnosis described what *exactly* Jeanette and I have experienced throughout the life of our marriage.

One of the negative patterns we discovered was that when tensions rise, Jeanette runs away, and I let my mouth get the best of me. In a typical fight (and neither one of us has to have any idea what we're fighting about), when anger spikes, all Jeanette knows how to do is leave, and all I know how to do is stand at the door and make sure she doesn't *go*. The longer we're fighting, the more upset I get and the more I fight for immediate resolve, whereas she needs time and space to cool down and come back with a head that's more level than either of ours is in the heat of the moment.

Identifying that pattern felt great because we finally had words to give to our experience. Learning, though, isn't the same as *implementing,* and if it isn't clear to you by now, I can be...bullheaded. The following week, Jeanette and I visited our counselor "friend" again, but she didn't want to discuss our results.

So, I told her we were done.

I told her that $175 per session needed to give me more than just a space to talk. The *results* had been helpful, then why didn't she want to talk about them *now*?

I got into an argument with her.

Which meant I got into an argument with Jeanette.

Which meant we entered back into our same old pattern again.

Ironically, we were hosting a marriage retreat shortly after that, and I started justifying my behavior with a classic game of comparisons. *We'll get through this because at least we're not in as bad a spot as some of these people.*

At least we're not going through *that couple's* hell.

In hindsight, I've come to realize another pattern: I always push forward under the assumption that "we'll make it through" (meanwhile, my wife loses more and more hope).

Of course, the irony isn't complete without telling you about who I booked to speak at our retreat.

Kay and Milan Yerkovich.

It was through their presence in our broken home – literally regarding our marriage and figuratively concerning our ministry – that I was led to a place of what I can only call "repentance."

That is: to identify a problem, about-face, and walk the other way.

Jeanette and I decided then and there that, no matter what, we were *going* to do this work.

Moving away from Pasadena was a part of it. Amid marital growing pains, I had also begun to identify the struggles I was having, personally, concerning my life and workload. We always talked about moving to the beach, and I streamlined the decision when I realized that I wasn't sure change would be possible for me if we stayed where we were. I'm not sure Jeanette believed it would be possible either way, but although our differences weren't resolved overnight, we were dedicated to change.

To healing.

We moved. I slowed down. We spent time with the Yerkovich's, went through their book and workbook together, and – to our excitement – even participated in one of their three-day counseling intensives.

It was the snowball that has since grown into an avalanche of self-discovery, personal healing, and rediscovering what it feels like to fall in love with one another all over again.

We dove into our parents' patterns, and what childhood was like for us. Jeanette was able to identify the root of her depression. She felt heard and understood, like she had permission to feel the way that she did day in and day out, and took comfort in knowing that help was available to her. She started taking Zoloft, and although both of us hoped that she wouldn't have to be on medication forever, I was proud of her for pursuing help.

Right around the same time, Jeanette grew to be more open about another awareness tool (and one that – if you've paid attention thus far – you're all familiar with by now): Cannabis. She suffered from a slight case of social anxiety and began to realize that Cannabis helped her be more outgoing and comfortable with people in her life. Our friends noticed it, too. I was overjoyed by the way it helped her because she began to remind me of the woman I fell in love with so many years ago – outgoing and carefree. She was starting to come out from hiding – the uninhibited Jeanette I knew existed beneath her armor.

As we explored our childhoods together, resentment and unforgiveness seemed to be resounding themes. <u>I have an entire website/talk dedicated to resentment (Resentment.org)</u>. Thankfully, I was able to work through a lot of my hurt when my dad and I reconciled, but Jeanette hadn't experienced that kind of restoration. Her mom left with her and her brothers when Jeanette was one, never to see her dad again. And she's never had the relationship a daughter deserves to have with her mom. There was so much hurt to work through.

At the time, a friend of ours had just attended a weeklong retreat at The Hoffman Institute in Napa Valley, California. If How We Love was our entry-point resource for this kind of healing and transformation, The Hoffman Process was all of it plus more, baked into a 7-day intensive retreat. Frankly, for all of the ideas that I'm continually throwing at the wall, I figured I'd get pushback from Jeanette when I suggested she attend, but by that point in her journey, she was ready.

Diving into the Hoffman Process is another chapter for another time, but the idea is that it *helps stuck people get unstuck* by making peace with their past, releasing negative behaviors, pursuing emotional healing, forgiveness, and authenticity and improving relationships.

Jeanette went. She did it all. And at the end, when I picked her up from the retreat, I met an entirely different human being.

I don't want to say that we're living happily ever after, because we still have plenty to learn. To work through, be aware of, and to understand.

But I will say that I'm in a different marriage now. I'm married to a different person. Everything has changed.

It's like falling in love again.

This has been the best, sweetest time we've experienced in our entire marriage.

The seasons that led to this place haven't been easy. Here again recently, with the start of our new venture, Christian Cannabis, we've had friends disappear, and ministry and business partners leave.

But Jeanette and I are finally united. Together. One. We're aware of the fact that none of what we fought about for the past 20 years had as much to do with one another as it did with the lingering pangs of broken childhoods that we never had the tools to work through.

As I write this, I am an hour away from Hoffman, myself. The transformation of my wife was too significant for me to ignore. She even got off of her medication and hasn't the slightest thought of returning to it.

Throughout this entry, I have talked a lot about *her* pain, her woundedness, and her need for healing.

But all of that exists in me, too.

The angry, irritable, and impatient patterns that define my love style? The Vacillator? That's my dad in me. When I was growing up, anger was the only emotion he allowed others to see. I've written plenty about our reconciliation in adulthood, but I realize more and more how much the negative behavior that I learned from him as a child is still ingrained in the man – and yes, the father – I am today. Admittedly, it's hard for me, approaching this next step of the journey, to even consider digging up old skeletons – especially knowing that he is already gone – but I know I still have the pain to work through, too.

However difficult, the sweetness of this journey – the fruit of this labor – has been too good to ignore.

Now that the clock is ticking, how do I wrap this up?

Put bluntly: we all have baggage to deal with.

It has been said that if "you're not growing, you're dying."

All of us have room to grow.

Jeanette and I are committed to growth. We want to *keep* growing. We know what the last 20 years of our marriage have looked like, and we know that we want to be intentional about making sure that the next 20 are significantly different.

Significantly better.

All has not been perfect, but all are being made new.

It wasn't easy. It still isn't easy, but learning who we are and identifying these negative patterns in the hope that we might break them has been the best work we've done together.

How We Love was the catalyst for it all. I can't recommend it highly enough. It helped us discover who we were before pain and neglect and success and ego and *life* happened, layered up on top of the little boy and girl buried beneath it all.

Do the work.

Dive in.

What will you find?

How will it change you?

*Watch Craig expand on this chapter by scanning the QR code below.

Chapter 34 – It Is Better To Give Than To Receive (On Bucket Lists)

"It is more blessed to give than to receive." – Jesus

Years ago, when my dad was still alive, my uncle wrote him a letter for Christmas:

> *Hey, Chip!*
>
> *Last year, we took a trip with the whole family. It was a bucket-list type trip. I want you and your family to take a bucket-list trip, too. Anywhere you want.*
>
> *Send me the details, and I will arrange what is needed.*
>
> *Bill*

I already wrote about what became of our trip to the 49rs vs. Giants Super Bowl rivalry in a previous chapter. The reason I revisit it here at all is that the gift my Uncle Bill was able to give my dad sparked something inside of me that said, *"I can't wait until the day I can do that for someone."*

One of my favorite authors is an entrepreneur named James Altucher. In 2015, he wrote a blog titled The Ultimate Guide For Becoming An Idea Machine and challenged his audience to write a daily list of "ten things," whatever they might be.

Ideas. Goals. Desires.

Fun things. Work-related things.

Realistic things. Absurd things.

It didn't matter. You just had to make a list, ten "things" long, every day.

I, of course, turned the challenge into a contest among my group of friends, to see who would do it for the most extended amount of time. Some people turned the challenge into a blog series. Some journaled their lists in a private notebook.

My wife chose the latter. She never shared her lists, publicly, and because they were more "out of sight, out of mind," I didn't read them until years later. When I finally took a peek, I saw lists titled *Ten Places I'd Want To Go* or *Ten Bucket List Items* and thought, "Wait, you want to do this stuff?"

Why didn't she ever tell me?

And then I thought, *"Alright, time to start fulfilling these dreams."*

Thanks to one list, I surprised her with a trip to Niagara Falls and SNL for her birthday. Thanks to another, I

discovered she wanted to watch the ball drop in Times
Square, NYC, for New Years. We turned that into a
family/anniversary trip last winter.

I just started knocking off as much as I was able to.

It occurred to me, through that experience, how fun it was
to *have a bucket list* at all. <u>I would never have given Nolan
his wristwatch had it not been for his list.</u>

I get excited about seeing other people get excited.

The trip my uncle afforded my dad and me inspired our
family to pay his kindness forward to one of our friends –
 David Dean. In 2016, the Cubs made it to the World Series
for the first time in over one-hundred years. I don't know a
bigger fan than David, so we sent him, his dad, and his son
to the game. His wife sent us a videotape of him opening
the letter with the tickets, and watching his disbelief turn to
joy stirred something inside of me that I'll never be able to
describe.

All I knew is that all I wanted was to give *that* to people as
often as I could. More and more. I wanted to keep fulfilling
people's bucket lists.

Our friend Sam Parsons lost his wife in May 2018. Days
later, he was diagnosed with stage four pancreatic cancer.
While we were visiting him and his family, I found out that
his daughter is a huge Steelers fan. During our
conversation, she said, verbatim, *"Heinz Field is a bucket
list."* At that point, it was settled: *they were going.* I knew

that I wanted to make that dream come true, and seeing the photos of father-and-daughter surprised with a trip to the game was *priceless*. Actually, "priceless" doesn't do it justice, either, but I'm not sure what word would.

When Jeff Bethke and I started <u>our mastermind group for social media influencers</u>, I met a couple who Jeanette and I offered to mentor. My thought – when meeting the husband, Neil – was, *"this kid is just like me."* Come to find out, not only are we similar, but so was his relationship with his dad much like mine had been – not much communication.

Neil lives in Toronto and is a Raptor's fan. When the team made it to the playoffs, my son said that he wished we could get him a pair of the Raptor's Air Jordan's. I said, "What do you mean, *'wish?'* We can do anything we want as long as we can afford it. Do you know what would be better than a pair of Jordan's, though? To send him to the game."

As it turns out, Neil's dad is a Raptors fan, too. We bought them tickets to the first night of the Toronto vs. The Golden State Warriors series, and even though I'm a NorCal fan, I loved Toronto for the first time in my life. Nolan and I sent them a video announcing our gift and received one in return, full of excitement and tears.

Then we got the video of Neil calling his dad to invite him to the game.

Then we watched the video of them at the game, together.

Then Neil watched every game of the series with his dad, sporting matching NBA Finals t-shirts. They spent more time together during those two playoff weeks than they had the entire year prior.

Then the Raptors won the NBA Finals. No one saw it coming.

I can't describe how sweet it is to see a son reconnected his father, thanks – in large part – to a bucket-list dream he never thought possible, fulfilled.

I went to a championship game with my dad when I was a kid. Lakers vs. Celtics. Neither of us even cared about those teams, but it was such a rivalry. Years ago, when he was still alive, I surprised him with Father's Day trip to the NBA Finals.

What I'm trying to say is: *it was incredible.*

I laughed telling Levi about all of these trips for this chapter, saying, "I don't know how to describe it to someone who isn't a sports fan." But he gets it. I've taken him to Coachella with Nolan and me three years in a row now. When the festival announced Eminem as 2018's headliner, he just about cried. He grew up listening to The Real Slim Shady and told me about the first time he heard Marshall Mathers' songs in a department store with his mom. When he was in high school, they'd drive around together, listening to Encore, while Levi described linguistics to her, and how Eminem's lyrical creativity and structure began to influence his journey into a career as a writer and performer. It was so good I surprised him with a trip to Bonarroo so we could watch him a second time during the summer festival circuit.

Levi said, "Eminem's been at the top of my bucket list for my whole life. I never thought I'd get to him live." He got to see him twice.

If Jeanette were to write about why she never shared her bucket list with me, she would say, "I never believed that what I wrote down was possible." But she's married to someone who believes anything is possible. I love instilling that belief in others.

It's never been about the trips or gifts. It's about the *why* or the *who* behind them.

To give to your friends, or your spouse, or your son, or your daughter, or your parents, or *whoever* it may be…there's nothing like it. There's nothing *better* than it.

And you never know what might happen. A basketball game might transform an entire family dynamic. It might just restore a broken relationship.

The point of this is not what I have done for others. The point is to reiterate, again and again, and again: *anything is possible*.

Dream big.

Share your lists.

Say them out loud.

Make dreams – and *fulfilling* those dreams – a part of what you're about. What your family is about. What your relationships are about.

Because at the end of the day, relationships are what it's all about.

I was pissed when Toronto beat the Warriors before I remembered Neil popping champagne and celebrating with his dad. Now that my dad is gone, I'm jealous of that kind of celebration but so thankful to know that they get to enjoy it together.

To be able to give an experience like that to someone, and to be in a marriage with a woman who is seeing dreams become realities-that's what it's about.

Find dreams that have the opportunity to bring people together and fulfill them.

Create experiences that excite and unite people.

Make a bucket list. Start fulfilling it.

Better yet, make someone else's dreams into realities. I promise it will be as much or more a gift to you as it is to the one receiving what you have to give.

It is more blessed to give than to receive.

*Watch Craig expand on this chapter by scanning the QR code below.

Chapter 35 – Enjoy the Moment (And Don't Record It)

Isn't it interesting that some of the best experiences are the ones we don't record?

The first time I saw Justin Vernon of Bon Iver play an intimate show at the Ace Hotel, I sat in the third row behind a woman whose phone seemed permanently stuck to her face. She took a photo of Justin, posted it to every social media platform under the sun, hashtagged it #frontrow, and spent the remainder of the evening scrolling through pictures of her friends having *"bath time with my babies!"* and frantically refreshing her feed to see how many likes she was getting on a photo of a private Bon Iver concert she couldn't possibly care less about.

Eventually, the lady whose glowing screen ruined both of our experiences received a comment from her *bath-time-with-the-babies* friend – a sarcastic "thanks for the invite…looks amazing" – and spent the remainder of the evening whispering about FOMO and how upset she was.

So much for an intimate evening at the Ace.

Our constant need to capture and share every waking hour of our lives is making us miss it entirely. Everyone wants to show everyone else what they're doing. We want to say we've been there. We've done it. In the process, we miss being there. We miss doing it.

We share the present at its own expense, scrolling through comments about a moment we posted but missed as much as everyone responding with their woes on our feed.

For the past three years, I've taken Levi, my son Nolan and a friend of his choosing to Coachella Music Festival. I wonder what it's like for the artists on stage to play for one hundred thousand phones? Levi knows more about that than I do, having toured full-time for the past ten years. I know it can feel gratifying to be the object of attention, but how strange must it be to perform for an audience who has paid for a "live experience" that is *still* watching you through a phone screen lifted in front of their faces, glancing down every ten seconds, deleting and frantically trying to catch the *best* segment of the *best* song that they're entirely missing for some arbitrary Snapchat following?

<u>Rolling Stone ran an article about musicians who are begging their audiences to put their phones away</u>. Entire businesses are being constructed purely for the sake of safely storing people's devices upon entry to an event where their phones are no longer permitted.

Do you know how much time people spend looking for an electrical outlet at music festivals? Do you know how many artists' sets people miss so that they can get their battery level back up to ten percent and record some jealousy-inducing clip of the headliner's show?

I have a growing affection for Childish Gambino. He headlined the opening night of last year's festival and

specifically asked the crowd to put their phones away.
Then, when they didn't, he exacerbated their narcissism. He
got right down into the crowd and gave them an
overabundance of everything they wanted more than what
he had to offer. Donald Glover is a smart dude. His art is
social commentary and frankly, I'm not convinced the
crowd was smart enough to receive what he had to say.
Sometimes the worst thing for us is to get what we ask for,
so he gave everyone indulgence. Boast, boast, boast. Watch
more and more and more of me, me, me.

It's a drug.

To hell with the phone-charging stations at Coachella. To
hell with the Instagram posts and the pics and the clicks and
our culture's obsession with its front-facing camera.

What are we doing to ourselves?

I'm not saying that taking a photo or recording a video is
inherently wrong, but it's still not the same as *being there*.
We've got to remember what it means – and what it *feels
like* – to *be present* with one another and with ourselves.
We're far too distracted and far too self-absorbed.

Recently, Nolan had the opportunity to meet one of his
favorite artists – Role Model. I asked him if he wanted me
to take a photo of the two of them together, and he
responded, "No, thanks. That's what everyone else is doing.
Maybe he'll remember me because I *didn't* ask for his
photo. Either way, I want to talk to him about his music."

He gets it. A picture with Role Model would have done "really well" – whatever that means. But Nolan's been friends with and watched enough of an entire culture of kids his age compete for a photo to know that all the "likes" in the world will only leave you wanting for more. He's just a fan of the guy's music, and that's enough.

Not everything needs a post. And not every post is worth seeing.

We keep staring at this screen, watching other people "have" the experiences we want to have, when in reality, the people who are "having" those experiences, aren't.

I wonder what it would be like to talk to Steve Jobs, were he alive today? Could he ever have imagined what his inventions would become? Did he envision it going this far?

Speaking of music, it was fascinating to watch the rise of vinyl records surpass digital sales over the past few years. Even Forbes ran articles on the phenomena that are physical sales skyrocketing in a digital age. We've seen the same type of thing when it comes to print journals and productivity resources as opposed to app-based systems. In his art, Nolan has found himself more and more attracted to film photography over and above his digital lens.

I'm convinced that it's all related. We're starved for *anything* other than digital *everything*. It's what happens when addictions – once so gratifying – curdle and turn sour.

Envy fuels us, and however cliche, "keeping up with the Joneses" is exhausting.

But how else are we going to know what's going on unless we're tapped continuously into Facebook?

How else are we going to prove to the world that we mean something unless we're always putting our best selves out there and pleading its attention?

We all bought into this hivemind that said: *You HAVE to post something.* But now that we *have* to, we're all tired, functioning out of deficiencies, and I'm convinced that none of us *want* to.

There's a saying that goes: *comparison is the thief of joy.* Well, I'd like to add something to that. Most of what we're comparing ourselves to are fake. Do you know how many older men and soccer moms are dressed up to take Coachella pictures in Off White and Yeezys next to Post Malone posters (an artist they've never even heard of before), flashing their VIP badges and adding thirty hashtags to the gram?

Please.

It's *fake*. At best, it's an attempt to escape. At worst, it's dishonesty. It's an entitlement and grasping for the vanity that another double-tap is on a picture that someone far away will stare at for long enough to wish they were you, and then scroll past, left wondering how the grass is so dead on their side of the fence (phone screen).

I know I'm going hard on this one. <u>Old Man Craig is back again</u>.

I can't help but wonder what it would be like for us to just *be*. Right here. Right now. We're always everywhere else with these computers in our back pocket. We are distracted and anxious, wondering what someone else is doing that we aren't, or whether they're seeing what we're doing when *they aren't*.

I know there's a flipside.

I'm fully aware that it's not *all* fake.

It's not *all* lies.

It's not *all* motivated by the need for validation.

It's not *wrong* to share a picture.

It's not *wrong* to be excited about an experience.

Mark Twain said, "To get the full value of joy, you must have someone to share it with," but that's part of the problem – are we really *with* the people receiving our "joy?"

Last year, Levi told me about a comedian named Bo Burnham. <u>He has an incredible Netflix special titled *Make Happy*</u>, with one bit in particular where he talks about social media, saying that the entertainment industry has become all of us, all the time, endlessly. He says this:

> *"I worried that making a show about performing would be too meta – it wouldn't be relatable to people who aren't performers.*
>
> *But what I found is that I don't think anyone* isn't.
>
> *They say it's a* 'Me Generation' *– it's not. The arrogance is taught, or it was cultivated. It's self-conscious. It is* conscious of self. *Social media is just market's answer to a generation that demanded to perform. So the market said,*
>
> *'Here, perform. Everything. To each other. All the time. For no reason.'*
>
> *It's prison.*
>
> *It is horrific.*
>
> *It is performer and audience melded together.*
>
> *What do we want more at the end of the day than to lay there and watch our life as a satisfied audience member?*
>
> *I know very little about anything, but what I do know is that if you can live your life without an audience.*

You should do it."

Perhaps what I'm getting at is that too much of a good thing can make you sick. It can make you sick as the "performer," and it can make you sick as the "observer" – and all of us seem to have become both. Last November, <u>the Anxiety and Depression Association of America published a fascinating article about social media obsession and anxiety disorders</u>, saying that our addiction to platforms like Facebook and Twitter "can greatly reduce [our] ability to enjoy real life," costing us relationships, jobs, and education.

Too much "medicine" is poisonous, and I'm convinced that our underlying need to "record the moment" –every single moment – is toxic.

What about simply being in it?

Is *here* and *now* so bad that we must continuously distract and filter and garner the approval of others to feel alright about who and where we are?

As a fast-moving, quick-starting achiever of a man, I know that changing habits is hard work. I know that social media feels like the epitome of bustling, noisy craziness. It's like the manifestation of what my head feels like all too often, and I know that I'm not blameless when it comes to overindulging in my feeds.

But I have also learned what it feels like to step away from the noise.

To sit in the mundane.

The slowness of real life.

The quiet that *is possible* if we will proactively mute the chatter.

The music that *does* move you if you're willing to pay attention.

The conversations that aren't cluttered if you're willing to engage the human being *in real life* across the table from where you're sitting.

The silence that *does* whisper when you're patient enough to hear it.

The stillness is where God is found.

*Watch Craig expand on this chapter by scanning the QR code below.

Chapter 36 – Refining Fires (And Saltine Crackers)

"There's no bridge for bypassing crucifixion." – Levi The Poet

---

Pain is an incredible teacher.

If only it didn't hurt so much.

It occurred to me while reimagining all of these journal entries for this project that I haven't written much about my mom.

The definition of "take for granted" is to *fail to properly appreciate (someone or something), especially as a result of overfamiliarity.* If the truth is that I've taken advantage of my mom, it certainly wasn't intentional, but it's painful, nonetheless. It's crazy to think that something as incredible as "*over*familiarity" could result in anything other than acknowledgment, appreciation, and praise. And yet, I sometimes wonder if it is precisely *because of* her consistent presence in my life that I haven't given her the credit she deserves.

She has been, simply, a given.

My mom lived with us for a while during a particularly painful season in our family's life. She needed to get out of the situation she was in, and we furnished the back house at our property in Pasadena to accommodate for her stay. I am thankful for that time, despite the circumstances, because it allowed me to love and serve my mom the way that she'd watched me love and serve my dad.

I hadn't realized, up until recently, that the relationship my dad offered to rekindle simultaneously sparked jealousy inside of my mom that made her feel as though I had chosen sides, and she'd been the one found wanting.

Again, it wasn't intentional, but it happened.

They say you don't know what you have until it's gone. Like the way that, once we decided to move, my mom and I didn't talk for months. I think we hurt one another in our silence. A mentor of mine asked if I remembered the same lesson I'd been paying forward ever since my dad called to reconcile before he died: *pick up the phone.*

It's amazing the way that a simple phone call can be such a catalyst for renewal. She's been down to visit a few times since then. <u>She got to see Elise dance to our song</u>. We've been able to discuss family trauma, redeem past pains, reconcile differences, and understand one another.

When I consider my relationship with my mom, I inevitably jump to my relationship with my kids. What pain will I pay forward that we'll need to work through when they're my age? Jeanette and I have done so much work lately when it comes to breaking familial patterns. We know that all parents leave some sort of imprint on their kids – for better or worse. Will I have done my job well enough that they take me for granted due to overfamiliarity?

Surely that is at least one definition of a job well done?

The opposite of *familiar* is *foreign*. Unacquainted. Unknown and unknowable.

How many mothers are *unfamiliar* to their children? I see Jeanette's pain as a result of her parents' absence, and my mom's constancy – her availability – shines brighter. I've always heard people say that motherhood is a thankless job. I wish it weren't so. I suppose this is an attempt at redeeming my silence.

After all, thank God I have a mother to thank.

This year, Levi decided that he was going to run a half marathon. He trained for months leading up to his race, and on the day of – at the end – he told me that his mom stood standing at the finish line, cheering.

Immediately, I knew, *"that's it."*

She's always been there, and she always will be.

My mom has had a funny way of showing it, at times. I remember the first morning I appeared on Good Morning America to talk about XXXchurch. She didn't say, "Good job, Craig." She said, "What's wrong with your hair?"

Either way, she's still been there for every "race," whether or not I've appreciated her commentary-even today. My mom was the first person to join the Christian Cannabis Facebook Group and Street Team.

She wrote to me the other day to say, *"My thought is that if you believe in something, you never let fear stop you. Case in point: XXXchurch. And now: Christian Cannabis. You always go for it. As your mom, I sometimes cringe, but I know that it's something God has put on your heart. I know you will succeed."*

I'm losing friends, business, and ministry partners left and right. Meanwhile, my mom wants to give me the last of her money to help invest in my next vision.

I suppose I've been fascinated by this idea of looking backward to go forward. My friend Dave treated me to a session with his breathwork coach not long ago. Even there, the instructor encouraged me to curl up into a fetal position, saying, "This is how you were for nine months in your mother's womb."

Return to it. Remember who you were and who she was before ego and all of this other garbage began to cake on top of your authentic selves.

It wasn't the only time, as of late, that the fetal position has reminded me of my mom.

During the past few months, I've experienced bouts of debilitating stomach problems. I've had to get a scope, clonic, and cleanse.

The pain there taught me something, too: not all physical pain is the result of physical problems. Sometimes, psychological turmoil manifests itself in bodily symptoms. I've flipped my entire world upside down over the past few months, and the stomach problems only started to subside with the resolve of all of my mental clutter.

It was as though the Lord was saying, "Dear Mr. Craig *Brain*, listen *not just to your head*, but also to your spirit and your gut-your *whole body* is telling you something."

So, I've tried to pay attention. And a few short days after the breathwork calm, I found myself back in the fetal position. This time, writhing and nauseous on the floor of a public bathroom. And it was while listening to my whole body that I was reminded of the purity of the relationship that is a mother's love for her son.

I thought of saltine crackers.

I lay on the cool of the tile in the bathroom stall for over two and a half hours with the worst stomach ache I've ever experienced in my life, crying and in pain unlike any I've ever known. I thought I was in hell. And when I saw myself doubled-over like that, I thought of being a kid in my parents' house, and the way my mom would care for me when I was sick.

I thought, "My mom would bring me saltine crackers in a heartbeat." And then I thought, "What would it be like if that wasn't a given?"

If you didn't know your mom would drop everything she's doing to bring a box of crackers, red Gatorade and a pan to your bedside?

If you didn't think your mom would show up at your race to cheer you through the finish line?

If you didn't have the luxury of taking your ever-available mom for granted?

At forty-three years old, curled up on a bathroom floor, I still just wanted my mom. And gratefulness overwhelmed me when I *knew* that, at forty-three years old, she'd still come if I called.

That realization does something to you. And I can only imagine that thinking (or knowing) you *don't* or haven't had that kind of support does something to you, as well.

That experience taught me compassion.

I knew then and there that I had to dedicate this project to my mom. Ideally, I'd rather have learned these lessons without having to shove my finger down my throat in an attempt to get the poison out of me, but I suppose pain is a better teacher than comfort. At the very least, it is an empathy-creator.

Growing up and getting old seems to shatter your preconceptions about the world. About what life is. About who your parents were, or are. The more I've suffered as one myself, though, the more anger has been replaced with empathy.

Levi writes a lot about suffering. He's experienced too much of it. One of the recurring themes that accompany his work–like a backbone–is the way that Christ describes himself as someone who can understand our plight, namely, through suffering. He often brings up Hebrews 4, where Jesus is described as a suffering, sympathetic servant. Even when you look up the word "passion," one of its definitions is *the suffering of Christ*. How else could He claim to relate to us had He not walked in our shoes?

Levi has a line in <u>one of his poems</u> that seems to fit well with my learning experience, so I thought I'd share it here:

> *You'll make it through. After your heart can no longer stomach the torture or the way the pain always expands to a weight that collapses on itself when gravity betrays the attraction of youth for the undress of age, you'll be able to breathe again.*
>
> *The thing is, there's no bridge for bypassing crucifixion.*

That last line rings true. It reminds me of the way that people have to "go through the fire to be refined."

I've written plenty about my family's brokenness throughout this season. My mom has been through the fire. As I go through my own, I see that more clearly. But I'm not sure I would have had it not been for the pain that teaches and unites us.

I have to believe that suffering is not pointless. Left unresolved, I know that it rots and robs us of joy. It can make us forget who we are and what we were made for. But worked through and learned from?

That process can transform us forever.

Perhaps that process is the culmination of what all of this has been for me. All of Craig Brain. All of the years between my Alaska Pilgrimage and The Hoffman Process. All of the search for medicine. All of the pursuit of quiet. All of the learning to listen inside of it. All of the trying to find me. All of trying to understand my parents, and who I am in light of who they were. All of trying to give my kids something different. All of reconciling differences between myself and my friends. All of learning what I am good at. All of letting go of what I am not. All of inviting Levi into this journey and asking him to clarify my intent. All of relocating and pushing for a better relationship with my wife and my family. All of understanding the pain beneath the surface and working on learning from and letting go of it. All of searching for God. All of allowing Him to redefine who I thought he was.

What is your pain teaching you?

And mom, thanks for always standing ready with saltines in hand, like water to douse the flames. I love you.

Craig

*Watch Craig expand on this chapter by scanning the QR code below.

Chapter 37 – Mind Chatter (& The True You)

Does your brain ever turn off? Can you check out of it? Is it telling you positive things or negative things?

It recently occurred to me that "normal" doesn't exist, because my normal isn't yours. My mind exploded when I realized that Jeanette could shut hers off when she cleans the house. She says that the activity replaces the thinking and quiets her head.

I have no idea what that's like. *You mean you can vacuum to quiet the noise?* No amount of activity ever does anything other than add to my internal chatter. Cannabis has helped me experience a bit more of that quiet, but my attempts to articulate it always devolve into some media outlet reporting the ways that *"Pastor Craig Gross says that weed makes him closer to God,"* twisting the narrative.

Levi has helped me write this entire book. I asked him to organize, edit and – in some cases – "ghostwrite" for me because I don't know anyone as able to get inside of other peoples' heads and articulate their experience the way that he can. I can give him a fragmented mess of a journal entry, and he can smooth its edges, helping me understand what the hell I'm saying while making it palatable for others at the same time.

But he has a hard time doing that for himself. He struggles to see the value that he has to offer the world, and it's largely because of what's "normal" inside of his head.

Part of the reason Levi and I get along, I think, is because of our ability to relate to one another's constant brain chatter. The difference is that mine usually propels me forward, creating more work than I know what to do with, whereas his paralyzes him, creating an inability to work at all. He struggles with condemnation, whereas I "struggle" with confidence. My mind doesn't know negatives. There's nothing inside of it that says, *"You can't."* It just starts and dreams and explores and plots and plans and goes and goes and goes and creates more and more and more work.

"The mind is a wonderful servant but a terrible master." My friend Chris is the only other person I've found who can resonate with the level of mind chatter that Levi and I experience.

"I don't meet a lot of people who get how relentless our heads are," Chris said. "We feel like it's our greatest asset. In some ways, it is. But it can also be the greatest impediment to our freedom, and our inner power and authority. I make my mind the master, but I'd rather make it the servant of my heart."

So I asked Levi, "Does your brain ever turn off? Can you check out of it? Is it telling you positive things or negative things?" Also – after having realized that *my* experience is not "normal" – I asked him to describe what he thinks of me. What does he think of how I function? Are our conversations normal? How do I compare to other people that he spends time with when it comes to the volume of conversation, thought, and activity he experiences with me?

With his permission, I've chosen to let you in on our conversation. We use a voice messaging app to track our discussions, so we decided – after trying and failing to describe our own heads – to translate and let you in on the dialogue wherein we attempted to answer these questions for one another. As you'll read below, I think this is an excellent means of getting there, because it was an attempt at articulation that happened in real-time, not filtered behind a computer screen, or an editor's censorship.

At the least, I hope it explains a bit of what I've tried to communicate throughout this season. Who knows, perhaps you'll read something of your own experience in what follows, as well:

Craig:

> Can you answer an honest question? I've never met anyone that can put words to how my mind functions. Does yours ever turn off? Can you check out of it? Is yours mainly saying negative things?
>
> And my second question for you is this: you've spent a lot of time with me throughout the years, how does our time together compare to everyone else you hang out with?

Levi:

> My brain never turns off. If I do hands-on stuff, like Jeanette, I can get into it. That's part of the reason art remains a desire I'd like to keep investing in. But

I sometimes think that I've got to figure out a new medium for it, outside of writing, because I'm always in my cognitive mind.

I sometimes feel like, "I don't *really* want to work a construction job, but maybe it'd be great for me. Or working in coffee. Something more hands-on and 'mindless' might be incredible for my mental health."

When I was in New Zealand this January, I experienced what it feels like for my mind to turn off for the first time in my life. I was just *present*. It was incredible. I was so *not* preoccupied in my brain with obsessive thoughts about all of the bad that I'm always projecting onto myself.

Unfortunately, lately, I've been having a hard time again. You talk about pain manifesting itself physically. I've got an ulcer, or a Hiatal hernia, or something. I don't know what's going on, but there's something wrong in my body. Stress-induced Hiatal hernias run in my family, and the worse it gets, the more stressed I get. On goes the cycle.

So, my brain doesn't shut off. That means I often feel like I can't be present with other people. It's all negative. Yes.

To your second question: you're doing more things than anyone else I know is capable of doing. Your capacity to handle a million things at once is something I envy. But I can also feel crippled by it because I don't think that I could ever do what you do. Self-pity starts to kick in. *"I wish…but I can't."*

As for the *volume* of conversation, I am capable of and enjoy having in-depth discussions with my friends. I create those opportunities with other people. So in that regard, our interactions/conversations aren't *more* than most, but of course, we talk about different things based upon where you're at in life.

That said, as for your question, "Am I on a whole different level?" *Yes*. I don't know anyone like you. I'm not sure how to describe it back to you, though. You think, talk, and move *so* fast. There's so much going on that you can't even complete sentences.

You seem fearless. You go, go, go.

I hear what you're saying about it being both a blessing and a curse.

I struggle because I *also* have a million ideas. They're not huge ideas like yours. They're small but could become something.

The difference, though, is that I get paralyzed by my ideas and never start. You delegate immediately and get it done.

One of the things that I struggle with is people who I perceive to be complacent. Their comfort with "the way things are" blows my mind. I'm not content. I always see what *could be*.

Unfortunately, though, I'm not seeing what could be from the perspective of a person who feels capable of going and *getting* what could be.

So, I wrestle with discontentment and covetousness about what could be, but then feel paralyzed by the possibilities, and get myself stuck.

Lately, I've been struggling with questions like, "What am I doing?" I feel purposeless. I lack direction and overall vision. It's making me spiral out.

I'm just trying to take one step at a time. Have a decent work day. Tack something else on top of that if I'm able to. I guess this is an example of my brain going from one unrelated thought to another to another.

I want a little less talk and a little more action.

One more thought, though. I talked about the complacency that bothers me. While that's true, it's also something I envy.

If I'm motivated or think I want to work on things – or if I can't help *but* work on things (which is, I think, what we're talking about) – I get annoyed by people who don't want to keep doing *more* all of the time.

But then there's another part of me that thinks, "Man, I *so envy* that ability just to *be content.*"

Getting to that place is extremely rare for me.

Maybe being content doesn't mean, "I don't want to do anything."

Maybe it just means, "I know when enough is enough." Whereas I'm stuck beneath: there's *always* more. So, I keep piling on *more*. And then when I finish one thing, there's never any sense of "done."

As much as contentedness *looks like* complacency to me, there is undoubtedly a lot of me that wants to be able to function from that place of contentedness. For me, that is a quality of mind. Or at least: a quelling of my obsessive mind, and the negativity continually running through it.

Craig:

Hey man, that was helpful. It also made me sad listening to what you deal with.

When I listen to these audio messages, and all we've gone back and forth about during this season, I think, "Is anyone talking like this, or are we only using junk drawer words like *mental health?* Do we understand it?"

What you just told me – I've experienced it. I was there for that thirty minutes the night I asked the Lord to reveal to me what your head is like. I hated it. It was horrible, and it messed me up for the entire next day.

You're a deep, empathetic writer. When I just heard you speak, though, it didn't feel as deep as it felt *clear*. I haven't read written words from you that are as clear as what I just heard you speak.

Have you ever told other people this?

Do we want to understand one another (not just you and me - but all people)?

I think my issue with many of the people and organizations that I see trying to champion the mental health discussion right now is that they all say a lot of things, but they don't go far enough. They're not explaining it in words specific to what's going on inside of them. I haven't heard anything from anyone like the voice memo you just sent. I see people post about going to counseling, but I wonder if they'd be willing to share a jumbled up mess of a recording about what is going on inside of their heads?

What are you thinking? What are you saying?

In <u>our Influencer Inner Circle mastermind</u>, there was a girl who I was convinced should do *this one specific thing*. But she was too scared to say that she was too afraid to do it. I asked the entire room if they all agreed that she *could*, and everyone raised their hands, and then she got to see that she *was* capable of the thing she'd been scared of.

But if we're too afraid to say what we're too afraid of, no one will have the opportunity to tell us that we shouldn't be.

Everybody's head game is different.

As your friend and someone who has gone before you on some of this stuff and has seen some progress, it would be awesome if you could grow out of this stuff, man. I'm old, and I'm just now making progress, but you've still got the gift of youth.
Keep working at it. Don't put it off. And if things need to change, then change them.

I asked Jeanette what she wishes I would have done sooner, and she responded, "Left XXXchurch. And it's not because life was *that bad*, but it's because now that you're so connected to your heart, life is *way better."*

That's where I go, *"Dude, you've got to figure out: how do I get back to New Zealand?"*

That journal entry you sent me after you got home, *that Levi,* is your authentic self. That's who you are.

Jeanette keeps saying, "I'm not going to let anyone steal my peace."

The peace is the gift.

And you can't keep living like this.

Whether your answer is medication, breath work, awareness, *whatever*. Start doing things. Ask yourself what works. Go after it.

When I talked to you after your trip to New Zealand – when I read your letter – I thought, *that's the true Levi.*

That's who you are, man. That's the Levi I know. Not the Levi that is in your head. Your head is not you. That's not who you are.

I'm sorry, man. I'm sorry about what it's like in your head.

Anyway – it's not *just* New Zealand – I've seen that in you since the day I met you. It's special. What you're wrestling within your head – at that capacity – has got to be scary.

Maybe it could be a type of medicine to be able to share/air some of this stuff. Be honest. Be honest as a reminder to yourself that what you're experiencing is *not who you are.*

Maybe that's the work for you in the season that you're in right now.

Love you man.

Of course, the conversation above is personal. It includes specifics and references that not everyone will understand in their entirety. Nevertheless, I wonder what of our dialogue – or the entire context of a season coming to a close – resonates with those of you who have chosen to follow along on this journey?

What kind of mind chatter do you deal with? Does it propel you? Does it paralyze you? Does it serve you, or does it impede your growth? Are you able to overcome it?

Chris talks about "practicing embodiment." I think we all have our own versions of this. For example, he loves breath work (think *Headspace* meditation plus breathing exercises) for the way it oxygenates his body and helps him "get out of his endless thought streams."

To admit the need for that kind of practice is not a failure.

For Levi, during his New Zealand trip that I kept referencing above, embodiment meant "vacation." Pressing a deliberate pause on his work to spend time with his wife, and working through *How We Love* in order to let go of negative patterns passed down from generation to generation inside of his family. Today, it means medication and leveling out chemical imbalances inside of his brain.

To admit the need for that kind of help is not a failure.

For me, it has meant spa days. It has meant cannabis. And it has meant contemplative prayer and practicing stillness in the midst of all of my activity.

To admit the need for this kind of rest is not a failure.

For all of us, I think – more than any mental health management – it has meant exploring the core of who we are and pursuing change from the inside-out. A lot of internal, fundamental healing has to take place for functional change to occur in a person's life...

Digging into the past.

Understanding where we've come from.

Extending and receiving forgiveness.

Working toward and being open to the pursuit of reconciliation.

Practicing acceptance over and above what "should be."

mewithoutYou has a song lyric that says, "A glass can only spill what it contains." Scripture says that out of the overflow of the heart, the mouth speaks. Jesus talks about the way that fruit can only be as good or bad as the tree that bears it.

Scripture also says that transformation begins in the mind, and I'm more and more convinced that if we want to change the narrative ours is speaking, we have to put in the hard work of understanding why it's saying what it's saying in the first place, and reminding ourselves of what the truth is.

Part of what that means for me is to recognize the lie that says *I'm not good enough* without whatever it is I stand to accomplish from all of the work I create for myself.

For Levi, perhaps that means recognizing the lie that says he's a failure if he *doesn't* accomplish all of the work he'd like to.

We're both accepted and inherently valuable with or without our work.

As we are.

(As are you.)

*Watch Craig expand on this chapter by scanning the QR code below.

Chapter 38 – Who The Son Sets Free Is Free Indeed (The Hoffman Process)

"You have turned for me my mourning into dancing; you have loosed my sackcloth and clothed me with gladness, that my glory may sing your praise and not be silent. O LORD my God, I will give thanks to you forever!" Psalm 30: 11-12

I saw this most clearly after they asked us to become as children for an entire day. Grown adults, playing games, gift-giving, feasting, and laughing that culminated in a dance party, where the weeping we'd done that morning was *literally* turned into dancing.

I felt all of the vindictiveness fall away from me. All of my anger and unforgiveness and self-pity and insecurity and overcompensation and the need to *prove* my worth…removed.

I buried it. I held a funeral for every negative pattern I've inherited, or created. Every generational curse I've embodied. I stood in a graveyard and delivered their eulogies.

Let me rewind.

In 2013, I flew to Anchorage, Alaska, to participate in a healing retreat an hour north of the city, in a town called Willow. It's beautiful. I dedicated the weekend to letting go of pent-up pain through a process called Rapid Transformation Therapy, allowing the guides to lead me through an experience designed to facilitate emotional healing and release repressed emotions. I spent time away from the constant buzz of the modern world. I even went salmon fishing.

I, Craig Gross, went salmon fishing. If that doesn't scream *transformative*, I don't know what does. Always a shock jock, I know.

At the end of my experience in Alaska, I felt as though the Lord told me that it was time to step away from XXXchurch. As I write this today, that was six years ago. I've spoken sparingly about that still, small voice (however loudly it continued to echo after the fact) since then, only telling a handful of people.

Whether it was care or ego that kept me here for another half-decade (let's be honest, it's been both), I couldn't see how it would have been possible for me to leave.

Today, though, I am finally free from my obligation to stay. Though it will be old news by the time anyone reads this chapter, I am completing this final draft on the same day that my departure from XXXchurch is announced publicly.

The official release went out about two hours ago. In it, I told whoever happens to pay attention that I feel as though the Lord has led me to take a step of faith even though I'm not quite sure where my foot is going to land. It is time to pass the torch, and one of the ways I know that to be true is because of the way God has reinforced his love for me during this season.

In many ways, I consider Alaska to be the bookend at the start of the journey that Craig Brain has been. From the moment I lay on the floor six years ago in some woman's mountain cottage – releasing emotional pain that had finally begun to bubble up – until now, having just completed The Hoffman Process and experienced the culmination of *letting go*, I am a drastically different person than the man I once saw in the mirror.

It is July 12, 2019, and this will be the last journal entry that I share for this project.

This is the bookend on the opposite side of the shelf that I began constructing so long ago.

Again, it is experiential. Again, it requires uncovering pain. Again, it speaks the truth.

I want to explain The Hoffman Process. While I was at their institute in Northern California, I was given a very clear mental image of a microphone, which I took as the Lord revealing my desire to share my experiences with others, particularly if I feel it will *help*.

I've referenced Hoffman here and there. An old intern of mine was the first to bring it to my attention. Then, one of my best friends flew across the country to experience it. Then Jeanette. Then his wife followed in their footsteps.

But now that *I've* had the chance to join forty other people for a week in Napa Valley, seeking transformation,

punching pillows, burying parents and rewiring our brains
together, I know that this experience is my conclusion.

Sound weird? It is. But *weird* doesn't mean *bad*, and I'd
like to conclude this journey by shedding light on a process
that feels as though it has only ever been shrouded in
mystery. I want this to exist for myself as much as anyone
else, and for the people close to me. The people who love
me. The people who I love. I want my kids and my mom
and my friends to be able to understand what it is, and why
it holds such a place of significance in my (and Jeanette's)
life.

To borrow their explanation, "The Hoffman Process is a 7-
day soul searching, healing retreat of transformation and
development for people who feel stuck in one or more
important areas of their lives." It is designed to help people
"make peace with their past, release negative behaviors,
experience emotional healing, and forgiveness, discover
their authentic selves, and improve their relationships."

Hoffman does this through something they call the Cycle of
Transformation, wherein *awareness* gives birth to
expression gives birth to *compassion and forgiveness* gives
birth to *new behavior*.

Thematically, I think *awareness* is the best one-word
summary of my inward journey during this long,
painstaking season. Over the years, I've added tools to my
belt – The Enneagram, How We Love, and other elements
that have lent themselves to self-understanding. The
Hoffman Process seems to both include and transcend them

all by giving people like me practical ways not just to understand, but to *change.*

The Apostle Paul, in Romans 12, asks that we would be "transformed by the renewing of our minds." After my week in Napa, I feel as though I have experienced the fruit of that labor for the first time in my life.

I'm not the first of my friends (or my family) to have attended the Hoffman Institute, but no one who had gone before me seemed comfortable clarifying – whether due to inability or unwillingness – what it actually is. A part of me wonders whether it is fear that drives people to silence, at least in the Christian bubble that I often find myself in. Hoffman is, admittedly, *not* a "Christian" process, but neither do they ostracize anyone for (or seek to replace) their faith. Instead, the process is holistic and integrative, and the language used is vague, and often more of a "fill in the blank with what you believe" – be it in Jesus or Oprah.

Knowing this, even though they discourage media in place of silence, I'm a rule-breaker, and I brought some of my favorite worship albums with me as a grounding presence during my time away. I am not afraid of interfaith experiences, but I also knew the object of *mine* and wanted to be sure I could take what I would learn as rooted in him.

The first of the seven-day experience is rooted in *awareness*. They start by asking about our patterns – learned, compulsive, automatic, and reactive behaviors – and just *how aware* we are of them in our lives-particularly negative patterns. The teachers help people trace their patterns back to what was ingrained in them by their parents, and their parents before them.

As for me and my negative patterns?

I'm impatient. I'm critical. I'm angry. I'm judgemental. I'm afraid of expressing myself. (When I consider that last pattern, in particular, it's a miracle that the words you're reading now exist at all.)

Hoffman doesn't just help a person dissect his or her mind, though. Instead, they focus on something that they call a quadrinity: four integrative aspects of what it means to be human, including your intellect, your body, your emotional self, and your spiritual self. As you begin the process on that first day, they ask you questions like, "Why are you here? What are you trying to let go of? Where are you trying to go?" They ask you to consider each of these questions with your *whole* being (which is easier said than done for a guy always stuck in his *brain)*.

It's fascinating. All of these patterns begin to come to life, and you realize, "Wow… I'm not my dad, but I sure do look a lot like him. I'm not my mom, but I sure do function in many of the same ways that she did."

After you've gone through the awareness portion of your stay, a person moves into *expression*. It's an immersive experience, and the staff walks the room through something that they call "bashing." As in: they give you a Wiffle ball bat and pillow and tell you to go to town. Imagine forty people in a room, full of rage, beating a pillow as though they were beating their past.

This was hard for me. Particularly when it came to expressing anger toward my dad. Not because my mom deserves more of it than he does, but because my dad is dead. He can't defend himself. Eventually, one of the teachers clarified their intent: "The idea is not to villainize your parents. You're *not* beating them. You don't have to hate them. But what about the negative patterns you inherited from them? *That* is what we're expressing today."

And that was all I needed. I demolished my pillow, and I think that if my dad were alive at my side, he'd have joined me. I believe that both of my parents would appreciate my putting the worst of what they gave me to death. They'd breathe a sigh of relief watching the chains they never meant to lock, loosed. They'd be glad to know I don't have to continue forward in the bondage they may not have been able to shake.

It's an incredible day. An exhausting day. A painful day. A healing day. A humanizing day. An honest day. A day that ends with appreciation and gratefulness as – perhaps for the first time in our lives – we have allowed our truest emotions to surface without fear or shame. And you realize in a new and beautiful way: the truth does set you free.

The truth is, the principal, core belief that I have functioned from for most of my life is this:

I am not good enough.

Because of that lie – one that I have believed as truth for as long as I can remember – I've spent most of my adulthood trying to prove the opposite. Working nonstop to be something other than a failure and walking a tightrope between my marriage and my need to be perceived as successful by an audience. Overcompensating. Overproducing. Oversharing. Proving myself. Working harder.

No more.

I heard the Spirit – clear as day – tell me that *"I am uniquely and wonderfully made."* I repeated it over and over and over and over and over again, and I believed him. How many nods of assent have I given to that truth as nothing more than a truism during my 43 years in this body? I finally believed it.

I am uniquely and wonderfully made. I don't need to prove my worth to *anyone*. I am accepted and loved not because of what I do, but because of who I am.

In all honesty, my intellect continues to fight against this truth. To reject it. But I felt forgiveness – *true forgiveness* – unlike any I've ever experienced in this life. Forgiveness for the ways that I've failed to be "good enough," and proceeded to whip myself day in and day out, trying harder to cover up my shame and feelings of worthlessness. Forgiveness for the ways that I have failed as a husband and a father and a friend and a son.

Forgiveness.

That night, as I lay in bed, I listened to my worship music, and the lyrics resounded, *"I am washed in the blood of the lamb, and through his scars, I am innocent."*

I believed it. I'm 43 years old, and I've been telling people this truth since I was a child, but I *finally* believed it for myself.

And I am convinced that I have never known peace like this before. Peace as it now rests upon me. I am washed in the blood of the lamb, and through his blood, I am innocent.

The following day, you give your unwanted, negative patterns and untrue beliefs a literal funeral. We were taken to a graveyard, told to separate from one another and find a tombstone that would act as our common burial grounds for the damaging imprints we've carried since childhood, and instructed to eulogize them.

Say farewell.

Mourn…

Perhaps even more beautiful than the awareness I've received through this process of self-exploration is the *compassion and forgiveness* that I've been allowed to experience. For myself, yes, but also for my parents. All of us have suffered, and I'm learning how to replace *blame* with *understanding*. The point of all of this childhood excavation is not to make an enemy of your mom and dad, but to understand that they, too, are a product of their parents' love (or lack thereof). When I "buried" their negative imprints that day, I wept every bit as much over the pain that they had to live with as I did over my own. While I rejoice that Jeanette and I have been relentless about pursuing healing from wounds and restoration in our marriage, I mourned the fact that my parents didn't have the tools to salvage theirs.

That day, I said goodbye to the patterns created by pain in the Gross family.

"I'm burying these patterns, mom. I'm burying these patterns, dad. They're not coming home with me."

My kids aren't inheriting them. I know I'm not perfect. I know Jeanette isn't perfect. I know we'll pass on our own set of problems to Nolan and Elise, but these generational lies stop with me.

They're in the ground.

The fourth and final step in Hoffman's Cycle of Transformation is *new behavior*. I can think of no better example, personally, than that with which I started this chapter: *dancing*.

I grew up a baptist. I wasn't allowed to dance. You should see me try, rigid as the Tin Man in The Wizard of Oz. (But what better analogy for a man like me, in search of his heart?)

During one of our dance parties at Hoffman, I watched a man dance with what I can only call reckless abandon. Maybe something like King David, embarrassing his wife as he danced before the Lord. I remember thinking, "I want to be free *like that.*"

Hoffman teaches something called *recycling*, which is – essentially – a way to change your brain. You visualize a scenario that you'd like to change because you know it to be associated with a negative pattern. You picture the moment as it occurred, and then "go back in time" to see where that pattern – which affected the way you acted on that occasion – came from. How does it make you feel? Then, when "recycling" that pattern, you replace the feeling with what you would prefer to feel and with who you would prefer to be.

Case in point, when I saw that guy dancing, I thought, "I could never do that," and immediately knew that if I was truly going to go *all-in* on The Hoffman Process – to truly put this experience to the test – I *had* to do *exactly* that.

As I mentioned earlier, one of the negative patterns I identified was a fear of expressing myself. So, in recycling, I took the fear, traced it back to where it came from, replaced it with *confidence* and visualized myself going wild, free from shame, embarrassment, not-good-enoughness.

I've never danced with such freedom in my life. And I knew, in all of my "undignified" rejoicing, that I was being made new.

I was being set free.

The next day – in my freedom – I broke a rule. I left the campground, and I brought my phone with me.

Months prior, a journalist named Jonathan Merrit wrote an article about some crazy "ex-pastor of pornography" who had undertaken some crazy new endeavor – *Christian Cannabis*. He hoped it might get picked up by The New York Times, but every scheduled opportunity kept getting pushed back, buried beneath more pressing news that took priority. That day, there was a possibility it would finally make headlines.

It did.

And I sat on the side of the road and cried.

I cried because the Lord's timing – like a cliché – is perfect.

I cried because six years ago, he told me that it was time for me to step away from XXXchurch and into something new.

I cried because I didn't know what that meant, or how to do it, and six years is a long time to feel stuck in limbo.

I cried because I still had so much to learn.

I cried because I still had so much to *unlearn*.

I cried because that article, posted like a finish line, represented the culmination of so many terrifying decisions taken in faith that this was a direction the Lord had been leading me.

I cried because my wife and I are more united than we've ever been.

I cried because Hoffman helped her learn how to forgive, and I cried because it helped me accept forgiveness.

I cried because the Lord took my shame away. Because he buried it and stands victorious over it.

I cried because he has made me new. Because of what that means for my wife. My kids. My family.

I cried because I knew that this was the bookend.

I could go home a new man.

I could breathe.

I was clean.

I don't expect everyone to understand, but I needed to write this out. I needed to articulate the conclusion to a long chapter of life, and turn the page.

I needed to speak "the end."

But I also needed to speak "the beginning."

For twenty years, I've defined myself by what I'm against. For the next twenty, I'm going to define myself by what I'm for. For twenty years, I've been trying to work to prove my worth. For the next twenty, I'm going to work out of the worth I know is inherent to who I am, fearfully and wonderfully made.

I am not running *away* anymore – I am running *toward*.

I left Hoffman that day with a promise, and I'd like to pay it forward to you, too:
"So if the Son sets you free, you will be free, indeed…"

I am.

You are.

Craig

*Watch Craig expand on this chapter by scanning the QR code below.

Chapter 39 - Epilogue – Jeanette Gross

I don't know where to begin this conclusion.

It feels like a daunting task. I am not a naturally gifted, empathetic writer like Levi. I don't have profound, deep thoughts like Craig.

One thing I know for sure, though, is that my husband is a different person from the nineteen-year-old I met in 1995.

Of course, he *would* be different in appearance. His hair was as long as mine when I met him. Later, when he proposed, he sported a bleached-out bowl cut. Then it was jet-black. Then highlighted and manicured. I think dreadlocks were the only style I never saw (thank God).

Over the years, one thing has remained the same: his clothing and shoe game. Craig has always been into appearance. He has always picked out my whole wardrobe, and I've gotten a talking to on the rare occasions when I've tried to venture out and away from his selections. To his credit, though, if my outfit is cute and someone makes a comment, it's because Craig bought it for me. I've come a long way from my roots as the Oregonian girl with no sense of style, thanks to him. Over the last few years, Craig finally settled into a consistent hairstyle. He even added sweatpants to the mix.

I said Craig has changed, but I am not really talking about his appearance.

I am talking about his *heart*.

After reading through each of these journal entries, you know by now that Craig always has a thought or opinion about...something.

Anything.

Everything.

This is how Craig has worked in his life up until now – in his head. I don't know anyone else whose mind functions the way that his does. If you know him, personally, then chances are you'd say the same.

All of that head chatter breeds both *reward* and *suffering*.

Craig has been involved in the non-profit ministry scene since 1998 – the year we were married. This *"Go! Go! Go!"* man is the only one I've ever known. The Craig who buys a gazillion domains. The Craig who offers his time to help other startup ministries succeed. The Craig who takes anyone's (and everyone's) phone call at any time – day or night. The Craig who figured out the tech game. The Craig who wants to see everyone's dreams come true. The Craig who has traveled to almost every state in the US to speak about pornography addiction. The Craig who stays up late to work and gets up early to work. The Craig who moved our family two times to different states for the ministry. The spontaneous Craig. The Craig who knocks things off people's bucket lists. The Craig who is always seeing a person's strengths. The Craig who is always pushing people to be better. The confident Craig. The Craig with an amazing sense of humor. The manifestor Craig. The thick-skinned Craig.

He is a man after God's heart. He is a social butterfly. Intelligent and optimistic. A risk-taker. An incredible friend.

A person whose mind doesn't turn off.

While each of these qualities is amazing, the wonder can take a sharp turn to exhaustion for those of us who live with him, work for him, and try to do life with him.

If you know Craig – if you've experienced some part of this life alongside him – then you know that he is the real deal, and you know that the descriptions above aren't just *"sometimes"* qualities…they're *nonstop-all-the-time* qualities.

When you allow your intellect to run your life – as opposed to your emotions, your heart, and your body – you exhaust both yourself and the people who love you.

The flipside – the negative to each of Craig's positives – produced anger and arrogance, criticism and impatience, and a lack of graciousness and compassion. Craig has left others in the dust and exhausted himself in the process. His speed can tire him out at the same time as it crushes others, making relaxation next to impossible and leading him right back to anger for the cycle to repeat itself.

We have been married since 1998. We've had our highs, and we've had our lows, and somehow, we have managed to stay together. We've prayed for the Lord's leading. We've prayed fervently for soft hearts. Craig resolved never to get divorced, and by the grace of God, we haven't. Both of us have experienced significant heart-changes during the past couple of years. At this point, I am so thankful to be *100% together* as we move into whatever comes next – on the same page, hearts beating together, in unison (insert cheesy phrase here).

The changes that I am seeing are reminding me of why I fell in love with Craig way back in 1995. It is nothing short of amazing when – after being married for so long – you can fall in love with someone all over again and experience a rich, deep relationship.

Here are a few of the changes that I love:

- Over the years, Craig has gotten over the fact that Elise is no longer interested in soccer and has tried to understand her deeper passion, instead: *dance*. He has always wanted her to dance and has paid a hefty price tag to make it possible.

- He has always helped pursue whatever Nolan has wanted to pursue. But this year, he trusted Dave to lead Nolan to his first love: *music*. He still can be "dadager" but he is excited to play a supporting role with Nolan's music career instead of leading it.

- He takes time to relax now.

- He hears from (and listens to) the Lord.

- He developed a filter he runs his decisions through (i.e., – he doesn't say yes to *everything* anymore).

- He has honed in on what he is good at and what work brings him life.

- He has found forgiveness for himself and his parents.

- He can clearly see when something is off with a person's demeanor.

- He is at peace. He isn't so frantic.

- He still has confidence, but it's in the Lord. He isn't as arrogant, and his ego is dissolving.

- He is more patient with others.

- He asks for what he needs and is clear about his emotions.

- He is in touch with his body now. He knows what it needs. He knows what *he* needs, like *food, exercise, and a decent night's sleep*.

- He walks slower.

- He has boundaries. He doesn't just answer every call and work all night long.

- He knows that everything is working together and has stopped using the phrase "it's weird."

- He gives great counsel to those who ask him for it.

- I don't see the anger in him when he expresses emotion.

The best part of all these changes I listed is that they are here to stay. They're not here today and gone tomorrow.

To anyone reading this: *change is possible.*

I have seen a marriage – *my marriage* – and *our lives* transformed right before my eyes.

I am so thankful that Craig chose to share his "brain" with all of us. It reminds me that this whole project isn't about his brain at all…it is about his *heart*.

And his heart is beautiful.

*Watch Jeanette expand on this chapter by scanning the QR code below.

Cliff Notes

Well, this is the end. Of a season. A series. A book.

Life as we know it.

I am just kidding. Sort of.

I've written and released *a lot* of content throughout this year and thought that a recap might be in order. Maybe you don't want to wade through an entire memoir, and so you wouldn't mind the cliff notes. Or maybe you can treat this as a sort of chapter glossary – a summarization of what I've attempted to put out into the world as the weeks have flown by.

To say that my life changed in 2019 is an understatement. In fact, as my wife and I watched the ball drop on midnight in Times Square, NYC, ringing in the new year, I knew that this year was going to be "the one." Granted, the spurring began long ago, and I suppose it was finally time to move forward. I'll tell you what, though, change comes with its consequences. I'm more aware than ever of life as a learning curve.

As I've shared this collection of journal entries, thoughts, family letters, prayers, business propositions, and whatever else we lumped into Craig Brain, it has been fascinating to interact with the people who have chosen to follow along. Though we originally connected the title of this project to my head, I have – in truth – shared more of my heart during this season than ever before. Indeed, if I am a product of its overflow, I guess that makes sense.

These chapters represent more to me than a mere exchange of ideas. These thoughts have become life, in some ways, and where appropriate, I've updated the post-published *action* I've taken since releasing certain chapters below. You'll also find a few addendums – like bullet points – that didn't seem to fit neatly enough inside of a particular subject to build an entire podcast or chapter around them, but do contribute to who I am. I thought I'd include them here for – if nothing else – the sake of context, just so that you can see where my head (and heart) have been at as I've processed these changes and made these decisions.

- I traded one million dollars for one million downloads. I wrote about that in my letter to Nolan. I couldn't have handled the money back then, and I know it. I couldn't have been the father I have been to my kids, and if I had to guess – had I gone the Covenant Eyes route – my marriage would be long over by now. Still, it's an eye-opening realization. My grandma said that she wished I'd have gone into business instead of ministry. I have no regrets, but I know that her desires mean more to me now than they did before I understood my father.

- I know that I love God, and I found him. Or, He found me. However it happens, through my relationships, I'm truly finding myself. I really discovered him the night I finished recording Craig

Brain. I night I will never forget and will be the first chapter in my next book.

- In 2013, everything fell apart. I have written about it several places, including a whole book that came out of it, titled *Go Small: Because God Doesn't Care About Your Status, Size or Success.*

- In Alaska – blindfolded on some mat during a process-session – I heard God tell me to step away from XXXchurch. I've never told anyone that, minus Levi. No one. I couldn't give myself the freedom to think about it. That's ego. I couldn't stand to think of what the ministry would be like without me. That was before I started to feel. I didn't experience it – I only heard it – so I had no problem ignoring it. I've started a few projects since then. All of them have had the potential for more, but I couldn't stand to think about quitting to pursue something new. It never occurred to me to think of changing positions as graduating. As if the ministry couldn't exist without me.

- Discovering cannabis was like a tool that God used to introduce himself to me. I had met him before, sure, but I didn't know him well until Spa Day, Vegas 2017. I got my medical card in 2013 but hadn't found real help through cannabis until three years later, in 2016, when a few mints changed my life.

  - I started to feel.

- o I slowed down.
- o I began to share more.
- o I began to love more.
- o I began to enjoy life more.
- o I moved to the beach.
- o I got a membership at a spa.
- o I started to go outdoors.

Cannabis in my system seems to put me in a more meditative space where I'm able to be more present with my physical, emotional, spiritual, and intellectual self (my whole self). My mind is sharper. I think more clearly and act more brightly.

During this season of life, I've taken risks like never before. And I think that's saying a lot, considering how much of a risk-taker I already am. These risks come more from my heart than my brain, and they're scarier because of it.

They're also more rewarding.

- I've begun to invest more deeply into Elise's passion for dance.

- I bought my son, Nolan, a bucket-list watch for his sixteenth birthday, and wrote him what was probably the most vulnerable letter he's ever received from me.

- My wife, Jeanette, has allowed me to speak into her life in new ways, and we've fallen in love all over again.

- I've learned what it truly means to experience forgiveness, and freedom.

Familially, the Grosses have continued to forego gifts for experiences. We still strive to be a family that "lives by design, rather than default." And I'm still trying to be a dad who pursues lifestyle over revenue. I don't think I've done it perfectly, but I know that I have – and my wife and our whole family has – experienced the fruits of this labor…it's just that *labor* has a whole different meaning to me now.

It seems ironic that the true work of these years has not been to toil *more*, but less. To relinquish control. How absurd that "rest" becomes more difficult than the grind?

And yet here I am, coming up on my mid-forties, learning how to *be*.

Ironically, it comes at the exact same time as I am learning how *not* to be. About halfway through Craig Brain, I released an episode about "saying *yes.*" Saying "yes" in spite of fear, or risk, or insecurity. I talked about how badly I want to impart that faith to my wife and kids. The faith that says, "this *is* where I'm supposed to go, no matter how daunting or unattainable it seems right now."

My God, if this year has been anything, it has been a challenge for me to put my money where my mouth is. To embody my desire to pay *trust* forward. Career-wise, my wife and children have watched me step away from next to everything I've ever known in order to do exactly that, and they've supported me every step of the way. I left my role at the ministry I founded and participated in for over eighteen years in order to embark upon a new journey – a new conversation. I've pressed ever-deeper into the mastermind group that I've found to be so life-giving. And, in what is probably the most rewarding job of them all, I've begun to help my son, Nolan, with his music career.

Maybe I should pause there for a minute.

My son has always been a performer. I knew it when he'd sing Justin Beiber to the family (or, to whatever audience came to hear me speak at events that he was in on). Since living in LA – the mecca of entertainment – and investing in his career here, Nolan has been both model and actor. Whether it's a shoot for Nike or a role for Aronofsky, I've watched him accomplish feats that most kids his age will never have the opportunity to attempt, let alone succeed at.

What we've discovered in recent years, though, is how much Nolan loves and thrives at *music*. Not only has music given us, as father and son, a world of opportunity to grow in our friendship – it has also given us a new means of creating together. When Nolan started writing songs, we got him connected with a friend and producer in Redding, California. As I write this, that was a few months back, at most. He's already got a full-length album *and* a music video to boot. He's talked to big-time Los Angeles creators – people I still can't wrap my mind around being in a room with, let alone working with my son.

I'm proud of Nolan. I'm proud of what he's chosen to sing about. I'm proud to hear his vulnerability, and his willingness to express himself through his songs. I'm proud to watch him act faithfully in the face of the unknown.

On a more personal note, we just signed a second lease for another year at our apartment in Huntington. We fell in love with the beach. These days, I even walk across the street to sit and look at it. These days, I've even come so far as to *actually* enjoy being outdoors.

We fell in love with the pace, too. Jeanette and I have experienced an indescribable amount of transformation in our relationship since making the move away from Pasadena, and much of it has been the result of slowing down. I wrote about my very first experience with "the stillness where God is God" at the very beginning of this endeavor, and while that journal entry was primarily about me, we've both come a long way since that day in January 2017.

In many ways, it was a day like a struck match that went on to light the rest of our lives on fire.

Since then, we've celebrated twenty years of marriage together (although, we renewed our vows next to a couple of alpacas at nineteen). We started working with awareness and healing tools like The Enneagram and How We Love. We both subjected ourselves to the life-changing (albeit, painful) experience that is The Hoffman Process. I've learned how to relax. To spend time *with* Jeanette rather than only spending time *for* her – a substantial difference that is as applicable to my relationships with the Lord, kids, friends and family as it is to my wife. And she's learned a lot, too. She learned that she is of inherent value, that her opinions matter, that her wisdom is needed. She remembered that she used to have a voice of her own before life and parents and pain and age came to strip it away. She's a brand new woman, and I'm a brand new man, and our relationship is vibrant and alive in ways we haven't experienced since we first met. Even our sex is better than ever. Which isn't the *main* thing, but it's definitely not *not* the main thing, either.

My family feels whole. Connected. I've even realized just how connected even the parts that sometimes feel broken have always been. And, I've been able to watch truly broken parts made whole. It reminds me of the way that Jesus says that he is making all things new. I'm just not sure that I ever viewed that truth in light of my having the opportunity to participate in it, here and now. The older I get, the more I realize how much intentionality it takes to actively participate in the redemption of things, or in the ongoing goodness of a thing that could easily be lost if left to flippancy and neglect. Be it friendships or be it daddy-daughter-dates or be it becoming one with the person you vowed to do so with, there are plenty of obstacles that stand in one's way, but they're not insurmountable.

As my wife wrote in her epilogue, "To anyone reading this, *change is possible.*"

As for me, "to anyone reading this," I would like to say:

Thank you.

The thing about vulnerability is that you never quite know what will come of it. At the risk of sounding as though I'm tooting my own horn, I took a step I'd consider *brave* when I decided to take this project as a dream and turn it into a reality. It's not a bravery I need *you* to applaud, but the decision itself – and seeing that decision through, come what may (and what has) – was a much a part of my healing journey as has been anything else along the way.

I'm proud of *Craig Brain*, and I'm grateful to say that – as goes the cliche – "Craig's brain" has experienced some of the change that the heart, eighteen inches south, has to offer it.

To call this "quite the journey" is an understatement.

To those of you who have chosen to walk this road with me, I hope that it has been as much of an honor to be here as it has been to have you.

I don't know what the future holds.

That's the thing about the future, conniving bastard that it is.

I do know that the present offers far more promise than what most of us are willing to believe about it. And I won't lie – the present is hard to learn to sit in. Levi has a line in one of his poems that reads, "let the silence be violent until it heals you." Perhaps you've heard it said that "darkness is

a good and necessary teacher." I've certainly had to face
my fair share of shadows in these journal entries, these
prayers, these letters.

This reflection.

Violent does feel like an apt description, but so has *healing*
been a promise, fulfilled.

I hope that, perhaps, some of what I've had to share has
been (or can be) a part of your healing, as well. I began this
entire endeavor with a prayer as simple as, *"I hope it
lands."*

And I hope it has.

Nevertheless, these pages are every bit as much about
making certain *I* don't forget as they are about giving *you*
something to remember.

It has been a deep honor to share them with you.

Craig

www.ingramcontent.com/pod-product-compliance
Lightning Source LLC
Chambersburg PA
CBHW051453030726
47592CB00006B/1909